CITIZEN AND
SOCIETY

CITIZEN AND
SOCIETY

SELECTED WRITINGS

M. HAMID ANSARI

Published by
Rupa Publications India Pvt. Ltd 2016
7/16, Ansari Road, Daryaganj
New Delhi 110002

Sales Centres:
Allahabad Bengaluru Chennai
Hyderabad Jaipur Kathmandu
Kolkata Mumbai

Copyright © M. Hamid Ansari 2016

The views and opinions expressed in this book are the author's own and the facts are as reported by him which have been verified to the extent possible, and the publishers are not in any way liable for the same.

All rights reserved.
No part of this publication may be reproduced, transmitted, or stored in a retrieval system, in any form or by any means, electronic, mechanical, photocopying, recording or otherwise, without the prior permission of the publisher.

ISBN: 978-81-291-3756-2

First impression 2016

10 9 8 7 6 5 4 3 2 1

The moral right of the author has been asserted.

Printed by Replika Press Pvt. Ltd, India

This book is sold subject to the condition that it shall not, by way of trade or otherwise, be lent, resold, hired out, or otherwise circulated, without the publisher's prior consent, in any form of binding or cover other than that in which it is published.

To
Salma
An exceptional human being
An unrelenting critic
A non-conformist par excellence

CONTENTS

Preface   ix

POLITY

1. The Moral Realm in Politics   3
2. Federal Policy   11
3. Virtue in Public Life   16
4. Some Questions on Elections, Representation and Democracy   22
5. Prudence and the Moral Imperative   28
6. Citizens and State Conduct   37
7. Democracy and Dissent   45
8. International Human Rights Day   51
9. Role of Women Legislators in Nation Building   57
10. Public Investment and Subsidies on Agricultural Inputs and the Upliftment of Agrarian Economy   61
11. Roles of Editors in Today's Media   68
12. Role of the Judiciary: Some Thoughts on its Criticality   73

IDENTITY

13. The Intellectual and Society: Role and Responsibility   81
14. Identity, Citizenship and Empowerment   92
15. The Art and Culture of Islam in India   102
16. Challenges for a Homeless Language: Urdu in Present-day India   108
17. Physical Integration and Emotional Inconsonance   116
18. Identity and Citizenship: An Indian Perspective   123
19. Patriotism, Nationalism and Social Peace: Some Aspects of Lala Lajpat Rai's Ideas   131
20. History and Historians   135
21. Indian Muslims: Quest for Justice   139
22. Mohammad Mujeeb: An Intellectual's Locution of Dissent   144

23. Literature, Art and Social Awareness 154
24. Faith and Interfaith: An Imperative of Our Times 158

SECURITY

25. Insecurity and the State: Emerging Challenges 165
26. Intelligence for the World of Tomorrow 174
27. India and the Great War 183
28. Golden Jubilee Commemoration of the India-Pakistan War of 1965 187

EMPOWERMENT

29. Science and Technology 193
30. Higher Education—Challenges and Imperatives for Change 199
31. Human Development and Inequality 206
32. Socio-Economic Parameters 210
33. Challenges in Indian Agriculture 215
34. Right to Education Forum 220
35. The Value of Scientific Temper 225
36. Social Innovation and Social Harmony 229

MATTERS GLOBAL

37. The Imperative of World Peace 237
38. What Might Be Happening In West Asia 245
39. A Century of Turmoil in West Asia: Some Pitfalls of Nationalism 253
40. Relevance of International Law 263
41. Some Thoughts on the Sacred and Secular in International Relations 268
42. Collective Security in the Persian Gulf: An Indian Perspective 273
43. Turbulence in West Asian State Systems: Road Blocks in the Quest for Participatory Governance 279
44. Accommodating Diversity in a Globalizing World: The Indian Experience 286
45. India and the World 292

Notes 298
Index 315

PREFACE

The human being is a social creature and—exceptions apart—lives in societies. The members of these societies, by birth or adoption, are designated its citizens and this membership bestows certain rights and obligations on them. Destined to live side by side, they have the duty of civic participation and need to 'come to terms with one another, and set up, maintain, and operate the legal frameworks that are necessary to secure peace, resolve conflicts, do justice, avoid great harms, and provide some basis for improving the conditions of life.'*

In other words, a citizen, *quo* citizen, cannot remain unconcerned since all aspects of public policy have a bearing on his or her conduct and wellbeing. In more specific terms, every citizen of India is a beneficiary of the *rights* bestowed by the Constitution of India and has the *duty* of shouldering the responsibilities emanating from it. Neither of these can be discharged meaningfully without an informed interest in civic affairs of our society.

This necessarily takes the discussion to the nature of the modern, post-20th century state, to the institutional mechanism that makes possible the citizen's relationship to it, and to the challenges—local and global—to the effective exercise of citizenship. The primacy of security is evident; its ambit now stretches beyond state security to comprehensive human security and, as an eminent sociologist has put it, becomes 'the conjoint concern of three pillars–state, market and civil society'. Societal security thus propels us towards a just and humane social order, necessitates equality of status and opportunity, and steers away from inequality in all its dimensions.†

It also takes us beyond tolerance, to *acceptance* of diversity.

---

*Waldron, Jeremy. 'Cultural Identity and Civic Responsibility' in Kymlica & Norman, *Citizenship in Diverse Societies*, New York, 2000, p. 155.
†Oommen, T.K. *Understanding Security: A New Perspective*, New Delhi, 2006, pp. 11–21.

Nor can the citizen, and the citizen body, remain oblivious to the imperatives of a fast changing world and to India's place in it. The first necessitates conformity in increasing measure to globally accepted standards that, in the ultimate analysis, cannot be restricted to economics and trade policy only and extends to all fields of societal activity. This, by implication, implies that the space for local peculiarities in behavioral norms is shrinking.

As we move to attain our stated ideals, the endeavour on all counts has to be unrelenting:

> *Mil hi jaaegi kabhi manzil-e-Laila Iqbal*
> *Koi din aur abhi baadia paimaai kar*

★

One of the duties of public office is to respond to requests from institutions or organizations to deliver lectures instituted to commemorate anniversaries or the contribution made in years gone by eminent individuals to society, its thought process in diverse fields and in the development of knowledge.

The lectures collected in this volume are one such effort to respond to these calls of office. The general theme of each lecture was at times suggested by the occasion, at others chosen by the speaker in an effort to relate it to a matter of public interest.

★

Writing is at times a journey in loneliness and at others the product of a thought process in which friends and colleagues give a helping hand. In some of the lectures collected here, three colleagues, S/Shri P. Harish, Nagesh Singh and Anshuman Gaur, all of the Indian Foreign Service, gave me at different times, invaluable support. Needless to say the approach and orientation, as also the shortcomings, are entirely mine.

I would like to place on record my gratitude to Rupa Publications India Ltd and to the diligent work of Ms Ritu Vajpeyi-Mohan and Mr Sayantan Ghosh that was so critical to the publication of this volume.

New Delhi   M. Hamid Ansari
April, 2016

POLITY

1

THE MORAL REALM IN POLITICS

TO BE CALLED UPON TO deliver the P.N. Haksar Memorial Lecture can only be a great honour at any time; it is to me, particularly because I belong to a generation of Indians who witnessed Haksar saheb's work in two phases of his life—of action and of introspection. Neither of these, let me add, was totally exclusive. By the time of his death in 1998, some of the major premises of his belief system—democracy, secularism, socialism, non-alignment—had come under pressure and were the cause of disillusionment.

In an editorial in *Man and Development* many years back, Haksar spoke of the need 'to hold aloft the banner of the moral universe' and opined that 'human passions' and 'permanent values' play a role in history. Elsewhere, he expressed surprise over the 'symptoms of utter confusion in its value system' displayed by the Indian society in a period of change. 'Preserving the moral health of [the] body politic and maintaining the ecological balance are conditions precedent to survival and growth not only of India, but of [the] this entire earth', he wrote.

It is my purpose today to probe these concepts and Indian responses to them.

A great revolutionary of the 20th century, Leon Trotsky, described the role of sentiment in critical moments in human history. 'The masses,' he wrote in his monumental *History of the Russian Revolution*, 'go into a revolution not with a prepared plan of social reconstruction, but with a

---

Note: Haksar Memorial Lecture, 30 November 2007, Chandigarh.

sharp feeling that they cannot endure the old regime'. He pointed to the difficulties encountered in studying 'the changes in mass consciousness in a revolutionary epoch'.

How then do we define the moral universe and the role of passion in it? The challenge for India, said Haksar, is 'to use its material, intellectual, cultural and philosophical resources to regenerate itself into a truly free, just and humane society, and simultaneously to strive for a similar world society. The two are different aspects of the same objective, for a humane and peaceable India is not possible if it lives in an aggressive world atmosphere'.

The operative words are 'free', 'just' and 'humane'. They relate to the domestic and the global scene. India became free in 1947 and gave itself a Constitution in 1950 that spelt out the dimensions of justice. It is to be social, economic and political. The sequence is not alphabetical and its logic is not difficult to comprehend. Distributive justice is writ large and has been so understood. It connotes the removal of injustice resulting from transactions between unequals in society.

The law does not define 'humane' or 'humaneness'. Its dictionary meaning—benevolent or compassionate—is in the realm of morality, ethics and philosophy. What is not defined in law is amplified in common usage. In America, a humane society is defined as 'as a group that aims to stop animal suffering due to cruelty or other reasons'; in fact, an American Humane Association for Protecting Children and Animals came into existence in 1877. From this, one could, in Socratic reasoning, perhaps argue on the one hand that humaneness could include prevention of cruelty to humans as a whole and, on the other, draw attention to the unavoidable link between humaneness and justice. On this logic, therefore, a just society has to be a caring society.

Other questions need to be considered before proceeding further. Is there a linkage between the social realm and the moral one? Is it possible to structure relationships on a political basis? Have societies existed that have defined their structures and relationships principally or exclusively on functional terms, devoid of value judgement? What has been the ambit of such societies in terms of inclusion and exclusion?

The debate goes back a long way in history. In the Mahabharata, the sage Vamadeva stresses the need to act righteously: 'There is nothing superior to righteousness. Those kings that are observant of righteousness succeed... That king who disregards righteousness and desires to act with brute force, soon falls away from righteousness and loses both Righteousness and Profit.'

The pervasiveness of the concept is evident in all periods and in all societies. Rousseau aptly posed the perennial question: 'I wish to enquire whether, taking men as they are and laws as they can be made, it is possible to establish some just and certain rule of administration in civil affairs.'

This is evident in our own times in Mahatma Gandhi's teachings and in Ambedkar's definition of 'dharma' as 'righteousness, which means right relations between man and man in all spheres of life', and which is, of necessity, social. It is also the essence of morality.

The Raj Ghat in New Delhi is visited reverentially by the public, ritually by public figures and out of curiosity by tourists. A little away from the Samadhi is a stone tablet with the inscription 'Seven Social Sins'. These are listed on the tablet:

- Politics without principle
- Pleasure without conscience
- Wealth without work
- Knowledge without character
- Commerce without morality
- Science without humanity
- Worship without sacrifice

Each of these is a statement of principle that can be comprehended, interpreted and implemented, individually and collectively. On my part, I would like to discern a pattern in the last words of each dictum: principle, conscience, work, character, morality, humanity and sacrifice. A similar pattern, summing up different forms of human activity, is discernable when the first words of the statements are put together.

In the Gandhian approach, therefore, conscience is motivated by considerations of humanity and sacrifice to develop a moral character that holds aloft in its work the banner of a principled approach. The reverse of it would be selfishness inducing an unprincipled, opportunistic approach to work. The latter would produce neither justice nor humaneness. On this thesis, the choice would be clear if the human being is a moral creature having a sense of right and wrong in his individual and group conduct.

Here we are confronted by a set of questions. Can the principles of public morality be different from those of private morality? Can a society have one set of ethical norms for governing conduct of public institutions and another set of norms for citizens in their individual capacities? Do these norms govern the conduct of the highest form of public institution—the state—(a) in relation to its citizens and (b) in interstate relations? In other words, is the state required to observe norms of behaviour in its functioning?

For purposes of our discussion, therefore, we end up with four possible categories of conduct norms: for individuals, institutions, the state within its domestic jurisdiction and the state in its dealings with other states. This raises a fundamental question: is such categorization desirable? Can virtue and righteousness be imbibed selectively? Is it not desirable to have a unified theory of morality?

The Gandhian, and the ethical, approach would be to insist both on a unified theory and on practice in consonance with it. In actual practice, however, selectivity is the norm. This approach concedes the desirability of morality in personal life but finds reasons for departing from it in public life. The proponents of this approach make a beginning with interstate relations in the comity of nations. An English statesman made a classic statement on this subject in the late 19th century. 'I am a great believer,' he said, 'in morality, public and private; you must however concede that the conduct of nations cannot be governed by it.' He did not add, but undoubtedly implied, that the state was above moral norms in its external dealings.

The argument had a limited time span. State misbehaviour contributed to it in good measure. The end of World War I saw the beginning of systematic efforts to circumscribe the unchecked conduct of states. World War II gave it an impetus and led to the Charter of the United Nations (UN). International covenants in the past seven decades have put paid to the doctrine of absolute sovereignty and to the unchecked behaviour of states. Practice, of course, lags behind but is not sought to be justified in principle.

A parallel evolution was witnessed in regard to the behaviour of the state within its domestic jurisdiction. The principle of rule of law, and of responsible and responsive governance, is no longer disputed and is being implemented in increasing measure. Before we delve into the particular domain of the current situation of our society and polity, I wish to briefly examine the instrumentalities that societal and political evolution has bestowed upon us for dispelling the darkness of moral ambiguity of states—the moral torchlights of our era. These are: (a) A globalizing civil society; (b) Fundamental and universal human rights; and (c) A global movement for enhanced transparency in the functioning of state actors.

We have seen periods in history where states have applied different standards or moral criteria: (a) in their domestic jurisdiction and (b) while dealing with states and peoples whom they consider as not deserving of equal treatment.

Yet, the horizon is not all dark. In our country, our region and beyond, we witness active civil society movements that have supported common peoples and have sought to bring back state behaviour to the moral realm. Advancement in communication and transportation has facilitated the process of globalization of this civil society movement. This development has been critical in emphasizing the primacy of fundamental and universal human rights, not only as a basic norm of state behaviour but also in the behaviour of individuals towards each other. Human rights, in varying degrees, have been internalized voluntarily or on account of external pressures.

The drive for greater transparency in state behaviour was intended to make state actors accountable. In our own country, the 'Right to Information' movement has had significant success and is seen globally as a pioneering effort. Good governance and transparency are being recognized as imperatives in corporate institutions and will be increasingly so in the future.

It is undisputed today that a free, just and humane society is one that respects fundamental human rights not only of its citizens but of all peoples, has a state structure that is transparent in its functioning and encourages the growth of a healthy civil society.

Step by step, therefore, the circle for unprincipled, immoral and amoral behaviour is being narrowed down to individual behaviour. The challenge lies in addressing it because individuals are the building blocks of societies. They are also the principal actors in political life of societies and determine its character by their principles and conduct.

A transition from the general to the particular is essential to carry the argument forward. The Indian society of today, despite its moorings in religion and tradition, is increasingly prone to be amoral in the behaviour of its individual and group components. A good instance is the case of corruption in public life.

Political corruption is defined as the misuse of public office for private gain. Mahatma Gandhi's outburst in 1939 is indicative of its presence even in the period before Independence.

In 1949, the Urdu poet Josh Malihabadi, in a poem entitled 'Rishwat', gave vent to public's perception of the prevalent bribery. A quatrain portrays its extent:

> *Log ham se roz kahte hain yeh aadat chore de*
> *Yeh tejarat hai khelaaf-e-aadmiyat chore de*
> *Is se bad tar lat nehain hai koye, yeh lat chore de*
> *Roz akhbaroan main chapta hai ki rishwat chore de*

A couplet, towards the end of the poem, was cynically expressive of disgust:

> *Illat-e rishwat ko is duniya se rukhsat keej ye*
> *War na rishwat ki dharalle se ijazt deej ye*

In 1951, the A.D. Gorwala Report made specific observations on this count. In 1964, the Santhanam Committee noted the 'widespread impression that failure of integrity is not uncommon among ministers and that some ministers, who have held office during the last sixteen years, have enriched themselves illegitimately'. It also talked of nepotism and 'other advantages inconsistent with any notion of purity in public life'. More recently, the published portions of the N.N. Vohra Report of 1995 spoke of 'the nexus between criminal gangs, police, bureaucracy and politicians [that] has come out clearly in various parts of the country. The existing criminal justice system, which was essentially designed to deal with individual offences/crimes, is unable to deal with the activities of the Mafia; the provisions of the law in regard to economic offences are weak'.

An observation by a former Chief Justice of India, in 1997, is telling. 'The element of deterrence,' he noted, 'is almost non-existent. The public perception is that the machinery for enforcement of accountability is itself controlled by those whose accountability needs to be enforced. All institutions of law enforcement lack accountability, the difference between them is only in the degree of culpability.' He pleaded for 'concerted efforts for infusion of ethics in public life'.

An official acknowledgement of the problem of corruption came from Prime Minister Dr Manmohan Singh in August 2004. Addressing a conference of state CBI and Anti-corruption Bureau officials, he said:

> The problem of corruption in public life is a source of great concern for all those who are interested in building a new India, an inclusive society, progressive society and a dynamic economy and a compassionate polity. In my Independence Day Address, I said that while the question of ethics in public life has repeatedly agitated our people, we have tried over a period of time, to find

constitutional, legislative and administrative devices to deal with the challenge posed by growth of corruption to our body politic. I said in my address that the time has come for us to evolve consensually a code of conduct for all political parties, a code of ethics for all individuals in public life, and a code of best practices for the Government at all levels.

This statement, from the highest levels of government, is indicative of the seriousness of the problem. It can be supplemented, in ample measure, by civil society perceptions. The Corruption Perception Index of Transparency International, based on public opinion and business community surveys, gave India in 2007 the score of 3.5 on a scale of 10 (highly clean). The corresponding figures for the preceding years were 3.3, 2.9 and 2.8. India was ranked 72 in a list of 179 countries.

This state of affairs has implications that are wide-ranging and multi-dimensional. The challenge is to comprehend, and confront, the question in its totality. Corruption is as much moral as a development issue. It tends to distort the decision-making processes on investment projects and other commercial transactions. It impacts on the foundations of the social and political fabric of society. It increases injustice and disregard for the rule of law. As such, it is to be viewed as a symptom of fundamental weaknesses in the institutions; the correctives, therefore, need to focus on a set of fundamental institutional determinants.

To what extent has the political system reacted to the malaise? A good example is the First Report of the Ethics Committee of the Rajya Sabha, in December 1998. It had this to say in its opening paragraphs:

> Moral and ethical concerns of the society weigh a great deal with those in public life as their behaviour is keenly watched by the people. At concerned quarters views are being expressed over the general decline in moral and ethical standards in public life. The Committee has itself noted the general decline in moral and ethical standards in public life. While the Committee felt that it was a serious trend, it did not, however, fully share the despondency...
>
> There is a general feeling that all is not right with our political system which is functioning under a great strain. In such a situation, the representatives of the people have to set high standards of behaviour in public life. Members of Parliament have not only to represent the society but have also to lead it. Therefore, they have

to function as the role models and this naturally casts on them a heavy responsibility...

The Committee notes that our freedom fighters and national leaders had set high ethical and moral standards in public life and they followed those principles scrupulously. This tendency, the Committee painfully observes, is now on a decline.

The Report addressed the question of criminalization of politics and felt it could only be tackled through self-regulatory mechanisms of political parties. It recommended a model Code of Conduct, of a general nature, for the members of the Rajya Sabha.

The Third Report of the Ethics Committee, in August 2002, opined that 'ethical questions are mainly matters of one's conscience' and therefore cannot be dealt entirely by legislation.

The argument thus returns to its point of commencement. The imperative of ethics in public life is eventually a matter of conscience, of morality, of a sense of values in relation to right and wrong, good and bad, just and unjust, humane and cruel. The perceived dichotomy between public and the private behaviour of individuals, therefore, does not exist in ethical terms and must not exist in practice. It follows that the individual, in relation to the state in any aspect of its functioning, must act in an ethical manner; it then becomes the duty of the state as well as of the civil society to ensure this through appropriate instrumentalities of law as also of social pressures. Only then would we see the day when the corrupt would not only be punished but also ostracized.

Conscience, in other words, may need to be jostled from time to time. The duty of the state, and of the civil society, is to be proactive in the matter. Only then would the moral realm in public life become meaningful and make India of the future truly free, just and humane.

2
FEDERAL POLICY

LATE SHRI SATYENDRA NARAYAN SINHA, or 'Chhote Sahib', as he was popularly called, was an important political leader of Bihar, a distinguished parliamentarian, and someone who had the interests of his state and people uppermost in his mind.

During his long public life of over six decades, Sinhaji made significant contributions in streamlining the education system of Bihar, motivated the youth and students to take an active role in politics and ensured their representation in political affairs.

As many readers would know, Sinhaji was also a strong votary of the rights of states in our constitutional scheme of things. As a chief minister, and as an eminent and long-standing parliamentarian, he was in a good position to appreciate the delicate balance maintained by our Constitution between the centre and the states.

This balance is dynamic and evolving. I therefore propose this afternoon to touch upon a few challenges to our federal polity in a period of great change, nationally and internationally.

Our Constitution was carefully crafted. It is a 'Union of States', having features of both a federation and a union with a systemic flexibility that has allowed it to becoming a three-tiered polity with a single citizenship, and with the capacity to be either unitary or federal, according to the requirements of time and circumstances.

The point was succinctly and authoritatively explained by the chairman of the Drafting Committee of the Constituent Assembly, Dr B.R. Ambedkar. 'The Drafting Committee,' he observed, 'wanted it to be clear that though

---

Note: Satyendra Narayan Sinha Memorial Lecture, 12 July 2011, Patna.

India was to be a federation, the federation was not the result of an agreement by the states to join in a federation,' adding that 'the federation is a Union because it is indestructible. Though the country and the people may be divided into different States for convenience of administration, the country is one integral whole, its people a single people living under a single imperium derived from a single source.'

While the Constitution does not use the term 'federal' or 'federation', the Supreme Court has spoken of the Indian Union as quasi-federal and deemed it to be a part of the basic structure. Eminent international authorities have characterized it as 'a centralized federation' and as sui generis.

Six decades of experience as a republic is perhaps long enough to assess the functioning of our federal structure that has been the principal instrumentality for accommodating the enormous cultural, linguistic, religious and ethnic diversity of India within the framework of a democratic polity.

It is possible to analyse the functioning of our democracy in three of its dimensions:

First, there is a need to assess its efficacy as an instrumentality of managing diversity, coping with political and social challenges, enhancing the scope of political participation of citizens, deepening their engagement with the state and accommodating various identities of our citizens;

Second, we should enquire if political federalism has served our democracy well by controlling extraconstitutional forces and enabling articulation of the aspirations of our citizens through a political process; and

Third, we need to examine the operation of fiscal federalism through the various tiers of our democracy and indicate required correctives.

It would be fair to assert that our democratic set-up has served us well in orienting our heterogeneous society towards its developmental goals, and including in this endeavour all segments of our citizenry. Our success is in sustaining a secular, pluralist democracy focused on the vision of our founding fathers. Our commitment to diversity and to upholding the varied identities of our citizens is unparalleled.

We have also shown that this commitment is not a fair-weather strategy to be discarded at the first sign of political or economic stress, but a fundamental value. Our federalism has enabled this achievement despite immense national and global transitions.

At the level of 'political federalism' it can be said with confidence that India has been a pioneer in moving from a dual federalism to a multi-level functional cooperative federalism through the 73rd and 74th Constitutional Amendments.

We thus have a multi-layered federal polity starting from the gram sabha, the gram panchayat, block and district panchayats, urban local bodies, the states and the Union. This transformation has brought a qualitative and quantitative difference to the nature of our political representation. From a small number of less than 5,000 political representatives from the Union Parliament and the State Legislatures, today we have the largest political representative base in the world of over two-and-a-half lakh local governments, comprising over three million elected representatives.

The experience of a series of coalition governments at the central level and in many states during the last two decades has changed the working dynamic of our polity. Today, having strong state governments pursuing their developmental goals with dedication and success need not depend on the dynamics of political force at the centre. The emergence of strong regional and sectional political parties who participate in governance at the local, state and central levels has further strengthened the federal impulse.

The constitutional scheme of distribution of powers continues to be the subject of argument, mostly rational, among political parties and constituent units of our federal set-up. Similarly, greater political and fiscal freedom to units lower down the political pyramid continues to be politically debated and negotiated.

Some of these issues are critical. The significant regional disparities in economic development focus attention on the important aspect of 'fiscal federalism'. It has been a difficult task of balancing the objectives of equity, efficiency and autonomy in federal transfers and to keep the process on track as envisaged in our Constitution. Finance Commissions have played a constructive role in harmonizing the revenue structures of the centre and the states and in resolving disputes with respect to distribution of revenues between them. Grievances regarding fiscal devolution mechanisms do exist, and continue to be aired and addressed through our polity. This dynamic of the political economy has strengthened the process and foundation of fiscal federalism in our country.

The question of eliminating fiscal barriers to interstate movement of goods and in the utilization of natural resources has raised political tension and adverse political mobilization. They pose a significant challenge for the management of our federal polity, especially as we move from a 'cooperative' to a 'competitive' federalism with constituent units competing for investments, job creation opportunities and grants from national and multilateral bodies to improve the standard of living of their peoples. A horizontal disparity in economic development among states coexists with intense competition, which at times also takes on political overtones.

Rapid economic growth, increased demand for commodity resources obtained from mining and buoyant commodity markets, and widespread poverty and underdevelopment in mineral resource-rich states have provided the backdrop for a debate on 'resource federalism' in the country. The polity has had to face questions about the functioning of our federal set-up in the context of resource development; the balance between political participation; protection of human, legal and fundamental rights; economic and developmental priorities; and local environmental and social responsibilities.

We are yet to find definitive answers to the question of independent regulators for offshore and onshore resource management, improving compensation and sharing of resource revenues, and improving the institutional capacity to utilize the revenues generated for public interest.

It also has to be admitted that the potential of the mechanisms suggested in the Constitution remains underutilized. A case in point is the Interstate Council under Article 263. It was established by a Presidential Order in 1990 but remains somewhat dormant. The March 2010 Report of the Commission on Centre-State Relations piously proclaims that 'cooperative federalism' is the key in which 'Statesmanship should lead Politics'.

Is this happening? Yet another area where cooperation rather than contention should prevail pertains to interstate water disputes and underlines the imperative need for better water governance on the part of all concerned.

Another issue that needs to be raised for consideration is that while there has been criticism regarding the manner and extent of devolution of finances from the centre to the states, the issue of further devolution to local government has not been adequately debated. India has one of the lowest shares of local government expenditure compared to total public sector expenditure at around 5 per cent, as compared to the Organisation for Economic Co-operation and Development (OECD) average of around 30 per cent, over 50 per cent in China and 15 per cent in Brazil.

Likewise, the share of local government expenditure in the gross domestic product (GDP) is less than 2 per cent in India compared to around 14 per cent in OECD countries, over 10 per cent in China and over 6 per cent in Brazil.

Thus, while political federalism has worked very well at the third tier of local government, through regular elections, granting of constitutional status, reservation for women and marginalized communities and the granting of responsibility for planning for economic development and social justice, these have been rendered without corresponding movement towards fiscal federalism. The institution of the State Finance Commissions has not been harnessed enough to achieve fiscal devolution to the local government and thus achieve a more inclusive and effective decentralized governance in the country.

The time for all the constituent units of our federal set-up to ponder on how to realize the full potential of our federal democracy for meeting the aspirations of our people has come.

The Canadian scholar W.S. Livingston, while writing in 1956, drew attention to the social forces that mould federal political institutions. 'The essential nature of federalism,' he wrote, 'is to be sought for, not in the shading of legal and constitutional terminology, but in the forces—economic, social, political and cultural—that have made the outward form of federalism necessary... Federal government is a device by which the federal qualities of the society are articulated and protected.'

Needless to say, this is all the more compelling in our changing world where the twin imperatives of globalization and identity have to be continuously reconciled to achieve our stated socio-economic and political objectives.

3
VIRTUE IN PUBLIC LIFE

BHIMSEN SACHAR WAS A FREEDOM fighter, a political activist, an administrator and above all, a person who advocated and practised the core values of our freedom movement. As the chief minister of Punjab, on more than one occasion in the early years of our republic, he shouldered the onerous responsibilities of putting in place administrative structures in the aftermath of a major disruption. He served with distinction as governor in two different states.

As a political personality occupying high public office, Bhimsen Sachar would have dealt with questions of governance of a perennial nature and have been posed in all periods and to all systems; each faced challenges, including those of probity; each sought to developed appropriate responses.

Societies throughout history have functioned mostly on the basis of an unstated consensus that provides the glue pertaining to social values, a set of dos and don'ts relating to the respective roles of the citizens and those entrusted by them with responsibilities of governance. The compact is in the nature of a trust. Record shows that points of tension arise whenever apprehensions develop about this relationship.

Many would agree that our society today, despite its firm moorings in religion and tradition, is increasingly prone to be amoral in the behaviour of its individuals and group components. Often, the connection between means and ends is being lost or side-tracked and the view is rampant that the end justifies the means, however devoid the latter may be of moral content.

The implications of this for individual and collective conduct are far-reaching. Good and not-good, good and bad, moral and immoral, virtue and vice are inclinations that determine individual and group action and

---

Note: Annual Bhimsen Sachar Memorial Lecture, 7 December 2012, New Delhi.

experience has shown that disregarding them inevitably leads to moral anarchy and eventually to social decay. For this reason, societies in all periods of history have sought to put in place, and observe, norms through which virtue is promoted and vice eschewed.

Can the norms be accepted or discarded selectively? If so, who makes this determination, and for what purpose, justification and duration? A good instance is the question of lack of probity in public life, a matter very much in our everyday discourse, though at times generating more heat than light.

The desire and need for a virtuous society is not just a metaphysical goal which lies in the ethereal realm of religion or philosophy but has tangible benefits for common good of humanity. Virtue in public life provides a necessary, if not sufficient, framework for sustained and harmonious political, economic and social progress in society.

Virtue in public life goes beyond the normal clamour for probity in government and public administration and covers the entire spectrum of a citizen's public activity. Similarly, virtue is not restricted to absence of corruption in financial or monetary terms, but includes values such as service, sacrifice, faith, trust, courage, justice and ethical conduct. As the philosopher Aristotle put it, virtue is a disposition for excellence in the human soul. This virtue can be acquired.

In an article in *Young India* on 22 October 1925, Gandhiji listed 'Seven Social Sins', which he considered to be spiritually most perilous for humanity, which together constitute a good point of reference for any discussion on virtue in public life. These were:

> *Politics without principles*
> *Wealth without work*
> *Pleasure without conscience*
> *Knowledge without character*
> *Commerce without morality*
> *Science without humanity*
> *Worship without sacrifice*

It is evident that each of the human activities listed here result in a socially relevant moral degradation if the concomitant virtue cited with it is absent. Hence the imperative need for imbibing and implementing them in social and personal behaviour patterns.

There can be other approaches to the problem. 'Virtue in public life', an American academic wrote a few years back, 'is less likely to be found in a clearer understanding of virtue and more likely to be found in a clearer understanding of public life', adding that 'virtue in public life is to be found not just in the individual propensity to be ethical but more in the development of organizational rules and procedures, in virtuous leadership, and in the development rules and procedures, in various leadership, and in the development of virtuous public cultures'.

Every society has in place a set of laws and regulations to deal with violations of rules, requiring proper conduct by those who indulge in public affairs. The adequacy of these remains a matter of unending debate.

Beyond these, however, and in terms of principles and commitments, there are two aspects of the requirement of probity in public domain. In the first place, I would like to draw your attention to Article 51A of our Constitution that prescribes, among the duties of citizens, the requirement 'to strive towards excellence in all spheres of individual and collective activity so that the nation constantly rises to higher levels of endeavour and achievement'.

This requirement, of a quest for excellence, cannot evade the seven principles prescribed by Gandhiji and necessitates a commitment for their implementation leading to probity in the everyday life of a citizen.

In the second place, and in our world of today, societies and states no longer have the luxury of isolation. Instead, we have a community of states and a globalization of values. National sovereignty is increasingly circumscribed by national commitments to global conventions. These, together, give teeth to the principles and behaviour pledges inscribed in the Charter of the United Nations.

Perhaps the most relevant of these international commitments, having a direct impact on an essential aspect of probity, is the UN Convention against Corruption, adopted in October 2003 and somewhat belatedly ratified by India on 11 May 2011. This is a comprehensive document, has a direct relevance to the question of probity in public life and its rationale and objectives therefore need to be considered carefully.

The Preamble of the Convention states that corruption poses threats to the stability and security of societies; undermines institutions, values of democracy, ethical values and justice; jeopardizes sustainable development and the rule of law; has international ramifications; and leads to organized crime and money laundering involving vast assets, thereby threatening political stability and development of the concerned states. It stresses that the prevention and eradication of corruption is a responsibility of all states, puts in place a framework for observance and urges in this endeavour international cooperation as well as support of individuals and groups.

The Preamble urges states to 'foster a culture of rejection of corruption'.

Given this requirement in terms of national and international norms and commitments, let's now discuss where we, in India, stand in terms of perception and action in regard to this ailment?

The matter is very much in the public domain. It has been said with much justice that 'evidence of corruption has moved from anecdotal to documentary'; that it is Indian democracy's 'inconvenient fact'; that it violates human rights, constitutional rights and Rule of Law; and that 'it undermines the very social fabric and the political and bureaucratic structure of the Indian society'.

Our ranking in the global Corruption Perception Index is, to say the least, distressing.

The disease is not of recent origin but, in an earlier period, carried a social stigma that is less evident today. In poet Josh Malihabadi's poem entitled 'Rishwat', one couplet sums up the public opprobrium attributed to the ailment:

Bhool kar bhi jo koi leta hai rishwat, chor hai
Aaj qaomi paagaloon main raat din yeh shour hai

The perception of widespread corruption has widened and deepened in the public mind. Furthermore, there is a nagging apprehension that the administrative and judicial mechanism in place is inadequate as a deterrent. In January 2007, the 'Ethics in Governance' report of the Second Administrative Reform Commission (ARC) concluded that 'anti corruption interventions so far made are seen to be ineffectual and there is widespread public cynicism about them'. This cynicism, it added, 'is spreading so fast that it bodes ill for our democratic system itself'.

It is evident that more effective corrective action is needed to restore public confidence. This has to be qualitatively different and must address three aspects of the matter simultaneously. These relate to: (a) propensity, (b) opportunity and (c) scope. It is essential to examine the role of each of these in the genesis and perpetuation of corruption:

- The *propensity* to resort to illegal or immoral means to achieve desired ends is increasingly pervasive in the wake of a sentiment that both traditional morality and constitutional morality have somehow become unnecessary and not in need of observance beyond the ritual of lip service. A culture of hedonism and of what Nehru called 'vulgar display of wealth' does of necessity lead to a culture of inequality, very different from the requirements of justice, equality and fraternity to which we swear allegiance as citizens. The only viable corrective to this would lie in a concerted effort, in the family, the school, the workplace and the civic domain to rejuvenate and reimbibe the required social values and, at the same time, put in place deterrents to ensure compliance.

- Propensity could, and does, also emerge from situational compulsion caused by real or created scarcity, by intentional delays in the delivery of public service and the resultant moral dilemma faced by the seeker of a public service. The petty corruption thus generated has a differential impact on the less privileged, whose capacity to resist is minimal. The ARC report cited above found that 'in a vast majority of cases of bribery, the citizen is a victim of extortion', and that 'experience has taught most citizens that there is a vicious cycle of corruption and they often end up losing much more by resisting corruption'.
- The same holds true for *opportunity*. Successive reports of government commissions over five decades have suggested reform of procedures that would facilitate public service delivery, introduce transparency and thereby reduce opportunity to go astray. The Right to Information (RTI) Act has helped rectify this in some measure; much still remains to be done. Rigorous training to inculcate the concept of service is essential so that it is rendered as a *duty* not a *favour*.
- The *scope* of what is considered corruption has to expand to cover the act as well as the actors—both the taker and giver of bribes. This is of particular relevance in cases that go beyond petty corruption. A paper presented at a World Bank workshop some years back observed that 'the problem of corruption lies at the intersection of the public and private sectors. It is a two-way street. Private interests, domestic and external, wield their influence through illegal means to take advantage of opportunities for corruption and rent seeking, and public institutions succumb to take these and other sources of corruption in the absence of credible restraints'.

A survey by the Swiss consultancy firm KPMG in March 2011 showed that 'in many cases corruption is induced by the private sector', adding that 'a large number of respondents believe that corruption is a two-way street and people who pay bribes are as much to blame for the current environment as those accepting such payments. The regulation in India tends to focus on the bribe taker rather than the bribe payer and hence corporates do not shy away from adopting corrupt practices'.

There are other dimensions to the problem. Given our social scene and traditions, nepotism in some form or the other is, tacitly or explicitly, considered a virtue. It is said to be 'a custom with infinitely more practitioners than defenders'. How is it to be defined in the Indian context of Kunba Parvari? When and where does it violate canons of probity and become a corrupt practice? Has any government or public body sought to develop a framework to check it?

Much of the debate on dealing with the perils of corruption has dealt with the legal framework and law enforcement and the effort to make it produce better results. This is essential, but not sufficient. An aspect of the fight against corruption, insufficiently addressed, is its impact on human rights and the extent to which it derogates the rule of law that ensures administration of justice by normal law courts, avoidance of arbitrary decision-making and abuse of discretionary power.

It has been argued in this context that 'the human rights approach to corruption control mechanism makes the people of India central players in the corruption resistance movement' and that 'the law enforcement work of the government to ensure corruption free governance ought to be perceived as a part of the right of the people of India to seek a corruption-free government. Concomitantly, it then becomes the duty of the government to ensure that all its affairs are conducted in a manner that promotes transparency, accountability, and integrity in public administration'.

One clear benefit of such an approach would be to link up different ingredients of good governance and thereby synergize the quest for better governance and substantive rather than formal political legitimacy.

In the final analysis, therefore, a fourfold approach to treat this deadly social ailment and promote probity would lie in the combination of (a) ethical training in norms incorporated in a legally enforceable code of ethics, (b) comprehensive protection of human rights, (c) a legal framework and regulatory practices that enforce clash of interest rules and (d) laws and procedures that forbid nepotism in all its manifestations.

These steps would assist the attainment of 'excellence' in terms of the 'Duties' prescribed in the Constitution. The endeavour is to be individual and collective. Here, as elsewhere, a Gandhian dictum is of relevance:

'You must be the change you wish to see in the world.'

4
SOME QUESTIONS ON ELECTIONS, REPRESENTATION AND DEMOCRACY

ONE OF THE PRIME ARCHITECTS of our Constitution, Babasaheb Ambedkar was a towering personality in the early years of our republic. He was a distinguished political leader, eminent constitutionalist, jurist, thinker and a radical social reformer. He was also a rationalist and an iconoclast. As chairman of the Drafting Committee of our Constitution, he is often called 'Father of the Indian Constitution'.

His exemplary work for the upliftment of marginalized and deprived sections of our society has given him a very prominent place in the pantheon of the founders of modern India.

Our founding fathers had the vision to comprehend that given India's ethos, diversity and requirements, a representative parliamentary democracy was the most suited form of political system. Today, we have emerged as the world's largest democracy, characterized by regular, free and fair elections, based on universal adult suffrage to determine the will of the people as to who should be entrusted with the duty of governance.

The entire exercise of an Indian general election is mind-boggling: in 2009 the electorate numbered more than 714 million; it was catered to by 10 lakh polling booths in which about 50 lakh personnel were deployed; 360 parties put forth candidates. The average voter turnout was 59.7 per cent.

As elections are the bedrock of any functioning democracy, a citizen is entitled to assess their efficacy in quantitative and qualitative terms and, for this purpose, examine the mechanism for their conduct and the adequacy

---

Note: 4th Dr B.R. Ambedkar Memorial Lecture, 17 December 2012, New Delhi.

of the end product.

The electoral methodology adopted and practised by us is the single member plurality system, otherwise known as the First-Past-The-Post (FPTP) system. The traditional arguments in its favour are that (a) it tends to provide a clear-cut contest between two or more major parties, (b) its working is easy for voters to understand, (c) it allows individuals who are not members of a political party to run as independents, (d) it tends to produce stable governments and (e) it is likely to produce a strong opposition party.

Despite the above, the system is not universal and critics have commented on its limitations. These relate to the disconnect between the vote share and the number of seats won, the propensity to over-reward major parties and under-reward smaller parties and the likelihood of smaller parties with a strong regional base getting a 'seat bonus' and winning more seats than their corresponding share of the popular vote.

Experience of six decades propels us to question the certitudes of the FPTP system, consider its limitations and acknowledge that there are a number of areas in the process that need to be looked at for corrective actions and improvement.

The changed context has to be borne in mind. There has been, since 1989, what Yogendra Yadav has called 'a fundamental transformation in the terrain of politics which in turn is anchored in the process of social change'. As a result, the participatory base of electoral democracy has expanded. There has also been a 'fractionalization of the political space'.

A number of government committees since 1990 have cogitated on the question of reforms relating to different aspects of the electoral process. These have dealt principally with criminalization in politics, funding of elections, election campaign procedures and reform of election expenditure laws. Their objective was to improve the efficacy of the system and attend to the lacunae that came to notice. Some of these, like the Law Commission Report of 1999 and the National Commission to Review the Working of the Constitution (2001), also touched upon the question of qualitative improvement in the degree of representative-ness of the elected candidates.

Useful suggestions have also emanated from civil society groups; think tanks and NGOs have likewise contributed to the discussions.

The most recent effort in this direction is in the shape of the Background Paper on Electoral Reforms initiated in December 2010 by the Ministry of Law and Justice and co-sponsored by the Election Commission of India. It confines itself to 'explore options for electoral reforms within the framework of the current system and will not address these larger structural issues'. Pursuant to it, a Core Committee has held regional consultation in seven state capitals; in some of these, views on systematic reforms have also been expressed.

The purpose of this chapter is to dwell on one aspect of this debate and probe the concept of the *representative-ness of the elected representative*. The question has a theoretical dimension as well as an empirical one. Dr Ambedkar's vision of 'one person, one vote, one value' is yet to be realized and may have to await a more egalitarian social milieu. In terms of existing reality, an elected candidate in our system is one who has secured a plurality, not a majority, of votes cast in his/her electoral constituency. Here, some questions arise:

- Did the candidate obtain a majority of total votes or a majority of the votes cast? If the latter, would it constitute a *majority* in terms of the democratic principle of 50+1? If not, and in case the electoral decision reflects the will of a minority of the total electorate, how and to what extent would the candidate be considered *representative*?
- If this pattern is repeated in a good many other constituencies, could a situation arise in which an elected assembly has a majority, or a good percentage of the majority party, or a combination of members elected on a minority vote in their own constituencies?
- Would such a body be considered representative of the electorate as a whole? Would such a situation derogate from the principle of majority rule?

A look at the empirical data provides some justification for raising these questions. In the first general election in 1952, the percentage of successful candidates who secured less than 50 per cent of the votes cast was 67.28. This figure went down to 58.09 per cent in 1957. In the 13th, 14th and 15th general elections in 1999, 2004 and 2009 respectively, it was 60.03, 75.87 and 82.68 per cent respectively.

The conclusion is inescapable that a majority of elected members of the Lok Sabha in recent years, and even earlier, won on a minority of votes cast in their constituencies. This is compounded by the absence, in our system, of compulsory voting. Thus, if a candidate is elected on 30 per cent of the votes cast and if the percentage of polling is the constituency is 60, then the positive mandate secured by the candidate is 30 per cent of 60 per cent, that is, just 18 per cent of the total electorate.

Such an outcome has a distorting impact on the composition of the elected legislature. This is vividly demonstrated by the vote-share seat-won data relating to all the 15 Lok Sabhas.

The situation is no better, perhaps worse, in state assembly elections with percentage of returned candidates on minority of votes cast going above 70 per cent in several cases.

What are the ramifications of such an outcome? Observers have noted that it induces candidates to focus on securing votes of a segment of the electorate and thereby accentuate or reinforce social divisions based on caste, creed, faith or language. For this purpose, and despite formal legal or regulatory constraints, candidates or their supporters do succeed in invoking narrower loyalties to further electoral appeal. The excluded or marginalized social groups 'then indulge in strategic voting'. Divisive tendencies and social conflict is necessarily the end product.

The foregoing would suggest a need to revisit the electoral procedures to ensure a greater measure of representative-ness in the elected representatives of the people. This is essential to achieve, in greater measure, the purpose of a democratic form of governance.

Suggestions have been made with regard to possible correctives to the present system. Principal among these are (a) Mixed Compensatory Proportional Representation on the German model, and (b) Second Ballot System to achieve a 50 per cent +1 result. Their merits need to be carefully assessed in terms of our conditions.

- The 'German model' or the List System requires that the overall representation of parties in legislature be based on the proportion of valid votes (at least 10 per cent of the total) obtained by them. 50 per cent of the legislators will be elected from territorial constituencies based on the FPTP system. This will ensure a link between the legislator and the constituents. The balance of 50 per cent will be allocated to parties to make up for their shortfall, based on proportion of votes. The party list for the latter will be selected democratically by its members. To operate this system, each voter will be required to cast two votes, one for each category. An essential prerequisite of this system is legal regulation of the internal functioning of political parties. It also requires a more literate electorate.
A diluted version of this model, suitable for 'Indian reality', was considered by the 1999 Law Commission Report on Electoral

Reforms. It suggested that recognized political parties obtaining at least 5 per cent of the total votes be considered to be eligible for allocation from 25 per cent of the seats earmarked for party lists.

- The Second Ballot system involves a run-off between the first two contenders in an election if neither of them obtains less than 50 per cent of the votes cast. It retains most of the advantages of the present system but would ensure that parties and candidates seek a wider mandate from the electorate, broaden their vote catchments and thereby minimize appeal to parochial sentiments, which is becoming a source of concern in terms of social cohesion.

The basic premise, and requirement, in a democratic election is to ascertain through the ballot the wish of the majority of voters in the constituency concerned. It cannot therefore be argued that the FPTP system now in vogue, whatever may have been the compulsions for adopting it, is theoretically valid or practically the most desirable. As a mature democracy, and one in which correctives in the electoral procedures continues to be work in progress, there is a need to debate the representative-ness of the representative, regardless of political convenience or administrative constraints.

This fundamental corrective in the electoral system can and must be added to other electoral reforms proposed by the Election Commission of India and others and are under consideration of the government, as indicated in the reply given by the government in Parliament recently. There is also a strong case for accelerating the process.

'Conditions Precedent for the Successful Working of Democracy' was the title of a lecture given by Dr Ambedkar in December 1952. He defined democracy as 'a form and method of government whereby revolutionary changes in the economic and social life of the people are brought about without bloodshed'. He listed seven conditions as essential for the successful functioning of a democracy and said there should be (a) no glaring inequalities in society, (b) a strong opposition, (c) no tyranny of the majority over the minority, (d) equality in law and administration, (e) observance of constitutional morality, (f) functioning of moral order in society and (g) public conscience.

Ambedkar concluded the lecture by mentioning some cases of failure of democracy and said, 'We ought to be very cautious and very considerate regarding our own future.'

Six decades later, we have to concede that the glass of democracy remains half-full. We have practised electoral democracy mechanically without making it fully representative. Our electoral procedures and practices have accentuated, rather than diminished, social cleavages. We have yet to succeed in eradicating electoral malpractices. We have allowed money power in all its manifestations to distort electoral outcomes. Our political process depicts ideological decadence and a declining observance of constitutional morality. Our society exhibits a disturbing disregard for moral order and public conscience and, in the words of an eminent academic, 'the lines between legality and illegality, order and disorder, state and criminality, have come to be increasingly porous'.

Are we on a slippery slope? There is, clearly an imperative need for rejuvenating our commitment to the values, objectives and the judicious balance of the Constitution.

5
PRUDENCE AND THE MORAL IMPERATIVE

GOPALASWAMI PARTHASARATHI, WHO WAS THE first vice chancellor of the Jawaharlal Nehru University, helped shape the institution both physically and spiritually, and this piece is a way of remembering his multi-faceted personality and diverse pursuits. He would have had no difficulty in concurring with an Arabic couplet of the classical period:

> *Tilka aathar-o-na, tadullu alaina*
> *Fa unzuru baad-a-na ilal aathar*
>
> These are our works, these works our souls display
> Behold our works when we have passed away

'GP', as he was popularly known, has been described as 'one of the most influential figures in our national life and a fine product of the Nehru era. His contributions were wide-ranging, solid and unadvertised'. President K.R. Narayanan called him 'an undeclared social rebel' who 'made no fuss about his radical social approach to life'. As the late A.K. Damodaran wrote in a memorial volume, 'he was never a Marxist, but he was personally a socialist'.

Parthasarathi was not a professional diplomat but diplomacy became his life. He did useful work as chairman of the International Commission for Supervision and Control in Indo-China; as ambassador to Indonesia, China and Pakistan; and as our permanent representative to UN in New York. Above all, as foreign-policy advisor and troubleshooter for Prime Ministers Indira and Rajiv Gandhi, he had a ringside view of events and his contributions were quiet but substantive. Like other humans, he could be fallible.

Note: First G. Parthasarathi Memorial Lecture, 25 March 2013, New Delhi.

He crossed the fine line between diplomacy and statecraft with ease; in the process, he contributed to both. He was an adroit practitioner of the art of negotiation and brought to it the required temperament.

Much has changed since his times but state actors continue to be on the global scene with age-old dilemmas. Hence the continuing need for diplomacy in a changed, and changing, world. The task of statesmen remains, as Bismarck put it, to travel on the stream of time, which they can neither create nor direct, but upon which they can steer with more or less skill or experience.

This skill and experience was present in the persona of GP. He believed in and articulated the Nehruvian approach to world affairs, premised on the search for security and stability in South Asia, promotion of world peace, de-colonization, non-alignment to power blocs, strategic autonomy, friendship to all and promotion of India's development and the hierarchy of national interests, as perceived from time to time.

In the post-Cold War world of our times, GP would have felt vindicated on some aspects and acutely unhappy about others. The diplomat in him would have relished responding creatively to the new challenges.

The quest for a cooperative, egalitarian and just world order was very much an ingredient of the approach GP subscribed to. The Purposes and Principles on the UN Charter, and various projects for the preferred world of the future, sought to move towards it, but without much success. The inherent inequality of states, and the structural violence between them and within them, ensured its failure, and at a high cost.

Two decades back and surveying the global turmoil on the eve of the 21st century, Zbigniew Brzezinski described the 20th century as a period of 'organised insanity', of mega-myths and meta-deaths. He suggested thinking in the direction of 'some shared criteria of self-restraint', of 'the political need of shared moral consensus in the increasingly congested and intimate world of the twenty first century'.[1]

The march of events, however, does not indicate improvement in the first decade of the present century. Instead of developing a shared moral consensus, the effort has been prescriptive, premised on political, economic and military power. The propensity to explore and realize new forms of dominance seems to continue unabated.

Last year, focusing on the emergence of Asia and the resultant dispersal of global power, Brzezinski opined that 'geopolitical equilibrium in the twenty-first-century Asia has to be based more on a regionally self-sustaining and constructive approach to interstate relations and less on regionally divisive military alliances with non-Asian powers', adding that 'the United States can and should be the key player in helping Asia avoid a struggle for regional domination, by mediating conflicts and offsetting power imbalances among potential rivals.'[2]

In other words, and in the absence of primacy, dominance in some shape or the other would still be the desired objective. The lessons learnt in the recent past, as the editorials in the *Financial Times* on 4 March 2013 and the *New York Times* on 19 March 2013 tend to show, are inadequately imbibed. This sustains Philip Windsor's observation that strategic thinking is 'too optimistic' and that many of its proponents 'cling to that optimism even in the face of disaster'.

Would this suffice for the world of the future that is unfolding before us?

Abba Eban, a consummate practitioner of the art of diplomacy, once observed that 'wisdom is born only when illusions die'. He cited with approval the historian Herbert Butterfield's observation that the underlying objective of the post-1945 era was to 'clarity the principles of prudence and moral obligation which have held together the international society of states throughout its history and still holds it together'.[3]

This combination of two seemingly discordant elements—prudence and moral obligation—is within the realm of possible. The critical question is about the proportions of the mix: at what point does one overwhelm the other? How morally valid is the resulting outcome? There is a view, articulated by Abba Eban, among others, that diplomacy should concentrate on practical goals like reciprocal self-interest, to the exclusion of arguments about virtue and conscience.

There are clear indications that in the coming decades we would witness both a diffusion of power and a shift in the nature of power. Alongside, there would be a change in the typology of challenges that would confront individual societies or humanity at large; these would include demographics, climate, urbanization and technology. The domain of self-interest would accordingly change. The process is already underway. Responses would thus need to be innovative, timely and appropriate. The objective would be to avoid self-destruction and preserve the world for future generations.

One other factor is relevant. For over a century and a half, in the words of Mr Pankaj Mishra, 'the West has seen Asia through the narrow perspective of its own strategic and economic interests, leaving unexamined— and unimagined—the collective experience and subjectivities of Asian people'.[4] The projection of an alternate version of modernity, drawing on this experience, as also on the limitations of the Western experience, is essential. It remains a work in progress.

The question that would have been posed to GP had he been around today is simply formulated: what should be the response pattern of Indian diplomacy—in terms of content and methodology—to the new challenges?

A simplistic response would be to protect national interest. The concept itself, however, is a slippery one, used to describe as well as prescribe policy. Citation of 'national interest' often becomes a closure clause. Its conceptual analysis necessitates dissection. What is national interest? Is it a monolith? Is it a constant? Is it synonymous with, or wider than, strategic interest? How, and by whom, is it determined? How is the validity of such determination assessed?

Some years back Peter Trubowitz analysed the sectional and regional dynamics at different points of time in American decision-making and concluded that 'national interest is defined by societal interests who have the power to work the political system to translate their preferences into policy' and that there is no single national interest when it comes to foreign policy. A similar study in terms of Indian impulses may yield interesting results.

The primary duty of the state in any society is to provide security, to protect it from external aggression and internal disturbance and to create conditions for the promotion of welfare and prosperity of its citizens. A few decades back, this was understood to mean physical security; today, it is focused on traditional and non-traditional, military and non-military, security, or comprehensive human security. More recently, Professor T.K. Oommen has expanded the ambit of security to make it 'the conjoint concern of three pillars, namely state, market and civil society' and argued that 'a society free from genocide, culturecide and ecocide may be conceptualized as a secure society'.[5] I can add to it 'hydrocide', a term that was mentioned in a waste water management seminar very recently.

Most readers would know well that concepts can be double-edged swords. They can and have opened the door for a modified, modulated definition of state sovereignty and national interest. The implications of these for the conduct of foreign policy are yet to be fully spelt out.

While new threats emerge, the older ones remain in place. This is evident from the typology of threats faced by us since Independence; these can be summed up in the following:

- Threats emanating from the nature of the international order: These include international arrangements that threaten our security, political or economic interests and thereby constrain our policy options.
- Ideological threats: These include external or domestic attempts to posit an alternate view to the basic structure of the Indian state and its core values of secularism, pluralism and peaceful coexistence of multiple identities within the framework of a union of states.
- Territorial and resource disputes: These relate to territorial and water disputes with neighbours.
- Internal threats: These range from ethnic, religious, regional and caste-based grievances; political dissatisfaction; separatist and secessionist agendas; ideological movements motivated by economic deprivation or injustice; traffic in narcotics and drugs; and terrorism in all its forms and manifestations.
- Threats emanating from environmental degradation and pandemics.

Each of these had, and continues to have, external dimensions. Given the geopolitical and socio-economic landscape, there is reason to believe that none of these would disappear in the immediate future. This highlights the need to muster all the resources of the state within the realm of diplomacy in quest of peaceful and acceptable solutions. It is here that the art and science of negotiation comes into play, a technique at which G. Parthasarathi was adept.

Negotiation in professional literature is described as the process of consideration of a dispute or situation by peaceful means, other than judicial or arbitral processes, with a view to promoting or reaching among the parties concerned or interested some understanding or amelioration, adjustment or settlement of the dispute or situation. For this reason, negotiations (even if they carry the threat of resort to violence), are cheaper than armed conflicts and less uncertain than arbitration. It can take different forms.

The value of a diplomat, therefore, lies in his ability to communicate, negotiate and persuade. Cardinal Richelieu, who knew a thing or two about the art, said the duty of a diplomat is 'to negotiate continuously, directly as in more devious ways, and in all place'. It requires patience, an ability to penetrate the thought process of the interlocutor and its limitations and a willingness to adjust and accommodate. Negotiations must be conducted without illusions. A negotiator, in Arthur Lall's words, must remember the general rule that each party to an international negotiation must emerge from it without having suffered a complete defeat. Revolutionary change through negotiation is therefore a rarity.

Beyond the methodology of negotiations lies the question of content. There has been much debate of late whether the earlier consensus about India's foreign policy still exists, whether it is still premised on a set of principles, whether it still advocates what has been called a 'particular ideology'. Much of this is based on, and reflective of, what the philosopher Gilbert Ryle called 'systematically misleading expressions'. Consensus does not imply unanimity, principles do not exclude realism and ideology need not imply the thought category only of a certain orientation.

A close examination of foreign-policy pronouncements in the past six decades would show general adherence to Nehru's early pronouncements: that India would pursue an independent foreign policy compatible with her own national interests, would keep away from power blocs, would cooperate with all who cooperate with us and work for world peace. Nor can the foresight of his observation of 15 August 1949 be overlooked:

> Our position in the world ultimately depends on the unity and strength of the country, on how far we proceed in the solution of our economic and other problems and how much we can raise the depressed masses of India.

Similar views were expressed by Indira Gandhi after a moment of triumph: prevent any erosion of our independence, assert of our freedom of judgement and action, friendship with every nation, no permanent estrangements, no interest in export of ideology.

In January last year, a group of scholars and strategic thinkers attempted 'to identify the basic principles that should guide India's foreign and strategic policy over the next decade'. Their stated purpose was to identify challenges and threat and define options that would enhance our strategic autonomy and maximize choices in a volatile and uncertain world, full of uncertainty as well as of great opportunity.

In this context, and premised on the unlikelihood of enduring coalitions based on fixed structural positions in the world economy, they sought to redefine non-alignment as 'skilful management of complicated coalitions and opportunities'. A prerequisite for this, they added, would be the need to maintain domestic power and legitimacy in more competitive and stringent conditions of transparency, good governance and accountability.

None of this, it would seem, is likely to contradict the basic premise and approach enunciated in different formulations in the past six decades, nor would it modify or change the content and objective of policy. A new top dressing, occasional deviations and variations in emphasis is nevertheless visible and so is the support base in terms of domestic politics.

A contributing factor for deviations is the pressure emanating from states. Some of these impinge on or constrict the centre's ability to conduct foreign relations. A serious student of Indian polity has observed that 'undermining the Centre's governance over its own jurisdiction does not do any service to the federal idea', adding that 'today the Indian federalism is gravely endangered by populist imperatives originating in the states which encroach so far into the Union's jurisdiction as to enervate Parliament and the Union Executive'.

After lifelong experience in the field and at the desk, Professor Muchkund Dubey has concluded that 'diplomacy operates on a very thin margin of practical possibilities. In the case of India, the margin is provided by outsiders' perception of the country's strengths and weaknesses. This perception depends more on what is happening inside India than what is happening outside'.

A last teasing question relating to diplomacy and morality inevitably arises. Morality is defined as conformity to principles concerning goodness or badness of human conduct. Diplomacy is traditionally credited with an amoral tradition. Yet, its practitioners have at all times claimed to espouse moral values. Sir Henry Wotton's adage about 'a good man sent abroad to lie for his country', or about another ambassador's comment of it being 'a nasty job', is reflective of the age-old dilemma between the personal sense of what is right and what 'may best serve the preservation and aggrandizement of his own state'. Henry Kissinger was asked last year about the interplay of morality and pragmatism. 'In philosophy courses,' he answered, 'you deal with absolutes; in statesmanship you deal with nuances.'

This dichotomy, real or apparent, raises a set of questions: is conformity to moral norms required of individuals only, or of groups and states? If the latter, what would be the point of reference and the minimal and optimal limits of this conformity?

Amartya Sen has cited with approval Aristotle's dictum that we have 'to look for precision in each class of things just so far as the nature of the subject admits'. He adds that 'imperfect obligation, along with the inescapable ambiguities involved in that idea, can be avoided only if the rest of humanity—other than those directly involved—are exempted from any responsibility to try to do what they reasonably can to help'.

Perhaps the international community is in a position somewhat analogous to this.

Human beings live in organized communities called states, and the totality of states constitute the international community. Each member of this community has crafted for itself a concept of justice which, as John Rawls put it, is the first virtue of social institutions. The community of nations, on the other hand, has been characterized as an anarchical society with a complex set of relations amongst its members. The maintenance of order in this community is through the identification of common interests aimed at facilitating organized interaction and avoidance of conflict.

For the greater part of the 20th century the effort was on 'maintaining and extending the consensus about common interests and values' that constitute the building blocks of wider areas of agreement. The process is slow and time-consuming; progress, nevertheless, has been made. A first effort took the shape of the Covenant of the League of Nations in 1919. A qualitatively different beginning was made with the Charter of the United Nations and the Universal Declaration of Human Rights, followed by a host of conventions and declarations relating to interstate relations as well as to behaviour of states within their own territorial jurisdictions. These include the conventions on elimination of all forms of racial discrimination, discrimination against women, conventions against torture, corruption, transnational organized crime, corruption, illicit traffic in narcotic and psychotropic substances, chemical weapons, etc. as also the conventions on the law of the sea, protection of ozone layer, and biological biodiversity.

While most of these are declaratory rather than mandatory, their cumulative impact on state behaviour and action is noticeable. They can be, and have been, invoked to bring pressure to bear on states who deviate from these norms. To that extent, it can be said that the ambit of common interests has continued to expand and, along with it, so has the propensity to confirm to a new set of norms. The effort, and the results achieved, is a product of an evolving vision assisted by diligent consensus-building. Diplomacy has been the handmaiden of this endeavour. Patiently but persistently, it has helped shape perceptions, bridge gaps, innovate solutions.

There is, however, another side of the picture. State entities, a product of history, acquire legitimacy in domestic terms and its recognition internationally. The international community too is a product of time and carries the scars of history. The quantum of legitimacy it bestows on itself, and on its decision-making processes, remains a matter of debate. Records would show that often the imperative is mendacious rather than moral.

There could be a third perspective, that of the visionary. In 1994, in a seminal lecture entitled 'Human Wrongs and International Relations', the political scientist Ken Booth urged the need to 'recognize the limits of state-centric perspectives' under conditions of globalization. He faulted the contemporary international community on five counts: (a) it is based on states that act as a shield when committing *human wrongs*, (b) it is not a real community because there is minimal reciprocity, (c) the governments that run it have a poor record when wrongs are committed by their friends, (d) most of them behave selfishly and (e) the system as a whole has not been normatively successful after three-and-a-half centuries.

Booth suggested, instead, the need for a global moral science or planetary societal morality, and argued that 'what is needed must have *moral* at its centre because the fundamental question of how we might and can live together concern values, not instrumental rationality'.[6]

A futurologist would revel in such a fascinating perspective. How would it impact on the earthly discipline of diplomacy? The experience of the past two decades, and the technological changes witnessed, would sustain Philip Bobbitt's thesis that 'the future is unlikely to be very much like the past' and that humanity is 'plunging into a new age of indeterminacy', which will upturn established notions of security.[7]

GP the humanist, the diplomatist, the policy planner, would not scoff at the idea. He would set up an interdisciplinary centre at JNU to study its implications for India, Asia and the world!

6

CITIZENS AND STATE CONDUCT

JUSTICE VITHAL MAHADEO TARKUNDE WAS a versatile man. An eminent judge whose calibre was acknowledged by the Supreme Court of India in a Full Court Reference, an ardent advocate of civil liberties and human rights, a supporter of causes fighting against injustice, a founder-member of the Committee on Judicial Accountability and the founder of the Centre for Public Interest Litigation. He kept alive, as he put it, 'the hope of the dawn of a new day' with the 'recognition of the inherent dignity and of the equal and unalterable rights of all the members of the human family as the foundation of freedom, justice and peace in the world'. His advocacy of secularism, his propagation of the philosophy of radical humanism and above all, his persistent efforts to highlight the fragility of individual liberty in the modern state as well as specific cases of injustice will be remembered for long. He was a passionate believer in the core values of the Constitution of India.

It has been said, over and over again, that eternal vigilance is the price of liberty, that power is ever being stolen from the many by the few and that the hand entrusted with power stands in danger of becoming the enemy of the people; hence the need for continual oversight to ensure that a people must be kept sufficiently awake to the principle of not letting liberty be smothered in material prosperity.

In a widely reported judgement in July 2011, the Supreme Court of India highlighted the imperative of ensuring 'conditions of human dignity within the ambit of fraternity'.[1] Thus, the operative concepts are *dignity* and *equal and unalterable rights to all*. With this in mind, I propose to explore

---

Note: Eighth V.M. Tarkunde Memorial Lecture, 21 November 2014, New Delhi.

the state of play with regard to the civil liberties and human rights in the context of what WE, the PEOPLE of INDIA, gave to themselves in the Constitution. The constitution-makers were aware that sovereignty to be commensurate with justice, had to be embedded in democracy[2] and, as an eminent jurist has observed, the Rule of Law cannot coexist with traditional conceptions of absolute sovereignty.[3] This, in fact, was the trend of informed opinion throughout the past century and, as early as 1914, Ernest Barker had penned an essay 'The Discredited State', in which he depicted sovereignty in internal matters as 'Poison—not to be taken internally', since it leads to a false view of the law.[4]

It is generally accepted that a pre-requisite of participatory governance is a commitment of the state to its own laws and to their uniform application. The term 'Rule of Law' is a part of our daily vocabulary and implies supremacy of law, equality before the law and fair and equal access to justice. As one jurist has put it, 'the Indian constitutional conception of the Rule of Law links its four core notions: rights, development, governance and justice'. This approach has been upheld in judicial pronouncements, with the Supreme Court describing the Rule of Law as 'a potent instrument of social justice to bring about equality in results'.

The debate over the core principles of the Constitution has stretched over six decades. Social philosophers, political scientists, jurists, courts of law, public personalities, political activists and informed citizens have been active participants. The explicit provisions are evident enough; the text also has, secreted in its interstices, many values that have been dilated upon and amplified in judicial pronouncements. These have been reinforced by international covenants to which India is a signatory and which have become a part of the law of the land.

The Constitution of India did not emerge in a vacuum. It was a product of the freedom struggle and of the values and principles enunciated and honed over decades. Issues of rights and liberties were of practical concern to the freedom fighters. Apart from individual acts of assertion of rights, perhaps the first initiative to form a civil liberties organization was taken by Jawaharlal Nehru in November 1936, when he founded the Indian Civil Liberties Union (ICLU) with Rabindranath Tagore as its president. Precision to the task on hand, and its pitfalls, was forthcoming from Dr Ram Manohar Lohia. 'The concept of civil liberties,' he said, 'defines State-authority within clear limits. It assigns well-defined liberties to the people. The task of the State is to protect these liberties. But the States usually do not like the task and act contrarily. Armed with the concept of civil liberties, the people develop an agitation to force the State to keep within clear and well-defined limits.'[5]

The quest for civil liberties did not cease with the end of colonial rule. The march of events after Independence brought into sharper focus the imperatives of sovereignty and nationalism and their implications for civil rights. Some of these became evident after 26 June 1975; in the words of a close observer, 'these events changed the basic relationship between the citizen and the State'.[6] It propelled the formation, later that year, of the People's Union for Civil Liberties and Democratic Rights (PUCDR), later to be named People's Union for Civil Liberties (PUCL). The purpose was to mobilize, not to stand outside the state, but to make the state more responsive and to recognize its constitutional obligations towards its citizens.[7]

The comprehension and advocacy of civil rights has undergone quantitative and qualitative changes in the past four decades. Debates over 'civil rights' have progressed into wider realms of 'democratic rights' and then to 'human rights'. Alongside, new dimensions have emerged as social movements focusing on women, Dalits, regional, minority and environmental issues came into focus. Each of these developed principally in relation to the state, since the state was the only conduit through which all segments of society related to each other.

In the final analysis, therefore, the focus is on the conduct of the state in relation to its own citizens, keeping in mind Rousseau's dictum that 'there will always be a great difference between subduing a multitude and ruling a society'.

A primary function of the state, in its most productive form, is to dispense justice to its citizens, since justice, as John Rawls rightly pointed out, 'is the first virtue of institutions' and 'in a just society the liberties of equal citizenship are taken as settled and the rights secured by justice are not subject to political bargaining or to the calculus of social interests'.[8]

Two broad categories seem to emerge in considering the failure of the state to deliver. In the first place, *act of omission*, or those matters where the state qua state should have acted in terms of its laws or constitution. Indications of this are readily available in various social development indices. Secondly, *act of commission*, or those acts that were plainly illegal or exceeded the legal or public morality limits prescribed by the law. These can be assessed in terms of the human rights norms present in our laws or subscribed to.

Credible documentation with regard to both categories is available nationally and internationally.

The obligations of the Republic of India towards its citizens have been stated in the Constitution, particularly in the sections on Fundamental Rights and Directive Principles of State Policy. A separate section delineates the Fundamental Duties of Citizens. Together, they amplify the vision and the principles enunciated in the Preamble namely, to *secure* to all citizens social, economic and political Justice; Liberty of thought, expression, belief, faith and worship; and Equality of status and opportunity; and furthermore *to promote among them* Fraternity assuring the dignity of the individual and the unity and integrity of the Nation.

A broad categorization of state responsibility in terms of constitutional obligations would relate to those matters that concern economic, social and cultural rights and the right to development in the first place. A second set of responsibilities would pertain to the provision of security and its achievement through the use of legitimately sanctioned force within stated parameters. In the third set, the state is required to ensure access to justice through appropriate mechanisms to redress grievances.

A set of questions seem to emerge:

- Has state responsibility been institutionalized for each of the above?
- What is its extent and efficacy?
- To what degree does the Indian state practice conform to global standards indicated in international instruments to which we have subscribed?

The answer to the first question is in the affirmative. The Constitution and the various rights-centric statutes prescribe the policy and institutional framework for human rights' protection; they also enjoin the concerned state institutions in discharging their responsibilities. The institutional safeguards for the rights enshrined in the Constitution include an independent judiciary and the separation of judicial and executive functions. Legislation and exercise of executive power is subject to judicial review with regard to its constitutionality. In the event of infringement of an individual's fundamental rights, the highest court in the land can be moved.

Our development objectives have been carefully spelt out in the 12th Five Year Plan. It is to seek 'a broad-based improvement in living standards of all sections of the people through a growth process that is faster than the past, more inclusive and also more environmentally sustainable'. This requires a carefully crafted strategy for management of resources, demographics, inclusiveness, rural–urban balance, energy security, environmental sustainability, a sustained period of social peace internally and absence of conflict abroad, particularly in the neighbourhood.

Much has been done to move towards the development targets for the country. Innovative legislation pertaining to right to food, education, information and rural employment has been put in place. However, a critical analysis of the results would show imbalance in implementation and insufficient attention to some other areas. We rank 134 out of 187 in the United Nations Development Programme's (UNDP) Human Development Index and while the poverty rate has shown a decline from 45.3 to 37.2 per cent in the decade ending 2004, the debate about nutrition levels and poverty line continues unabated. The average growth rate in 2007–2011 was 8.2 per cent but the decline of poverty in the same period was 0.8 per cent. A poet may well say:

> *Roshan kahin bahar ke imkaan huai to hain*
> *Gulshan main chaak chand garibaan huai to hain*
> *Ab bhi khizan ka raj hai lekin kahin kahin*
> *Goshe rahe-chaman main ghazal khwan huai to hain*

[Though autumn remains dominant, prospects of spring have brightened and flowers have started to bloom.]

At the international level, India is a signatory to the six core human rights covenants. It is committed to the rights proclaimed in the Universal Declaration of Human Rights, 1948. We have signed and ratified Human Rights Conventions which inter alia include the International Covenant on Civil and Political Rights; International Covenant on Economic, Social and Cultural Rights; Convention on the Elimination of all forms of Racial Discrimination; Convention on the Elimination of all forms of Discrimination against Women; and the Convention on the Rights of the Child. In 2005, we ratified the two Optional Protocols to the Convention on the Rights of the Child and thereafter the Convention on the Rights of Persons with Disability.

We have signed, but not yet ratified, the Convention against Torture and Other Cruel, Inhuman or Degrading Treatment or Punishment.[9] The same holds for the Convention on Enforced Disappearances.

It is relevant to recall that Section 2(d) of the Protection of Human

Rights Act, 1993, defines 'human rights' as the rights relating to life, liberty, equality and dignity of the individual guaranteed by the Constitution or embodied in the International Covenants and enforceable by courts in India. This definition is in conformity with the accepted interpretation of human rights. The Supreme Court has, in its concern for human rights, also developed a highly advanced public interest litigation regime.

It is thus clear that the requisite intellectual, legal and institutional framework for protection and promotion of human rights is in place. Questions, however, do arise in regard to their efficacy in actual implementation, as cases of discrimination based on religion, caste, language, ethnicity, work and economic status continue to be reported. These relate both to violation or denial of rights by state agencies and to violation or denial of rights by individuals and groups to individuals and groups. The weak—individual or group—is invariably the victim.

What is most concerning is the state conduct resulting in violation or denial of rights of citizens. It has been observed that there is a 'profound disenchantment with the State at the popular level' where 'the lines between legality and illegality, order and disorder, State and criminality have come to be (viewed) as increasingly porous'.[10]

The most serious human rights violations by the state vis-à-vis its citizens pertain to Article 21. Some of these are abuse by the police and security forces, including extrajudicial killings, custodial deaths, torture, arbitrary arrest and detention, enforced disappearances; poor prison conditions that are frequently life-threatening; lengthy pre-trial detention; and widespread corruption at all levels of the government, leading to denial of justice. This is particularly acute in areas of internal conflict, such as Jammu and Kashmir, the Northeast and the Naxal belt where serious complaints about the misuse of laws like the Armed Forces Special Powers Act (AFSPA), the Disturbed Areas Act (DAA) or the Public Safety Act (PSA) continue to be made. Much of this is credible, has been carefully documented and reflects poorly on the state and its agents.[11]

According to the latest Annual Report of the Ministry of Home Affairs, during the period 1 January 2013 to 31 March 2014, the National Human Rights Commission (NHRC) conducted investigation of 6,834 cases, including 4,450 cases of death in judicial custody, 448 cases of death in police custody and 186 cases of police encounter deaths.[12] These figures speak for themselves. The situation is exacerbated by the fact that the judiciary is overburdened and court backlogs cause lengthy delays or the denial of justice.

Despite the constitutional and legal guarantees, religious minorities continue to be the target of violence and discrimination from time to time. Patterns of systematic mobilization of hate and divisive politics are discernable; in many cases these have been pursued with impunity. The same holds for other weaker sections of society including Scheduled Castes and Scheduled Tribes, women, children and persons with disabilities. Credible data on these is available in government, academic and civil society reports. These cut at the root of the constitutional principle of equality of opportunity and equal access to justice, and highlight the failure of the state to act appropriately. As we embark on the path of rapid economic growth and development, the issue of finding a balance between traditional rights of citizens, with environmental imperatives and economic objectives, will have to be addressed by the state; else, social tensions will undermine the development agenda.

A particular area of concern is the inadequacy of state action in relation to women. The UN Special Rapporteur on Violence against Women has reported that it is systematic and occurs in the public and private spheres. It is underpinned by the persistence of patriarchal social norms and inter- and intra-gender hierarchies. Women are discriminated against and subordinated not only on the basis of sex, but on other grounds, such as caste, class, ability, sexual orientation, tradition and other realities. The manifestations of violence against women are a reflection of the structural and institutional inequality that is a reality. An eminent former judge had not too long ago observed that 'even today, most women in India neither have freedom nor liberty to take decisions'.[13] The need for greater social awareness, and correctives at all levels of society, is imperative.

Record shows that a number of progressive legal and policy initiatives have been taken by the government. Equally true is the fact that implementation is tardy, that 'mindset' obstacles and social prejudices are formidable, that allocation of resources is inadequate and that contradictions persist between economic policies, 'development priorities' and national and international human rights commitments.

To conclude, let me draw your attention to two sets of impulses. The first suggests dogged defence of the status quo; the second, a measure of introspection. A plural society, and a mature system of governance, would opt for the latter, more so because we stand committed to constitutional and global norms. Pursuant to this, India is a party to, and has participated in, the Universal Periodic Review of Human Rights held by the Human

Rights Council in May 2012. The Status Report prepared by the Working Group on Human Rights after the second review summed up its assessment, inter alia, with the following observation:

> Despite a number of progressive and policy initiatives taken by the Indian Government, the continued prevalence of human rights violations across the country poses manifold challenges. The claim of rapid economic development does not hold any value when it fails to include the excluded. Lack of proper implementation of government policies due to the bureaucratic lethargy, inadequate allocation of resources, contradiction between different policies, other development priorities and the so called national and international interests continue to hinder to the full realisation of human rights for India's most vulnerable. The ever-growing trend of atrocities against religious minorities, women, children, SCs & STs, apathy towards the disabled and other disadvantaged people, constitute a scar on the face of Indian democracy...

In a foreword to the Report, the convenor suggested that:

> India must meet the human rights accountability challenge defined by the contents of its Constitution, the international human rights instruments it has ratified, and the recommendations that have emanated from the UPR I and UPR II processes at the UN as well as from other UN treaty bodies and special procedures. To meet this enormous challenge, nothing but a radical shift in economic, social and security policies is needed—both at the central and state levels.[14]

We, as a people, need to awaken our collective conscience, strive for fulfilment of national norms and global standards and induce fuller accountability into the system of governance at all levels, so that the culture of impunity ends, and the state and its functionaries are held accountable for every act of omission or commission.

7

DEMOCRACY AND DISSENT

NO SINGLE ADJECTIVE, OR SET of adjectives, can adequately describe the personality of Ram Manohar Lohia. For over two decades he was the 'stormy petrel' of Indian politics. He was erudite and had a passionate interest in all matters relating to human freedom, justice and dignity. He earned recognition of his knowledge of law from none other than the British magistrate trying him for preaching against the war effort in 1939. Earlier, in November 1936, he joined Jawaharlal Nehru when the latter founded the ICLU with Rabindranath Tagore as its president. The concept of civil liberties, Lohia said on that occasion, 'defines state authority within clear limits. The task of the State is to protect these liberties. But States usually do not like the task and act contrarily. Armed with the concept of civil liberties, the people develop an agitation to force the State to keep within clear and well defined limits.'[1]

Dr Lohia was an idealist and had identified his icons in the early period; Mahatma Gandhi represented his 'dream', Nehru his 'desire' and Subhas Bose his 'deed'.[2] This idealism led him to request Gandhiji to propose to world leaders a four-point programme: (a) cancellation of all past investments by one country in another, (b) unobstructed passage and the right of settlement to everybody all over the world, (c) political freedom of all peoples and nations of the world and constituent assemblies and (d) some kind of world citizenship.[3]

Gandhiji was indulgent, but did not act on the suggestion.

Lohia was a socialist and an avowed anti-communist. He was amongst the

---

Note: First Ram Manohar Lohia Memorial National Lecture, 23 September 2015, Gwalior.

few who struggled with the difficulty of transferring the ideology of socialism from Europe to non-European cultural locations.[4] He differed with the Congress leadership on a whole range of issues. These included the acceptance of the decision on Partition in 1947 and he wrote a detailed monograph entitled *The Guilty Men of India's Partition* (1960). He had pronounced views on the caste system and the damage it has done to the Indian psyche. These were candidly, albeit brutally, expressed in another monograph, *The Caste System* (1964). At the same time, he was realistic about ways of modulating it, as is evident from the following passage:

> To stop talking of caste is to shut one's eyes to the most important single reality of the Indian situation. One does not end caste merely by wishing it away. A 5000 year long selection of abilities has been taking place. Certain castes have become especially gifted. Thus for instance the Marwari Bania is on top with regard to industry and finance and the Saraswat Brahmin in respect of intellectual pursuits. It is absurd to talk about competing with these castes unless others are given preferential opportunities and privileges. The narrowing selection of abilities must now be broadened over the whole and that can only be done if for two or three or four decades backward castes and groups are given preferential opportunities [sic]. I must here make distinction between opportunities for employment and those for education. No one should be turned away from the portals of an educational institution because of his caste. Society on the other hand would be perfectly justified in turning those away from its employment whom it has so far privileged. Let them earn their living elsewhere. Society is required alone to equip them with the necessary educational ability.[5]

Despite the adulation of the earlier years, Lohia's criticism of Nehru and his policies after the early 1940s was trenchant. His articulation of the principles of the Congress Socialist Party transmuted itself in the 1950s into the Praja Socialist Party which, as he put it, 'is as distant from the Congress party as it is from the communist and the communalist parties'.[6] He had a nuanced view of the parliamentary form of government and advocated alongside the option of direct mass action. He told his party colleagues in 1955 that instead of an insurrectionary path they ought to choose a balanced mix of constitutional action and civil resistance where necessary.[7]

Lohia's advocacy of issues relating to farmers took practical shape in

1954 when the Uttar Pradesh government increased irrigation rates for water supplied from canals to cultivators. In his speeches in the area, he incited cultivators not to pay 'the enhanced irrigation rates' to the government. He was severely critical of the state government. He was arrested and charged under Section 3 of the UP Special Powers Act, 14 of 1932. In a habeas corpus petition in the High Court, he contended that the Act, and particularly Section 3 of it, stood repealed under Article 13 of the Constitution on account of it being inconsistent with the provisions of Article 19. The Court, in its judgment, addressed two questions: first, that Section 3 of the Act, making it penal for a person by spoken words to instigate a class of persons not to pay dues recoverable as arrears of land revenue, was inconsistent with Article 19 (1)(a) of the Constitution and second, that the restrictions imposed by this section were not in the interests of public order. The Court ordered that he be released, and costs paid.[8]

Throughout the 1950s and the early part of the 1960s, Lohia's critique of government policies was unrelenting. He was elected to the Lok Sabha in August 1963 and, a few days later, delivered a sharply focused speech in an adjournment motion, expressing dissatisfaction with the government's policies and postures. He even used some archaic expressions: 'Parliament,' he said, 'is the master whereas the prime minister is its servant. The servant has to behave modestly and politely with his master.' He utilized the parliamentary platform to express powerfully his views on what he considered were shortfalls in domestic and foreign-policy issues. At the time of the presidential election in 1969, in which he was an ardent supporter of the former Chief Justice of India, Subba Rao, he called upon the youth to think about politics focused on five principles: socialist unity, unity of all opposition parties, joint demonstrations, single purpose platforms and hard work.[9]

Ram Manohar Lohia's political legacy, and the impulses generated by it, are very much in evidence today and have been so for over two decades. 'In the world of politics,' as one of his ardent scholar-activist followers has put it, 'Lohia is remembered today as the originator of OBC (Other Backward Classes) reservations; the champion of backward castes in the politics of north India; the father of non-Congressism; the uncompromising critic of the Nehru-Gandhi dynasty; and the man responsible for the politics of anti-English.'[10]

Commentary on this graphic summing up is unnecessary. Time and experience will tell if Lohia would have urged a greater measure of flexibility in the strategies of affirmative action currently underway. My purpose is to focus on the principle of dissent in democracy that Dr Lohia personified and its relevance for the continuing success of functioning democracies anywhere in the world.

In 1950, the people of India gave themselves a Constitution that promised to secure to all citizens, inter alia, 'liberty of thought, expression, belief, faith and worship'. This was given a concrete shape by the specific rights guaranteed by Articles 19 and 25 and the associated framework ensuring their implementation. The past six-and-a-half decades have witnessed the manner, and the extent, of their actualization.

The Constitution was not crafted in a vacuum. It was preceded by the freedom movement and the values enunciated in it. These were formally encapsulated in the Objectives Resolution of 22 January 1947. At the same time, the Constitution-makers, or some amongst them, were not unaware of the pitfalls. In his speech at the end of the drafting process in the Constituent Assembly, Ambedkar had warned about the impending 'life of contradictions'.

Ambedkar spoke of the danger posed to political democracy by focusing on the disconnect between political equality and socio-economic inequality. A few decades later, two eminent sociologists commented on some of its underlying aspects. They noted the backdrop of two competing narratives: 'the civilisational history of co-survival of communities and the political history of ethnic competition and conflicts'. They said, 'the use of the coercive power of the State for effecting homogenization in the society and the counter-violence by the political-cultural entities resisting such incursions by the state constitute *the* problem of the political system in India today.' They enquired 'whether the institutional imperiousness of the liberal state can be effectively countered by the popular movements' and felt the challenge in India 'is to discover and press on the softer edges of the space within which the transformative, democratic movements find themselves enclosed. In this sense, the challenge for these movements is as much intellectual as political'.[11]

The quest for correctives often found expression through assertions relating to freedom of expression and its concomitant, the concept of dissent. It is a concept that contains within it the democratic right to object, oppose, protest and even resist. Cumulatively it can be defined as the unwillingness in an individual or group to cooperate with an established authority—social, cultural or governmental. In that sense, it is associated with critical thinking since, as Albert Einstein had put it, 'blind faith in authority is the greatest enemy of truth'.

It has been observed with much justice that the history of progress of mankind is a history of informed dissent. This can take many forms, ranging from conscientious objection to civil or revolutionary disobedience. In a democratic society, including ours, the need to accept difference of opinion is an essential ingredient of plurality. In that sense, the right to dissent also becomes the duty of dissent, since tactics to suppress dissent tend to diminish the democratic essence. In a wider sense, the expression of dissent can, and does, play a role in preventing serious mistakes, arising out of what has been called 'social cascades' and 'group polarization', which act as deterrents on free expression of views or sharing of information.[12]

Dissent as a right has been recognized by the Supreme Court of India as one aspect of the right of the freedom of speech guaranteed as a Fundamental Right by Article 19(1)(a) of the Constitution. The court has observed that 'the restrictions on the freedom of speech must be couched in the narrowest possible terms' and that the proviso of Article 19(2) is justiciable in the sense that the restrictions on it have to be 'reasonable' and cannot be arbitrary, excessive or disproportionate.[13]

In the globalizing world of today and in most countries having a democratic fabric, the role of civil society in the articulation of dissent has been and continues to be comprehensively discussed; so does the question of its marginalization or suppression.

Despite the unambiguously stated position in law, civil society concerns about constraints on the right of dissent in actual practice have been articulated powerfully. 'On the surface,' wrote one of our eminent academics sometime back, 'Indian democracy has a cacophony of voices. But if you scratch the surface, dissent in India labours under an immense maze of threats and interdictions.' Referring to the then new reporting requirements for NGOs, he said:

> 'Nothing is more fatal for disagreements and dissent than the idea that all of it can be reduced to hidden sub-texts or external agendas... The idea that anyone who disagrees with my views must be the carrier of someone else's subversive agenda is, in some ways, deeply anti-democratic. It does away with the possibility of genuinely good faith disagreement. It denies equal respect to citizens because it absolves you of taking their ideas seriously. Once we have impugned the source, we don't have to pay attention to the contents of the claim...This has serious consequences for dissent.'[14]

This was written in 2012. It is a moot point if, given the Pavlovian reflexes of the *Leviathan*, things would have changed for the better since then. Informed commentaries suggest the contrary.[15] Every citizen of the republic has the right and the duty to judge. Herein lies the indispensability of dissent.

8
INTERNATIONAL HUMAN RIGHTS DAY

THE INTERNATIONAL HUMAN RIGHTS DAY is one of those dates in the calendar that is remembered by all who care about humanity and wish to propel it away from brutality and towards humaneness in greater measure.

The concept of human rights is of ancient vintage. Until quite recently, however, it was selective rather than universal. Here lies the uniqueness of the date—December 10—that we have gathered to commemorate and celebrate.

It was on this day in 1948 that the General Assembly of the United Nations adopted the Universal Declaration of Human Rights, which recognized 'the inherent dignity and the equal and inalienable rights of all members of the human family' and declared it to be 'the foundation of freedom, justice and peace in the world' for 'all human beings' and 'a common standard of achievement for all peoples and nations'.

Subsequent documents adopted by the international community amplified the principles enunciated in the Universal Declaration and now cover basic civil, political, economic, social and cultural rights that all human beings should enjoy and that all societies should respect and protect.

Three characteristics of these rights need to be highlighted: (a) they are 'natural' and accrue to us by the virtue of being humans, (b) they are 'universal' and pertain to all human beings irrespective of nationality, place of residence, sex, national or ethnic origin, colour, religion, language or any other status, and (c) they are inalienable and cannot be taken away except in specific situations and according to due process.[1]

Pursuant to these basic principles enshrined in the Universal Declaration,

---

Note: Speech delivered at the inauguration of the event to commemorate the International Human Rights Day, 10 December 2015, New Delhi.

a number of covenants and declarations have been subscribed to by most—though not all—members of the international community. Their stated objective is to reinforce the commitment of member states as 'being intrinsic element of their obligations of sovereignty'. This principle emanates from the very nature of humans as social beings living in societies in which justice becomes the first virtue endowed with inviolability.

The most recent manifestation of this is the United Nations Human Rights Council set up by the UN General Assembly in March 2006 to strengthen the promotion and protection of human rights around the globe and for addressing situations of human rights' violation and making recommendations on them. Its operational mechanisms include the Universal Periodic Review to assess the human rights' situations in all member states and special procedures to examine, advise and publicly report on thematic issues or human rights' situations in specific countries.

Thus, the responsibility of national governments to uphold and implement international human rights standards is not in doubt. And yet, as T.S. Eliot wrote,

Between the idea
And the reality
Between the motion
And the act
Falls the Shadow[2]

The effort to bridge this gap continues. The question has been considered in the International Law Commission's work on the Responsibility of States for Internationally Wrongful Acts and in conjunction with implementation of the International Covenant on Economic, Social and Cultural Rights.

Over the past two decades, a consensus has emerged that with respect to human rights, states have a threefold responsibility: to respect, to protect and to fulfil their obligations. This has been expounded upon by the Office of the UN High Commissioner for Human Rights:

- The obligation to respect means that states must refrain from interfering with or curtailing the enjoyment of human rights.
- The obligation to protect requires states to protect individuals and groups against human rights', abuses.
- The obligation to fulfil means that states must take positive action to facilitate the enjoyment of basic human rights.

The extent to which these principles and international mechanisms based on them can, and do, go, as also the question of their universal applicability without exceptions, is the subject of vigorous debate and much controversy on international forums, premised as these are on the Westphalian principle and where the effort—genuine as well as motivated—to reconcile law and morality is unlikely to be fruitful in the foreseeable future.

While persisting in the effort to attain the desirable, it is somewhat easier to focus on the doable. I refer here to the human rights' commitment and performance of our own country.

The framers of our own Constitution were aware of the Universal Declaration of Human Rights. The Fundamental Rights enshrined in the Constitution cover most of the rights that had been articulated in the Universal Declaration. Article 14 establishes the Right to Equality, creating the basis of non-discrimination, a corner stone for the application of human rights.

Over the years our courts have dwelt on the notion of Fundamental Rights in the Constitution and have expanded their scope and nature. It can thus be argued with justice that many of the rights articulated in the Universal Declaration have now been subsumed under the expanded meaning of the Fundamental Rights. Article 21 in particular has seen intervention by courts to expand the meaning and scope as something more dynamic than the meaning attached to life and liberty. Right to Life now includes right to human dignity and quality of life.

Similarly, the Directive Principles of State Policy in Part IV of the Constitution go beyond the International Covenant on economic, social and cultural rights.

A mechanism, in the shape of The Protection of Human Rights Act, 1993, and the constitution of the National Human Rights Commission, the State Human Rights Commissions and Human Rights Courts, has been put in place for the enforcement of these rights. Certain other legislations, which may be referred to in the context of human rights, including Protection of Civil Rights Act, 1955, and Rules, 1977, as well as legislation providing for care and protection of especially vulnerable groups, have also been enacted.

Thus, the institutional structure for the attainment and enforcement of human rights is firmly in place. Our quest, therefore, needs to focus on:

- The extent to which the desired objectives have been attained;
- The practical impediments to their achievement;
- The efficacy of the governmental efforts to overcome them' and

- The civil society's role and its assessment of the human rights', situation in the country.

A perusal of reports from government and non-government organizations—both domestic and international—provides an overview of the human rights' monitoring and safeguard mechanisms in India.

The Annual Report of our National Human Rights Commission for 2011–2012 (the most recent one available) indicates the typology of human rights' violations: (1) custodial deaths; (2) police high-handedness, firing, encounters; (3) illegal detention, torture or firing by military, paramilitary forces and police; (4) violation of rights of Scheduled Castes and Scheduled Tribes; (5) atrocities on women and children; (6) bonded labour and child labour; (7) Right to Health; (8) cases of suo moto cognizance taken by NHRC.

The Annual Report of the Ministry of Home Affairs for 2014–2015 states that in this period, the NHRC's investigation division dealt with 5,439 cases of custodial death, including 3,707 cases of death in judicial custody, 326 cases of deaths in police custody and another 1,406 fact-finding cases. The number of cases of custodial death in 2011–2012 stood at 1,302.

The Universal Periodic Review on India for 2012–2016 by the Special Rapporteur in the Office of the UN High Commissioner for Human Rights carries a number of observations that need to be noted:

- A significant role has been played by the Supreme Court in interpreting the Constitution with a view to achieving justifiability of economic, social and cultural rights. The functioning of the judiciary however was hampered by a backlog and significant delay in administering cases of human right violations due to lack of capacity, manpower and resources.
- While welcoming the continuing work of the National Human Rights Commission, and the establishment of National Commission for the Protection of Child Rights, it expressed concern that the investigation of human right [sic] abuses continue to be conducted by the police who, in many cases, were also the alleged perpetrators. It urged the government to consider enacting special legislation to protect human rights defenders.
- Expression of deep concern that 'despite the Constitutional guarantee of non-discrimination, as well as the criminal law provisions punishing acts of discrimination, widespread and, often, socially accepted

discrimination, harassment and violence persisted against members of disadvantaged and marginalized groups, including women, Scheduled Castes and Tribes, urban poor, informal sector workers and religious minorities.'
- Expression of concern that the anti-torture bill (2010) introduced in the Indian Parliament following India's ratification of Convention against torture, was much diluted. Even this was eventually not approved by the Parliament.
- India was one of the few countries retaining the death penalty and in 2010 had voted against UN General Assembly resolution 65/206 on the *'Moratorium on the use of the death penalty'*.[3]

The *Global Citizenship Country Report Card*[4], which covers human rights, indicators, as well as transparency and good governance, in its latest report on India, calls India a 'climber', ranked fifth among its list of 12 pilot countries, behind Germany, Brazil, Peru and the United States. It noted that India had ratified six of the International Human Rights Convention and also ranked India high on account of the performance in right to self-determination indicator due to large-scale participation and conduct of free and fair elections in 2014. It, however, ranked India poorly on the non-discrimination index, particularly due to the continuing criminalization of homosexuality.

The Human Rights Watch World Report for 2015[5] criticized India for continuing with state censorship and imposition of certain restrictions on Non-Governmental Organisations (NGOs). It noted that caste-based discrimination, neglect of marginalized communities and violence against women continued. It expressed concern on what it called 'the lack of accountability of security forces', and recommended urgent police reforms to increase capacity and accountability. It also expressed concern at the continuation of the AFSPA in several parts of India.

It applauded the January 2014 judgment of the Supreme Court commuting the death sentence of 15 prisoners and establishing guidelines to safeguard the rights of prisoners on death row, but expressed concern at India's continuing use of the death penalty. The Report commended India for continuing to accept refugees from Tibet, Mayanmar and Afghanistan while noting that India had not ratified the UN Refugee Conventions.

The Amnesty International Report 2014/15[6] noted that despite 'progressive legal reforms in court rulings the state authorities had failed to prevent crimes against Indian citizens, including children, women, Dalits and Adivasis'. It expressed concern on the human rights' abuses by armed insurgent/terrorist groups, which killed and injured civilians and destroyed property. It regretted India's failure to pass a strong anti-torture bill, noting that torture and other ill-treatment continued to be used in state detention.

Many of the shortcomings mentioned in these reports have also figured in periodic reports of some national NGOs, in the media and in Parliament. It is evident, therefore, that there is, at times, a gap between what the official agencies project and what is perceived to be the situation on the ground. One reason for this is wider public awareness of human rights' norms; another is the extent and speed with which defaults or alleged violations are brought to public notice.

Many new issues have become part of the human rights' agenda and will remain crucial in the coming decades. The conflict over natural resources; the issue of gender equality and the increasing incidence of gender violence and of caste; communal, ethnic and sub-national conflicts among communities; and environmental implications of some developmental projects are some examples. Human rights abuses by non-state actors, such as violent insurgent groups, terrorists and extremists, both from the left and right, has also emerged as a major challenge.

Faced with these candid assessments, how should we, as a society, react to them? One possible reaction is to dismiss them as devoid of veracity or denounce them as the work of hostile elements, even consider their work as 'detrimental to national interest'. The other is to respond to them in a mature fashion.

In a vibrant and robust democracy like ours, there is no shame in acknowledging the faults and the lacunae that exist in the policies and institutions pertaining to human rights. Our point of reference should be the Constitution of India and the principles, rights and duties enunciated therein. On this basis, we are duty-bound, legally and morally, to address these challenges through firm and unbiased corrective actions by the state, civil society and other stakeholders. It is, and should be viewed as, a societal duty.

It is here that education in human rights' culture becomes critically important in educational institutions. Citizens and civil society institutions must, therefore, take a lead in helping us meet the moral challenges of our times.

We as a nation have to awaken our collective conscience. We also need to strive for global standards.

9
ROLE OF WOMEN LEGISLATORS IN NATION BUILDING

THE THEME 'ROLE OF WOMEN Legislators in Nation Building' is appropriate and timely, to reaffirm that women are entitled to their rights and freedoms without any discrimination.

There are primarily two matters of high priority on the national agenda. The first relates to women's political representation and the second to the performance of the women legislators in the legislatures. The two need to be considered together, sequentially, so that assessments and correctives are based on ground realities.

Women's vital role was unequivocally recognized in our freedom movement under the leadership of Mahatma Gandhi. The women of our country were drawn out not only to participate in large numbers, but also to play an important role in the non-violent struggle against colonial rule.[1] In 1929, championing the cause of women's rights, Gandhiji said: 'Women must have votes and equal legal status, but the problem does not end there. It only commences at the point where women begin to affect the political deliberations of the nation.'[2]

The framers of our Constitution had the wisdom and foresight to realize that without political equality between men and women, we cannot rightfully claim ourselves to be a true representative democracy. That is why equality before law was granted to both genders in the Constitution.

Giving women constitutional rights to suffrage is one thing, but its tangible impact in raising women's power and influence in polity and society

---

Note: First Conference of the Women Legislators in India, 5 March 2016, New Delhi.

is an altogether different matter. Notwithstanding the fact that almost 47 per cent of the total voters were women during the last Lok Sabha elections in 2014,[3] patriarchy and social norms have hindered its full reflection in positions of power.

More than two decades earlier, in 1993, the need was felt to give greater representation to women in elected bodies. This took shape in the 73rd and 74th Constitution Amendment Acts regarding membership and chairpersonships in panchayats and municipalities. This initiative redefined gender representation in the decision-making process at the grass-roots level. At present, there are 1.27 million elected women representatives in panchayats, which constitute 43.56 per cent of total elected representatives.[4] This is perhaps the largest ever representation of women in elected bodies anywhere in the world.

Despite the challenges of 'proxyism', women representatives have performed exceptionally well in the local bodies. In recognition of the good performance of women in local bodies, as many as 16 states have introduced 50 per cent reservation for women in panchayats. Other states may follow suit. However, the introduction of statutory requirement of meeting new eligibility conditions, such as a certain level of education, number of children or other criteria to fight panchayat elections in many states, is loaded against women. This calls for serious reflection.

Here, a paradox confronts us. The increase in women representation at local bodies has not led to a commensurate increase of women members in legislatures, both at the centre and the state. Today, our Parliament's gender profile is woefully unbalanced, with women constituting only 12 per cent of the total membership.[5] As such, the average number of women members in Parliament has never been more than 12 per cent since the first Lok Sabha[6]. In the states, too, the average share of women legislators is only 9 per cent in the Legislative Assemblies and only 6 per cent in Legislative Councils.[7]

This does not compare favourably with global trends. Apart from the Nordic pattern of around 40 per cent women's representation, a recent survey[8] by the Inter Parliamentary Union (IPU) shows a world average of 22.7 per cent in national parliaments.

A closer look at the participation of women parliamentarians lends weight to the notion that most, though not all, only cover issues related to women. This also seems to be sustained by data on their membership of parliamentary committees, though the responsibility for this state of affairs is to be shared by party leaderships who, in the final analysis, do the nominations. A few instances sustain this impression:

- There are just two women members in three Financial Committees out of their total strength of 74 members. While the Committee on Estimates has two women members from the Lok Sabha, there is none in the Committees on Public Accounts and Public Undertakings from both Houses.
- The Department-related Standing Committee on Finance does not have a single woman member, while the Committee on Railways has only one. The Committee on Home Affairs has got two women members whereas the Committee on Defence has four. In all, there are seven women members in these four committees out of their total strength of 124 members, thus constituting approximately 6 per cent.
- The 30-member Joint Committee on Insolvency and Bankruptcy Code, 2015 has only one woman member.
- Even the Committee on Security in Parliament Complex does not have any woman member other than the speaker as its chairperson.
- In contrast, however, the Joint Committee on Empowerment of Women has 28 women members out of the total strength of 30 members, constituting a whopping 93 per cent.

These facts call for some correction.

The first corrective has to be made by political parties. To shore up women's political representation, all political parties need to extend their support to ensure that the Constitutional Amendment Bill to provide for 33 per cent reservation to women in the Lok Sabha and State Legislative Assemblies is not delayed further.

Until then, they need to expand their pool of women candidates at least. If we see the track record of the six national parties in fielding women candidates during the last general elections (2014) we find that out of a total of 1,591 candidates fielded by them, only 146, constituting 9.17 per cent were women[9]. This is certainly not very encouraging.

Besides, the respective political parties must broad base their nomination while nominating their women members to the committees, statutory bodies as also while selecting speakers to participate in the debates in the House on other areas of public concern.

The leaders and whips of parties in the House need to overcome their own gender bias in engaging the women members in different parliamentary roles.

Above all, the women members themselves need to show their interest and contribute meaningfully to the debates.

The fact that women members, within the limited opportunity available to them, have demonstrated their concern over other issues of national interest, must tilt the balance in their favour.

The task of nation building is an arduous exercise and a complex process. It involves women as much as men. Several studies show that women's political participation results in tangible gains for democratic governance, including greater responsiveness to citizens' needs.[10] Women are also often the strongest voices for peace and non-violence. Women's leadership and conflict resolution styles embody democratic ideals and they tend to work in a less hierarchical, more participatory and more collaborative manner than their male counterparts.[11] Thus, women's contribution is crucial to building a strong and vibrant nation. We can ignore it at our own peril.

10
PUBLIC INVESTMENT AND SUBSIDIES ON AGRICULTURAL INPUTS AND THE UPLIFTMENT OF AGRARIAN ECONOMY

WE GAINED OUR INDEPENDENCE IN August 1947. Freedom came in the wake of the great, man-made Bengal Famine of 1942–1943, which claimed about three million victims. In the early years of freedom, food shortages were rampant, dependence of food imports was perennial and food rationing was regularly resorted to. For this reason, Jawaharlal Nehru said in 1948 that 'everything else can wait but not agriculture'. In 1951–1952, the total grain production was 52 million tonnes. Today, it is over 264 million tonnes.[1]

The centrality of agriculture in the socio-economic fabric of India is thus self-evident. As a source of livelihood, agriculture—including forestry and fishing—remains the largest sector of Indian economy. While its output fell from 28.3 per cent of the economy in 1993–1994 to 13.9 per cent in 2013–2014, the numbers employed have declined only from 64.8 per cent to 48.9 per cent. Therefore, almost half of the workforce in India still remains dependent on agriculture.

Agriculture is also a source of raw material to a number of food and agro-processing industries. It is estimated that industries with raw material of agricultural origin accounted for 50 per cent of the value added and 64 per cent of all jobs in the industrial sector. At $38 billion, agricultural export in 2014–2015 constituted 10 per cent of our exports.

Note: National Seminar on 'Public Investment and Subsidies on Agricultural Inputs and the Upliftment of Agrarian Economy', 5 March 2016, Hyderabad.

After Independence, we undertook special programmes, such as the Grow More Food Campaign and the Integrated Production Programme, focused on improving food and cash crops' supply. Land reforms were undertaken with two specific objectives. First, to remove impediments to increase in agricultural production arising from the inherited agrarian structure; and second, to eliminate elements of exploitation and social injustice within the agrarian system, to provide security for the tiller of soil and assure equality of status and opportunity to all sections of the rural population.[2]

Successive Five Year Plans stressed self-sufficiency and self-reliance in foodgrain production. Concerted efforts in this direction did result in substantial increase in agricultural production and productivity. This was the 'Green Revolution'.

Today, India is the largest exporter of rice in the world, and the second-largest exporter of buffalo meat and cotton. India is the largest producer of milk, and the second-largest producer of fruits and vegetables, rice, wheat and sugarcane.

However, there are indications that the Green Revolution benefits have plateaued. There is criticism that the input-intensive approach has largely been irrelevant for 60 per cent of India's cultivable land, which is unirrigated. These rain-fed areas have failed to benefit from public spending despite the fact that 90 per cent of the country's oilseed, 81 per cent of the pulses and 42 per cent of food grains are produced here.

Since the early 1990s, liberalization and globalization have become central elements of the development strategy of the government. This has also had an impact on Indian agriculture. Such measures were aimed at creating a potentially more profitable agriculture sector, which could 'bear the economic costs of technological modernization and expansion'[3].

The reforms appear to have improved terms of trade for agriculture, but growth in agricultural sector has been weak and well below that of non-agricultural sectors. The gap between rural and urban incomes has widened. While national income has grown at above 6 per cent over the last five years, agricultural income grew by a mere 1.1 per cent during 2014–2015.

A survey commissioned by Bharat Krishak Samaj on 'The State of the Indian Farmer' in 2014[4] reported that some 62 per cent of agriculturists were willing to quit farming to move to cities and that only 20 per cent of the rural youth was keen on continuing farming. The survey found that more than 40 per cent of farmers were dissatisfied with their economic condition. The figure was more than 60 per cent in eastern India. These are disturbing trends.

Since 1995, some 300,000 farmers have committed suicide in the country. According to P. Sainath, 'suicide rates among Indian farmers were a chilling 47 per cent higher than they were for the rest of the population in 2011.'[5] The issue of farmers' suicides is, no doubt, a complex one but it brings into sharp focus the stresses that the agricultural sector in India is now subject to. The recent mobilization in support of demands for caste-based reservations in government jobs, and not for betterment in the agricultural sector—by communities that have traditionally benefitted from agriculture—also indicates the growing stress within Indian agriculture.

Some policy experts have noted that public fund allocation to agriculture remains substantial. Of the five concerned ministries related to agro-sector—Agriculture, Chemical and Fertilizers, Consumer Affairs, Food and Public Distribution, Food Processing Industries and Water Resources—for 2015–2016, the fund allocation was roughly Rs 2.3 lakh crore.[6] This is not a paltry sum.

Why is the Indian agriculture under such stress despite the quantum of public investments it appears to be receiving?

It has been observed that small farms in India are superior in terms of production performance, but weak in terms of generating adequate income and sustaining livelihoods.[7] Small and marginal farmers, whose land holdings are below 2 hectares, constitute almost 80 per cent of all Indian farmers, and more than 90 per cent of them are dependent on rain for their crops. Their participation in the agricultural market remains low due to a range of constraints, such as low volumes, high transaction costs, lack of markets and information access.

This disparity is illustrated starkly by the experience from Punjab—a state which has undergone substantial modernization of the agricultural sector. There was consolidation in the land holdings and the subsidization of fertilizers and electricity for irrigation. Per hectare consumption of fertilizers increased and water-intensive crops like cotton and rice were adopted. Studies have shown[8] that the total operational cost of rice and wheat production increased by around 50 per cent between 2000–2001 and 2005–2006, while rice yields increased by only 12 per cent and wheat yields actually declined by 8 per cent. Thus, while farmers invested more on growing their crops, their total output, and therefore their profit, continued to decline. As the water tables have fallen, only farmers who were able to afford more powerful, and more expensive, equipment have been able to use the subsidized electricity for irrigation. The subsidies on fertilizers have also resulted in the unrestricted use of chemicals, leading to salinization and nitrogen-nutrients' imbalance in formerly fertile soils.

The Economic Survey for 2015–2016 includes a detailed analysis of fertilizer subsidy and its associated inefficiencies and misuses. Rs 73,000 crore, amounting to 0.5 per cent of the GDP, was budgeted for fertilizer subsidy. However, the Survey highlights three types of leakages for urea alone. First, it points out that 24 per cent of the urea subsidy goes to inefficient producers of urea manufacturers; second, of the remaining urea subsidy, 41 per cent is diverted to non-agricultural uses and is smuggled to neighbouring countries; and third, most of the remaining 24 per cent is consumed by large farmers. So, in a nutshell, only 35 per cent of the urea subsidy goes to intended beneficiaries—the small and marginal farmers. The Survey suggests taking the direct benefits transfer (DBT) route via Jan Dhan, Aadhaar and Mobile (JAM) and de-canalizing imports of urea. Agricultural experts agree that this is a 'fertile candidate for reform'.[9]

Agriculture in India intersects with almost every development agenda, be it human development, poverty elimination, rural development or environmental protection. Agricultural capacity has a direct impact on the food security situation in the country. It also helps in initiating and sustaining demand in other sectors. A progressive agriculture sector, thus, serves as a powerful engine of economic growth.

The 12th Five Year Plan growth target for the agricultural sector had been set at 4 per cent. The Gross Capital Formation in agriculture and allied sectors as a percentage of total GDP has remained stagnant at less than 3 per cent. Public spending on agricultural research, education and extension is presently about 0.7 per cent of the agricultural GDP—much lower than the international norm of 2 per cent. This raises concern that the inadequacies of the provision of the critical public goods for agriculture may dampen the targeted growth.

In a recent essay, Ashok Gulati, former chairman of the Commission on Agricultural Costs and Prices, has noted,

> Agriculture needs massive investment, for irrigation, agri-R&D and to build faster and more efficient value chains between farmers and retailers. Irrigation alone may need more than Rs 3,00,000 crore if it has to be provided to every farmer. But the Ministry of

Water Resources was allocated only Rs 4,232 crore for Financial Year 2016, less than the revised estimate of Rs 6,009 crore for the previous year... At this pace and with such allocations, irrigation for all farmers by 2022—promised to them by the PM—looks like a distant dream.'[10]

Enhanced public expenditure in agriculture—in the form of increased investments, rather than un-targeted subsidies—is thus required to bring about technical change in agriculture and higher agricultural growth. In addition, concerted reforms are needed to achieve equity in terms of higher growth in disadvantageous regions like rain-fed and tribal areas and benefit small and marginal farmers.

Some of the areas for policy intervention may include the following[11]:

1. Land market reforms are in need of a new impetus. As holdings are becoming fragmented and uneconomical, marginal farmers need flexibility in leasing out the land. There is, perhaps, a need to have a framework for operation of land markets but with sufficient safeguards to protect the interests of small and marginal farmers.
2. Agricultural price policy has been facing challenges. The practice of announcing minimum support price based on variable costs before sowing season could be looked into. Similarly, procurement price based on total costs may be used to procure food grains needed for public distribution system (PDS) and for food security purpose.
3. We need to consider a rational approach to pricing of agricultural inputs such as irrigation, power and fertilizer. However, any such measure, while providing timely delivery of the required inputs, must ensure that the small and marginal farmers are not adversely affected.
4. Farm and food subsidies need to be rationalized and better targeted to benefit the poor and the needy. Direct cash transfers offer a possible mechanism. While ensuring transparency and preventing leakages is important, these subsidies are justified as they benefit not only producers but the society at large. Large subsidies continue to be provided by developed countries that has distorted the international food prices. The Organisation for Economic Co-operation and Development (OECD) data shows that their members spent around $258 billion to subsidize agriculture in 2013. European Union spending on farm subsidies accounts up to $58 billion annually.
5. Although flow of agricultural credit has increased significantly in recent

years, we need to address distributional aspects of agricultural credit, including better access to small and marginal farmers, strengthening rural branches and reducing significant regional and inter-class inequalities in credit.

More than 800 million of India's 1.3 billion people live in rural areas. One quarter of this population lives below the official poverty line. The search for economic justice for a population of this magnitude cannot be addressed by relying on migration to the cities. Rural–urban migration and absorption of labour in the urban economy has been slow due to the slow growth of employment in manufacturing. The rural labour force will, therefore, have to find a way to improve their incomes in situ. Strengthening of agriculture, thus, becomes a national imperative.

Amartya Sen in his seminal 'Development as Freedom' argues forcefully that democracy plays a pivotal role in ensuring that indicators of abject poverty, such as famines, do not occur in such societies due to the presence of a free media and a political class that has to be necessarily responsive to citizens' needs. Harvard Professor Ashutosh Varshney raises some questions as to why the Indian farmer, despite having the democratic numbers, failed to secure a better economic deal from the Indian state. Varshney attributes this to the 'self-limiting' nature of rural politics in India:

> ...for rural power to push the state in economic policy more in its favour, it must present itself as a cohesive force united on economic interests—higher producer prices, larger subsidies and greater investment. Rural India has chosen not to construct its interest entirely economically. While politics based on economic demands is stronger than before, politics based on other cleavages—caste, ethnicity, religion—continues to be vibrant. Politics based on economic interests potentially unites the villagers against urban India; politics based on identities divides them, for cast, ethnicity and religion cut across the urban and the rural. There are Hindu villages and Hindu urbanities just as there are 'backward castes' in both cities and villages. Until an economic construction of interest completely overwhelms identities and non-economic interests, rural power, even though greater than before, will remain self limited.[12]

Describing the developmental challenges in our rural sector, Rajiv Lall had noted that:

The truth is unfortunately more complex and less comforting. As impressive as the ongoing transformation of rural India seems to be, a number of old challenges remain unaddressed and have become even more daunting, and new challenges have emerged.[13]

We, therefore, need a social corrective, along with the economic correctives, to redress these challenges. Mere infusion of funds might not be enough unless the underlying social gaps and divisions remain in place. Barriers growing from caste and other identities, that have seemingly hampered progressive measures, such as the farmer's cooperative movement in most parts of the country barring a few regions, need to be dismantled and ground created for collective action.

We have the resources and the ability to bring happiness to the lives of our farmers. It would take persistent and continuous action but it is not impossible. The government needs to take bold steps to translate the good intentions into action to tackle the deficiencies. This would, however, require a strong political will and the need to develop a wide political consensus.

The time has perhaps come for us to consider putting in place a 'Grow in India' programme to transform the socio-economic fabric of our agricultural sector, since it's as much in need as a 'Make in India' programme.

11

ROLES OF EDITORS IN TODAY'S MEDIA

IT IS SAID THAT AN editor's is a thankless job. He is respected, feared and even hated. A story goes that Napoleon once shot at a magazine editor, missed him and killed the publisher; the narrator added that Napoleon's intentions were good!

So how should we judge a member of the species? The Press Council of India Guidelines on Ethical Norms deal at some length with Editors' Discretion. It recognizes that in the matter of writing an editorial, the editor enjoys a good deal of latitude and discretion. It is for him/her to choose the subject and to use the language considered appropriate, provided that in the process the boundaries of the law and norms of journalism are not transgressed and the views are couched in sober, dignified and socially acceptable language. The guidelines uphold the editors' discretion in the selection of the material for publication, but in the expectation that, on a controversial issue of public interest, all views are given equal prominence so that the public can form an independent opinion in the matter.

These are substantial powers.

The media has a transmutative capacity. It not only portrays reality but can alter the perception of reality itself. The editor thus holds the key to forming public perception, and by extension public opinion, and thereby sets the agenda for the national debate. It is not unheard of for a powerful editor to take on the government of the day, and occasionally, even to bring one down.

There was a time, not long ago, when newspaper editors were intellectual stalwarts who acted as the brain trust of the country. The editor was the

---

Note: Seminar on the 'Roles of Editors in Today's Media' organized by RSTV, 19 March 2016, New Delhi.

personality of the newspaper, setting its tone and tenor, as well as determining its philosophical and political line.

Does contemporary reality correspond to this ideal of a liberal democracy? A political editor recently confided that credibility, which often takes years to build, is being treated as a commodity by media houses, and that part of it is being bartered for immediate economic gains. Such an observation, serious in itself, dents the requisite professional standard of journalism and impinges on an essential prerequisite of a free press in a free society.

The philosopher John Rawls has noted that substantially equal access to the media was to prevent politics being captured by concentrations of private economic power, which would make it impossible for equally able citizens to have equal opportunities to influence politics, regardless of their class. Much the same was said by Amartya Sen when he observed that 'it is not hard to see why a free, energetic, and efficient media can facilitate the needed discursive process significantly. The media is important not only for democracy but for the pursuit of justice in general.'

In an article investigating the charges of editorial bias carried by a newspaper, A.S. Panneerselvan wrote that journalism has two central functions, the credible-informational and the critical-investigative-adversarial, and that it operates to fulfil two social requirements—'what is in public interest and what the public is interested in—in a manner where issues of public interest is not subsumed by the dictates of what the public is interested in.'

Thus, to uphold journalistic ethos and values, an editor must:

- Ensure that the content is accurate and relevant: In a fluid, 24X7 news environment, the speed in providing news stories is important. However, the need to guarantee accuracy is even more important in the information frenzy we seem to be experiencing. Our own recent experience has shown how erroneous reports exacerbate social and communal divides. There have been cases when news groups have aired content—with disastrous effect—whose veracity and antecedents were doubtful. While such content may, in the short run, increase visibility or serve preferred political patronage, it eventually detracts from the credibility of the press and eats into the civil liberties. In every society, information plays a key role in empowering citizens to form their own opinions and play an active role in society. This is a duty that the news mediums have. The reporting thus has to be accurate and mistakes corrected quickly.

- Be impartial and independent: Trust is at the heart of the relationship that a news medium has with its readers. The content carried has to be a proof of this precious relationship. The editor has to be an independent observer of power. This independence is a cornerstone of reliability. In their book, *The Elements of Journalism* (2001), Bill Kovach and Tom Rosenstiel write that journalistic independence is not mere neutrality: 'While editorialists and commentators are not neutral, the source of their credibility is still their accuracy, intellectual fairness and ability to inform—not their devotion to a certain group or outcome. In our independence, however, journalists must avoid straying into arrogance, elitism, isolation or nihilism.'
- Be fair and respectful: Of the readers and the audience. The news medium should be open about its objectives and approach its subject with respect. Victims of violence, crime, war, conflicts, accidents or disasters should be treated with utmost respect. The aim should not be to sensationalize.

It has to be admitted regrettably, that examples of editorial daring and demonstrating the high professional and ethical standards are now few and far between. Even some of the newspapers that have strong reputations of quality have been open to serious allegations on issues of accuracy, empathy and maintaining ethical standards. Correctives are few, far between and insufficiently enforced.

Over the years there has been a change in the role and the position of the editor.

- The first big change came with the advent of television. Initially, the television was an empowering tool allowing the editor to see the news as it broke, without relying only on his journalist in the field. However, the 24X7 agitation that defines news television today has put tremendous pressure on the editors. Now they have to compete with this instantaneous medium in grabbing 'eyeballs' and at the same time deliver quality content to the readers.
- In this cacophony, the pressure on the editor to be heard and seen has increased. In the constant tussle between upholding the values and ethics of journalism and being fair and impartial—and the need to keep the newspaper operation financially viable—the editor is increasingly forced to prefer a healthier bottom line over neutrality and fairness.

- Not only do editors have to acquiesce to the owner/business person on following lines that would generate public interest/controversy, but many times they have to become 'event managers' for various sponsorship drives. To attract star participants and ensure attendance of the high and mighty newsworthy personalities, editors have had to make compromises.
- The sharp demarcation, between the editor's responsibilities in determining the prioritization of news hierarchy and the domain of the owner in running a profitable venture, has become increasingly blurred. There appears to be a distinct reluctance on the part of the owners to have a visible, independent and opinionated editor. The owners have also started playing a larger role in determining the news content and orientation of the newspaper or the television channel. This situation further subordinates the editor's position and ability to take independent stands. In the age where large corporates are also the owners of media outlets, this development becomes particularly challenging. The lines between an editorial and an advertisement should be drawn in bold.
- The evolution of the digital space and social media has had a further impact on the position of editors. This age of Twitter and Facebook feeds, where the newsmaker is able to directly communicate with the audience and the masses, is redefining the whole concept of journalism as we understand it. The editor's role, in this situation of surfeit information, has become limited to trying to filter the information and acting as a goalkeeper to prevent incorrect information from going out through his medium to the audience.

So is the era of tall editors over?

Perhaps not. In the very technology that brought about a rapid change in the position and role of editor lies perhaps the salvation. The digital medium today provides space for independent thought and contrarian views. We have seen some recent examples where prominent editors of well-known print dailies have moved completely to a digital medium in order to preserve their space and independence. With the digital divide in India narrowing, this might provide a way out for the editors. We have already seen this happen in the United States, where, as the news and readers both moved to the digital medium, so did the editors.

The challenges before editors arising from ready access that readers have to alternate sources of information and the increasing expectation on editors to focus on marketing and revenue, even as a larger proportion of the editorial staff gets deployed to revenue-raising work, is daunting.

A few years ago, when I was in the National Minorities Commission, I had come across a writing that included the following pithy comment:

> The administrative truth was passed on to the media; media took the official truth and transformed it into 'media truth'. The judiciary accepted the official and the media truth and transformed it into judicial truth; media praised the judicial truth, without attending the trial.

I am sure your deliberations would help bring into focus challenges that editors face in doing their jobs today while keeping alive the ethical and public good expectations of journalism.

12

ROLE OF THE JUDICIARY: SOME THOUGHTS ON ITS CRITICALITY

OUR FOUNDING FATHERS GAVE US a Constitution that encapsulates, in its text, the ideals and values of the people of India. The first among these is justice and, as John Rawls put it, 'rights secured by justice are not subject to political bargaining or to the calculus of social interests'. To ensure this, Article 32 of the Constitution gives us the right to move the Supreme Court, which has the power to take corrective measures for the enforcement of these rights. A similar power is conferred, within their area of competence, on the High Courts, under Article 226.

From this emanates the centrality of the judiciary in securing for citizens the rights bestowed by the Constitution. In our own times, as an eminent judge elsewhere noted some years back, 'people increasingly turn to the judiciary hoping it can solve pressing social problems'.[1]

An essential concomitant of this is accessibility of the judiciary; another is affordability; a third is the confidence that justice will be dispensed speedily. The latter is contingent not only on the technicalities of the law but also on the unstated major premise underlying the thought process. It is said that the judiciary is above, but not beyond, the issues of the day. 'We may try,' said the American judge Cardozo, 'to see things as objectively as we please; none the less [sic] we can never see them with any eyes except our own.'[2] 'And yet,' he continued, 'the training of the judge, if coupled with what is styled the judicial temperament, will help to broaden the group to which his subconscious loyalties are due.' Hence arises the need 'of constant

---

Note: 16th Convocation of the University of Jammu, 2 April 2016, Jammu.

checking and testing of philosophy by justice and of justice by philosophy'.[3] To this may be added Lord Bingham's caution about the need for judges to 'neutralize any extraneous considerations which might bias their judgement', or else decline to make the decision in question.[4]

Judge Albie Sachs of South Africa expressed the needed balance differently. The required approach is 'neither [a] purely libertarian one, nor simply communitarian. It was dignitarian. Respect for human dignity united the right to be autonomous with the need to recognise that we all live in communities'.[5]

This is precisely what is prescribed in the last part of the Preamble to the Constitution of India. The operative principles are *fraternity, dignity* and *unity* to be sought through justice, liberty and equality.

One of the matters in the societal domain that figures prominently in public discourse relates to the constitutional ideal of India being a 'secular' republic having a 'composite culture'. The former expression is in the Preamble and the latter in Article 51A(f).

Any discussion of these constitutional values has to be premised on the existential reality of our society. It is characterized by heterogeneity; a population of 1.3 billion comprising over 4,635 communities, 78 per cent of whom are not only linguistic and cultural but social categories. Religious minorities constitute 19.4 per cent of the total. The poet Pandit Kailash Narain Kaul Bedil Dehlavi expressed it finely in a couplet:

> *Ilahi lutf kya aata jo sub mai-khwar hi hote*
> *Teri duniya ki raonaq barh gai sheikh o barahman se*

Our democratic polity and its secular state structure were put in place in full awareness of this plurality. There was no suggestion to erase identities and homogenize them.

Political scientists and sociologists have written a good deal on the Indian perception of secularism. The three generally accepted characteristics of a secular state, namely *liberty* to practise religion, *equality* between religions as far as state practice is concerned and *neutrality* or a fence of separation between the state and religion, have been invoked but 'their application has been contradictory and has led to major anomalies'.[6] Commenting on the debate on secularism, Amartya Sen observed that 'secularism is basically a demand for symmetric political treatment of different religious communities' but that leaves open 'the choice between the forms that symmetry can legitimately take'; he added that 'there is a real difference between achieving symmetry through the sum-total of the collective intolerances of the different communities rather than through the union of their respective tolerances.'[7] Very recently, Soli Sorabjee has reminded us of the *Emmanuel v. State of Kerala* and of Justice Chinappa Reddy's remarks on the subject of tolerance.[8]

The challenge, then, is to reduce, if not eliminate, these anomalies.

This leads us to the question: how has the Indian Sate, in principle and practice, given shape to the essential ingredients of the secular principle and composite culture?

Apart from the principles enshrined in the constitutional text and policy pronouncements of public figures, often nuanced to suit the occasion, judicial pronouncements shed useful light on the matter.

The Basic Structure doctrine relating to our Constitution is now settled law.[9] One of its ingredients is *secularism*. This is accepted in principle by most segments of opinion (barring advocates of some version of theocracy). It is more than a passive attitude of religious tolerance; it is a positive concept of equal treatment. Its most emphatic assertion in a pronouncement came in the set of judgments in the *Bommai* case:

> Secularism has both positive and negative contents. The Constitution struck a balance between temporal parts confining it to the person professing a particular religious faith or belief and allows him to practice profess and propagate his religion, subject to public order, morality and health. The positive part of secularism has been entrusted to the State to regulate by law or by an executive order. The State is prohibited to patronise any particular religion as State religion and is enjoined to observe neutrality. The State strikes a balance to ensue an atmosphere of full faith and confidence among its people to realise full growth of personality and to make him a rational being on secular lines, to improve individual excellence, regional growth, progress and national integrity... Religious tolerance and fraternity are basic features and postulates of the Constitution as a scheme for national integration and sectional or religious unity. Programmes or principles evolved by political parties based on religion amount to recognizing religion as a part of the political governance which the Constitution expressly prohibits. It violates the basic features of the Constitution. Positive secularism negates such a policy and any action in furtherance thereof would be violative of the basic features of the Constitution.[10]

The principle so laid down is emphatic. Despite its clarity, however, different interpretations were placed on it and 'there is no real consensus within the Court on what secularism entails'.[11] It has been opined that what the Court *said* is different from what it *did*.[12] Observers have noted that subsequent pronouncements of the Supreme Court have 'effectively vindicated the profoundly anti-secular vision of secularism' of some quarters. For this reason, it has been argued 'whether a more complete separation of religion and politics might not better serve Indian democracy'.[13]

The difficulty lies in delineating, for purposes of public policy and practice, the line that separates them from religion. For this religion per se, and each individual religion figuring in the discourse, has to be defined in terms of its stated tenets. The 'way of life' argument, used in philosophical texts and some judicial pronouncements, does not help the process of identifying common principles of equity in a multi-religious society. Since a wall of separation is not possible under Indian conditions, the challenge is to develop a formula for equidistance and minimum involvement. For this purpose, principles of *faith* need to be segregated from contours of *culture*, since a conflation of the two obfuscates the boundaries of both and creates space to equivocalness.[14] Furthermore, such an argument could be availed of by other faiths in the land since all claim a cultural sphere and a historical justification for it.

Within the same ambit, but distinct from it, is the constitutional principle of equality of status and opportunity, amplified through Articles 14, 15 and 16. This equality has to be substantive rather than merely formal and has to be given shape through requisite measures of affirmative action needed in each case so that the journey on the path to development has a common starting point. The Kundu Report on Diversity Index in 2008 had drawn attention to the 'Inequality Traps' that prevent the marginalized and work in favour of the dominant groups in a society and had concluded that 'unequal economic opportunities lead to unequal outcomes which in turn lead to unequal access to political power. This creates a vicious circle since unequal power structure determines the nature and functioning of the institutions and their policies. All these result in persistence of initial conditions'.[15]

The same absence of homogeneity holds good for 'composite culture'. The freedom movement recognized this existential reality of immense diversity on the ground. The *Bommai* judgment said that 'this cultural heritage in India shaped that people of all religious faiths, living in different parts of the country are to tolerate each other's religious faiths or beliefs and each religion made its contribution to enrich the composite Indian culture as a happy blend or synthesis.'[16] Thus, secularism and composite culture are two sides of the same coin. A historian has analysed it in some detail:

> The social and cultural life in India incorporated within it a multi-regional and multi-religious form and content. This interpretation of cultural influences was neither uniform nor equally intense in all regions. Yet their presence is marked all over. As a result, although historically cultural transactions and social negotiations embraced the entire subcontinent, they led to variety and plurality rather than to homogeneity. In almost all realms of cultural production—music, drama, painting, architecture, and so on—as well as religion, different influences made their mark, imparting to them a composite character. As a result, historically India developed as a colourful cultural mosaic and not as the manifestation of cultural practices inspired by a single source. The dynamism of Indian culture is derived from this diversity, which moulded the cultural practices of the people. It is in this sense that culture was embedded in national identity.[17]

Furthermore, and to revert to the same author,

> ...the cultural implication of this historical process is not limited to diversity and plurality at the national level, but within each region itself as well... The coming together of people of diverse cultural moorings and traditions had several cultural consequences. These have been variously conceived as synthesis, assimilation, acculturation, and eclecticism...Whether India developed as a melting pot of cultures, or only remained a salad bowl is no more the issue. The crucial question is whether Indian culture is conceived as a static phenomenon, tracing its identity to a single unchanging source, or a dynamic phenomenon, critically and creatively interrogating all that is new.'[18]

To Jawaharlal Nehru, India was a palimpsest on which many had written their contribution and none were to be disowned. The poet Raghupati Sahay Firaq expressed the process in a couplet:

> *Sar zamin-e-Hind par aqwam-e-aalam ke firaq*
> *Karwaan aate gaye, Hindostan banta gaya*

It is evident from the foregoing that despite the clarity of enunciation in some of the *Bommai* pronouncements, political perceptions have sought to interpret its intended meaning for their own purposes.

Some years back, in a volume published on the occasion of the Golden Jubilee of the Supreme Court, two eminent jurists had observed that 'as we transit into the next millennium, the Supreme Court has a lot to reflect upon, and not least on how to protect the minorities and their ilk from the onslaught of majoritarianism'.[19] So, as an acknowledged authority on the Constitution put it, 'unless the Court strives in every possible way to assure that the Constitution, the law, applies fairly to *all* citizens, the Court cannot be said to have fulfilled its custodial responsibility.'[20]

Is it therefore bold to expect that the Supreme Court may consider, in its wisdom, to clarify the contours within which the principles of secularism and composite culture should operate with a view to strengthen their functional modality and remove ambiguities that have crept in?

Indian secularism has been described as *ameliorative* whose spiritual core is incrementalism.[21] A citizen could well hope that this incremental approach is used to enhance social cohesion and social peace.

IDENTITY

13
THE INTELLECTUAL AND SOCIETY: ROLE AND RESPONSIBILITY

AS A PHILOSOPHER, SARVEPELLI RADHAKRISHNAN, unquestionably one of the great Indians of the 20th century, interpreted Indian thought to the world in what has been called the 'battle of consciousness'. The republic bestowed on him the highest offices of the state and he in turn added lustre to them. A constitutional head of state in a modern democracy cannot, with justice, lay claim to Plato's ideal of a 'perfect guardian'; despite that, the philosopher in Radhakrishnan did inject a deeper perspective, drew attention to values and helped the system, as he put it, 'do the right thing'. Inaugurating the Indian Institute of Advanced Study, Shimla, in 1965, he cautioned against the deification of error and becoming 'prisoners of the status quo'.[1]

Three centuries earlier, another man of philosophy, Baruch Spinoza, had prescribed for himself a rule of communication: 'to speak in a manner intelligible to the multitude, and to comply with every general custom that does not hinder the attainment of our purpose'.[2] Radhakrishnan would have readily endorsed this. Less reverential is Bertrand Russell's observation[3] that philosophers are, for the most part, constitutionally timid, dislike the unexpected and therefore invent systems which make the future calculable!

Given Radhakrishnan's intellectual stature, it would be beneficial to explore his views on the role of the intellectual in public life. These make interesting reading and retain a contemporary relevance.

He addressed the question in his 1942 lectures, delivered at the University of Calcutta and at the BHU; these were published in 1947 as *Religion and*

Note: 13th Dr Radhakrishnan Memorial Lecture, 16 April 2009, Shimla.

Politics. The imperative, spelt out in the first lecture, was the 'very rapid' pace of change:

> Everywhere round about us we hear the sound of things breaking, of changes in the social, in the political and economic institutions, in the dominant beliefs and ideas, in the fundamental categories of human thought. Men of intelligence, sensitiveness and enterprise are convinced that there is something radically wrong with the present arrangements and institution...[4]

He traced the cause to 'the serious distemper' between social institutions and the world purpose of bringing about a cooperative commonwealth resulting in dignity, noble living and prosperity for all. The way out, he suggested, was 'the restoration of the lost relationship between the individual and the eternal'; hence, the relevance of religion. Established religions, however, cannot meet the world's need for a soul.

Having sought to establish a balance between the ideal and the practical, Radhakrishnan spelt out a role for the intellectual in the final lecture. The relevant passages are noteworthy:

> The final ends of political action are to be considered by the thinker and the writer. In them society becomes conscious and critical of itself. They are the character of a society. Their business is to educate us to a consciousness of the real self of society, and to save guardians of the values of a society, the values which are the real life and us from spiritual callousness and mental vulgarity...
>
> The intellectual need not take an active part in politics or in the actual affairs of administration. It is their primary function to serve society with intellectual integrity. They must create social consciousness and sense of responsibility which transcends the limits of the political community. Those who can serve society in this way have a duty not to engage in politics. For every society there will be a few for whom participation in political activity would be a perversion of genius, a disloyalty to themselves...
>
> If the intellectuals abandon the interests of culture, and repudiate the primacy of spiritual values, we cannot blame the politicians who are responsible for the safety of the state.[5]

Two-and-a-half decades later, and while replying to a farewell address by the members of Parliament, he put forth a more benign perception of men of politics:

> Politicians do not mean people of twisted tongues or cold hearts. They are men with warmth of feeling, who have compassion for the suffering of humanity. We should, as politicians, exert our utmost to alleviate the sufferings of humanity. Politics should not absorb all our life; it is indispensable, but not the whole life.[6]

Embedded here are perceptions of intellectual activity and the role of intellectuals, as also of politics and the purpose of political activity. Each has a bearing on life, in society and on the meaning of citizenship. For this reason, it remains relevant.

The debate on the linkage between thought and action, and the moral imperative for action, is a perennial one. Neither exists in isolation. It has been argued that the notion of pursuit of knowledge for its own sake, in contrast to knowledge pursued explicitly for some particular end, is misleading. The intellectual's responsibility, admittedly, is to think, but thinking in itself is an activity and as such is linked to the activity which is the implementation of thinking; a refusal to see it so, is to be morally culpable. The intellectual thus becomes a critical element in the value system of a society.

A definition of the intellectual and his role was provided by the sociologist Edward Shills:

> In every society there are some persons with an unusual sensitivity to the sacred, an uncommon reflective-ness about the nature of their universe, and the rules that govern their society. There is in every society a minority of persons who, more than the ordinary run of their fellow men, are enquiring, and desirous of being in frequent communion with the symbols which are more general than the immediate concrete situations of everyday life, and remote in their reference in both time and space. In this minority, there is a need to externalize the quest… This interior need to penetrate beyond the screen of immediate concrete experience marks the existence of the intellectual in every society.[7]

The intellectual is thus entrusted with a special responsibility. It necessitates corresponding action. Such an approach would lend credence to Marx's observation that 'philosophers have only interpreted the world, in various ways; the point is to change it'.[8] Nor was Marx alone in urging a linkage. 'The intellectual,' wrote Vaclav Havel in 1986, 'should constantly disturb, should bear witness to the misery of the world, should be provocative by being independent, should rebel against all hidden and open pressure and manipulations, should be the chief doubter of systems of power and its incantations, should be a witness to their mendacity'.[9] By doing so the intelligentsia risks, in Toynbee's telling phrase, becoming an outcaste, born to be unhappy because his or her very existence is a reproach to the society concerned.[10]

In a celebrated essay in 1967, Noam Chomsky had asserted that in considering the responsibility of intellectuals 'our basic concern must be their role in the creation and analysis of ideology' and to see events in their historical perspective.[11] The same point was made by Edward Said in his Reith Lectures in 1993, when he urged the contemporary intellectual 'to speak the truth to power', and do so by 'carefully weighing the alternatives, picking the right one, and then intelligently representing it where it can do the most good and cause the right change'.[12]

At the other end of the spectrum, the intellectual is viewed as a dangerous creature capable of poisoning minds, destabilizing order and creating chaos. Paul Johnson, in a selective survey, has questioned the 'moral and judgmental credentials of intellectuals' and cautioned about 'the heartless tyranny of ideas' emanating from them.[13] Such perceptions have been used to create or sustain closed societies, including some masquerading as open ones. We have enough examples in our own times of dictatorships of the right or the left, and of societies imposing a monopoly of control anchored on race, religion or atavistic claims.

The debate on what the intellectual can, and should, do, and in what manner, has taken place in most societies. The impulses and imperatives vary, so do the constraints. It is of particular relevance in a society like ours where, to echo Edward Said's caution, 'easy certainties provided us by our background, language, nationality… so often shield us from the reality of others'.[14]

On the basis of the role played by intellectuals in different societies, it is possible to develop a typology. They can be academics, writers, artists or activists. Creativity and courage are the two essential conditions for their public role. There is also a symbiotic relationship between the ideas generated within a society and its institutions of social sciences. Nor can external influences or linkages be overlooked; researchers have spoken of the impact on national perceptions of international 'epistemic communities', defined as network of professionals and experts who share normative beliefs, lay claim to policy-relevant knowledge and impact policy perceptions.[15]

Where, then, do we locate the role and responsibility of the intellectual in contemporary India?

India, it has been said, is a political and economic paradox: a rich-poor nation with a weak-strong state. Persistent centrism, and continuous realignment, are two of its striking features. This has accommodated a wide spectrum of interests, classes, status groups, regions and communities in the political process and development structures. This accommodation has not always been equitable. The Constitution provides the point of reference; its Preamble is the key to its social, political and economic philosophy, and to its core value system. It has been described as a moral document embodying an ethical vision; this compels attention to Ambedkar's observation that constitutional morality is not a natural sentiment and has to be cultivated.

On Radhakrishnan's parameters, therefore, amongst the primary responsibilities of the intellectual would be to educate the society on these values and to assess the extent to which they are being adhered to. An unavoidable concomitant of this would be the necessity of 'speaking the truth to power'. The challenge before the intelligentsia, wrote Rajni Kothari six decades after Radhakrishnan's lectures, is 'to keep alive the flame of hope and resurgence, and to continue offering ideological alternatives to the struggling segments of the mass public'.[16] The role of the intellectual thus becomes integral to the healthy functioning of a society.

The nature of the society in question, and the relationships secreted in its interstices, provide the starting point of analysis. Any critique of the Indian polity would thus involve scrutiny on multiple axes and require threefold examination of the relationship of the state and society, the state and democracy, and the polity and the economy. Our quest would focus on the role of the intellectual in the furtherance of this critique.

Since time constraints come in the way of a comprehensive analysis, I shall endeavour to confine my remarks to five specific areas, namely: institutions, economic amelioration, corruption, rights and environment.

Institutions: The structure of our polity took shape through intensive debates during the freedom struggle and in the Constituent Assembly. The Constitution bestowed centrality on the state and impacted on the relationship between it and the society. A good deal of social activity came to be focused on ways and means of impacting state perceptions and activity. Interest groups in society thus came to focus on elections as the first and logical step in this endeavour; the excellent work in this field done by Lokniti has been widely acknowledged. In the process, however, the democratic functioning of the society came to be considered by most as synonymous with the electoral process. Ashish Nandy has termed it 'psephocracy'. The study of the actual functioning of the institutions received inadequate attention and the wider implications of this for public debate and discussion were, exceptions apart, insufficiently scrutinized by the intellectuals. Its impression on public perceptions is all too evident today and raises questions about the health of our institutions and the state of governance. There are some exceptions to an otherwise pervasive neglect; Pratap Bhanu Mehta and Rajni Kothari, amongst others, are illustrative of these.

Mehta's critique is on the failure of the state in the removal of inequality. There is, he asserts in an eloquent passage, a deepening of democracy on the one side and its corruption on the other: 'It would be a rare citizen who has not felt the force of both narratives directly. The difficult question is how to bring the two together.' Democratic practice has, in effect, meant advancement of group interests through competitive negotiations rather than through the diffusion of democratic norms. This has led to 'a profound disenchantment with the state'. The Indian state, in its day to-day transactions, is often 'neither feared nor loved: incapable of having the rule of law secured either through an effective set of institutions, nor the eliciting of allegiance to its dictates by inspiring a sense of obligation'. One reason for this disenchantment with the state, he concludes, is the perceived failure of the instruments of accountability, since democracy has become non-deliberative. The deliberative capacities and oversight functions of the Parliament are in decline and elections are rarely fought on policy issues. Political parties are in disarray. Mehta's solution lies in correctives to statism through a new politics of redistribution, arising out of the policy of economic liberalization: 'What Indian democracy needs is a new sense of the relationship between the public and the private.' He accepts that this will require an extraordinary effort. No blueprint, however, is put forth, except the suggestion that the proceeds of disinvestments should be earmarked for poverty alleviation and human resource development.[17]

To Rajni Kothari, democracy 'as a system has not been realised in practice' and remains an aspiration. The turbulence in India compels attention to the 'deeper psycho-spiritual dimensions of Indian reality', to societal perspectives rather than political ones. The Indian scene is characterized by a tradition of tolerance of pluralism, dissent and opposition. An unwelcome consequence of it is tolerance of 'ambiguity, deprivation and humiliation'. The consensual polity that emerged in the early decades of the republic was supported by 'charismatic power and pliable tradition'. The strength of the consensus was unavoidably contingent on the organizational skills of the elite and on the levels of discovery. When both faltered, new sets of actors emerged to redefine the contents of politics in terms of a new agenda of aspirations. These new movements are 'no longer limited to economic or even political demands, but seek to cover women's issues and questions of public health as well as ecological and cultural issues. They include a sustained attack on sources of internal decay and degeneration'. They demand new instruments of political action, non-party and party-like. This necessitates a review of ideological positions on the nature and content of democracy.[18]

One aspect of the institutions of democracy pertains to the Rule of Law. A few years back, a senior law officer of the government posed a candid question: have the three organs of the state discharged their constitutional obligations and functioned within the limits set forth by the Constitution? His own answer was that the Rule of Law is 'under serious threat' arising out of 'cancerous developments eating into the fabric of each institution' and 'each is destroying itself from within'.[19] Others, too, have spoken of the under-reach of some institutions and overreach of others, both resulting in disturbing the balance visualized in the Constitution.[20]

There is little or no evidence to suggest that the requisite correctives are underway; nor has any concerted effort been made by public intellectuals to turn the grievance into a movement.

'Sixty years after Independence', writes the historian Ramachandra Guha, 'India remains a democracy. But the events of the last two decades call for a new qualifying adjective. India is no longer a constitutional democracy but a populist one.'[21] A report published by the Centre for the Study of Developing Societies (CSDS) last year on the 'State of Democracy in South Asia' calls for a new political imagination to build democracy that would 'meaningfully accommodate minority and marginal groupings'. It calls for a reworking of political institutions to free democracy from the stranglehold of dominant caste and class elite.[22]

Economic amelioration: These views on institutions, reflective of a widespread frustration on one plane over their demonstrated shortcomings, have not prevented civil society movements led or supported by intellectuals advocating correctives in some areas of social life, and putting some of them in place through changes in the institutional framework. I refer, in particular, to the processes leading to the enactment of the RTI Act and the National Rural Employment Guarantee Act (NREGA), both in 2005. The first has led to the empowerment of the citizen vis-à-vis the state and is unquestionably the first major step towards transparency. We have, as Aruna Roy put it, 'an obligation to those who are denied access to shrinking public spaces' adding that 'campaigns have repeatedly demonstrated the power of collective participation to change the direction of governance'. The origins of NREGA go back to the Right to Food campaign initiated in 2001 with the writ petition in the Supreme Court that developed into a movement thanks to what Jean Dreze has called 'skilful activism'. Despite uneven implementation by state governments, and some criticism by the World Bank lately, NREGA's uniqueness as an instrument of ameliorating the condition of the rural poor by helping them avoid hunger and distress migration by providing opportunity to earn a living wage in a dignified manner cannot be questioned. The process is assisted by the monitoring mechanism established by the Supreme Court; the Eighth Report by Commissioners N.C. Saxena and Harsh Mander in August 2008 is indicative of the scope of the initiative and the extent of intellectual-activist involvement in it.

Public opposition to specific instances of acquisition of agricultural land for special economic zones (SEZs), and the related discussions on approaches to industrialization, continues to propel the debate about alternate models of development strategy. This has received an impetus in the wake of the global financial crisis. The need for financial stimulus and the re-emergence of the public sector as the engine of the economy has reinvigorated many intellectuals to question the premises of 'neo-liberalism' and the policies arising out of it. Prabhat Patnaik is a case in point.[23]

On a wider canvas, Amartya Sen has stressed the need for 'ideas about changing the organization of society in the long run'. 'Do we', he enquires, 'really need some kind of "new capitalism" rather than an economic system that is not monolithic, draws on a variety of institutions chosen pragmatically, and is based on social values that we can defend ethically? Should we search for a new capitalism or for a "new world" that would take a different form?'[24] **Corruption:** In a paper written in 2004, Peter deSouza called corruption 'Democracy's inconvenient fact'. The Approach Paper to the 11th

Five Year Plan considered corruption 'endemic in all spheres'. Former Central Vigilance Commissioner N. Vittal characterized it as 'financial terrorism', as antinational, anti-poor and anti-development, and as 'the root cause of very poor governance in India'. More disturbing is the perception that 'as crass individualism makes its way, the social attitude towards corruption is more forgiving'.[25] Corrective movements like Parivartan have based their effort on effective use of the RTI, and the mechanism of social audit and Jansunwai have received support of intellectuals and civil society groups; they have produced results in specific cases. This is acknowledged in the Report of the Administrative Reform Commission on 'Ethics in Governance'. ARC's specific recommendations would need, for implementation, political will and focused public support in much greater measure than is forthcoming at present.[26]

Rights: The doctrine of rights has evolved in recent years. A conscious effort, as yet uneven, has been made to give content to concepts of equality and justice. The role of the judiciary, and of the Public Interest Litigation (PIL), has contributed substantially to it. The ambit of rights has been amplified by the 1997 judgment of the Supreme Court in the *Vishaka v. State of Rajasthan* ruling that 'provisions in the international covenants pertaining to human rights can be read into the domestic law in the absence of any inconsistency between the two, as a canon of construction'.[27]

The position taken by a wide cross section of intellectuals on communal, economic or regional issues, like the Babri Masjid demolition, the 2002 Gujarat riots, or the happenings in West Bengal on land acquisition, in Odisha and Karnataka on security of minorities and on regional chauvinism and communalism in Maharashtra, are indicative of an awareness that is to be welcomed.

In regard to actualization of group rights, intellectual, public and governmental initiatives have been taken to ascertain the factual situation on deprivation and discrimination 'in production, distribution and social sectors'. The problem has been summed up by Amitabh Kundu: 'Unequal economic opportunities lead to unequal outcomes which in turn lead to unequal access to political power. This creates a vicious circle since unequal power structure determines the nature and functioning of the institutions and their policies. All these result in persistence of initial conditions.'[28] Exploratory efforts have been initiated by the government to put in place a Diversity Index and create an Equal Opportunity Commission. Intellectuals have contributed to both in good measure. Both would need a wider degree of public support to allow these to pass the test of legislative approval.

Environment: Movements to protect and safeguard the environment have an older vintage and fall into two broad categories: micro movements based on result-oriented efforts on specific issues and with wide public participation, and macro movements to influence policy. The most famous in the first category is the Chipko movement of the early 1970s. Other movements have related to opposition to the construction of major dams and hydel projects and to instances of environmental disasters; examples of these are the Silent Valley, Tehri Dam and Narmada River Valley projects and the Bhopal gas tragedy. Despite the involvement of eminent activists, large-scale public support on a sustained basis was often lacking and only the movement to oppose the Silent Valley project was fully successful. On the other hand, grass-root level efforts in Maharashtra, like the Pani Panchayat and Ralegan Siddhi, associated with Anna Hazare, have been more successful.

At the level of activist-intellectuals, and despite the good work done by environmentalists like Sunita Narain and Vandana Shiva, public awareness of environment issues is still in its infancy and there is merit in Vandana Shiva's observation that 'the environmental movement can only survive if it becomes a justice movement'.

The instances cited in this very brief survey present a varied picture ranging from frustration to success and to a mix of both. The latter may induce the optimist to advocate, as a hard-nosed realist put it in another context, patient accumulation of partial successes. The intellectual, admittedly, must speak truth to power; the manner of speech, however, cannot be that of the angry poet expressed so eloquently by Majaz:

> *Barh ke is Inder sabha ka saaz-o-saaman phoonk doon*
> *Is ka gulshan phoonk doon, uska shabistaan phoonk doon*
> *Takht-e-sultan kya, main saara qasr-e-sultan phoonk doon.*

It is now time to revert to the role and responsibility question, in regard to intellectuals. Most would accept the need to speak truth to power and do so by advocating the correct alternative. In doing so, awareness and analysis of the major and minor premises of proposed approaches become unavoidable. T.K. Oommen has taken the argument a stage further and, in the context of our constitutional values, developed the 'perspective from below' that helps 'institutionalisation of equality and justice' in contrast to the view from above that assists 'perpetuation of hegemony'. The response of the state to social movements, he adds, 'does not fall into unilinear patterns; (it) is dictated by the nature of the mobilisation attempted by a movement. Conversely, the character of the party in power is [a] critical variable in determining state response.' This could range from facilitation to toleration and discreditation, even repression.[29]

Where then do we conclude? The answer is neither easy nor simple. A position, nevertheless, needs to be taken. The journey, of necessity, is a lonely one. I cannot help recalling a passage from that most indomitable of intellectuals, Edward Said:

> Nothing in my view is more reprehensible than those habits of mind in the intellectual that induce avoidance, that characteristic turning away from a difficult and principled position which you know to be the right one, but which you decide not to take. You do not appear too political; you are afraid of seeming controversial; you need the approval of a boss or an authority figure; you want to keep a reputation for being balanced, objective, moderate; your hope is to be asked back, to consult, to be on a board or prestigious committee, and so remain within the responsible mainstream; some day you hope to get an honorary degree, a big prize, perhaps even an ambassadorship. For an intellectual these habits of mind are corrupting par excellence. If anything can denature, neutralize, and finally kill a passionate intellectual life it is the internalisation of such habits.[30]

Gandhiji would have put the point across in his own way. 'I know the path', he said. 'It is straight and narrow. It is like the edge of a sword. I rejoice to walk on it. I weep when I slip.'

14
IDENTITY, CITIZENSHIP AND EMPOWERMENT

MAULAVI MOHAMMAD BAKHSH AND HIS son, Khuda Bakhsh, are known to us by their simplicity, dedication to a cause and single-mindedness of purpose. The Khuda Bakhsh Oriental Public Library in Patna is amongst a handful of its kind in the world. It is a unique collection of Persian and Arabic manuscripts, described by a visitor as 'an enclosed garden of precious things'. These testify to the richness of the civilization of Islam, to which India and Indians contributed in no small measure. One characteristic of it is the diversity of the cultural dialogue conducted over centuries between peoples of diverse stocks and traditions and the interaction between Islamic values and the historical experience of Muslim communities.

The late Professor Mohammad Mujeeb concluded his monumental work *The Indian Muslims*, published in 1967, with what he termed 'a note of warning'. 'Generalisations about the Indian Muslims', he wrote, 'can only be partial statements of truth and would, therefore, be misleading'.[1] Commenting on the inadequacy of prevailing historical perception, he added that 'the Indian Muslims are judged by the non-Muslims and, vice versa, the non-Muslims by the Muslims, as if the historical record of one party could be separated from the record of the other, and each party answerable only for itself'.

Equally relevant is Richard Eaton's observation about the 'diverse variety Indian Islamic traditions' that reflect 'both the dynamism of Islam and the fluidity of Indo-Islamic identities'.

Both judgements signal uniqueness. They were arrived at after

---

Note: Speech delivered at the Khuda Bakhsh Oriental Public Library, 12 December 2009, Patna.

encyclopaedic surveys of a thousand years of political, intellectual and cultural history in which the past journeyed into the present. Every stage of this journey was marked by debate and dissent, reflective of what were perceived to be prevailing challenges. It is, therefore, of critical relevance to the India of today that counts 160 million Muslims amongst its citizens who constitute 13.4 per cent of the population of the country.

There is also an external dimension to this identity. India is not a part of the 'Muslim World' but is not away from it; not a Muslim-majority state in statistical terms, yet home to the third-largest community of Muslims in the world; not a society focused on Muslim welfare only but one in which the Muslims, as an integral part of a larger whole, constitutionally claim the attention that every other section does. The Indian Muslim community also has a history of engagement with the larger Muslim world and has contributed in intellectual, cultural and material terms to its enrichment.

The two aspects of the interaction that has characterized the Indian experience can be listed as:

- Have the Muslims allowed their parameters to be frozen in time and taken too much for granted?
- Have they been sufficiently critical? Is there a need for newer impulses to respond to new situations?

Both relate to the debate within the community, as also to interaction with the wider national and international community. Both have contemporary relevance. Both are emotive and could be evaded if the instinct of caution were to prevail:

Udhar mashkook hai meri sadaqat
Idhar bhi badgumani kam nahi hai

The effort, nevertheless, must be made.

The discussion needs to be posited in the contemporary Indian reality. Ours is a pluralistic society, a secular polity and a state structure that is democratic and based on Rule of Law. Plurality is an existential reality; responding to its imperative, the founding fathers of the republic crafted the Constitution endowed with the values enunciated in its Preamble: a sovereign, socialist, secular and democratic republic dedicated to the achievement of justice, equality, liberty and fraternity. Each of these enunciates a comprehensive agenda; some objectives have been achieved; others remain a work in progress. These political virtues are, in essence, interlinked and interdependent and cannot be considered as replacements or substitutes. Some are of older vintage, other are of recent origin.

The Indian reality pertaining to its Muslim population has another dimension. This was portrayed in the Sachar Committee Report of 2006 that examined the ground situation pertaining to identity, security and equity, highlighted facts emanating from official data and made recommendations for corrective and affirmative action.

What conclusions do we draw from our experience of six decades in terms, firstly, of the conceptual framework, and secondly, of the actual experience?

Let us begin with plurality. It is a social reality that has manifested itself in different ways in different periods of our long history. It was cherished and relished:

> *Gul haai ranga rang se hai zeenat-e-chaman*
> *Ai Zauq is jahan ko hai zaib ekhtelaaf se*

Pluralism indicates the presence of differences and marks a departure from policies aimed at annihilating the other; it however remains silent about the public status of these communities. Cultural pluralism of the past thus existed within acknowledged structures of authority and did not seek to place it in a framework of equality. The contemporary constitutional framework of equality and secularism, however, provides it a different enabling atmosphere. 'In today's India,' writes Asim Ray, 'tolerant pluralism is totally meaningless and impotent unless it is thoroughly rooted out of its traditional mores, and is relocated on the basis of equalitarian and egalitarian principles.'[2] Such relocation, he adds, can only be achieved if all religious groups dedicate themselves to an overarching spiritual ideal of living together. This brings forth 'three interconnected ideas: repudiating the idea of the state as belonging to the dominant group; replacing assimilationist and exclusionary nation-building policies with policies of recognition and accommodation; and acknowledging historic injustice and offering amends for it'. This imposes obligations on the state to promote equal treatment. It must, as Gurpreet Mahajan puts it, acknowledge and accommodate diverse cultural communities as equal partners: 'Only when the diversity that comprises the totality is reflected in the universal can communities have a sense of identity and equality.'[3]

The same holds for secularism. The concept itself, mentioned though not defined in the text, is accepted as part of the basic structure of the

Constitution. It pertains to three sets of relations in a society: between religion and the individual (freedom of religion); between the state and the individual (citizenship); and between the state and religion (separation of state and religion). The basic debate in India on the meaning and content of secularism has ranged on two principal approaches, namely (a) neutrality of the state vis-à-vis religions to ensure a basic symmetry of treatment between citizens of different religious communities and (b) prohibition of religious activities in the functioning of the state. The former implies respect for, and implementation of, rights given to religious minorities. The record of six decades shows that flawed practice has at times tended to dilute these principles. The devil, as always, lies in the detail of implementation and the 'major premise' in the functioning of state machinery. There is also a need to probe Asghar Ali Engineer's observation that 'increasing democratisation should have meant more secularisation, but increased democratisation is resulting in greater communalisation'.[4] The inevitable conclusion is that patterns of political mobilization in the country have not always adhered to our constitutional ideals and have exacerbated societal fault lines.

In regard to state structure, the Constitution prescribed the form of political democracy. This has produced good results and empowered the citizenry. However, the working of the democratic process has lent weight to Ambedkar's foreboding about the contradiction between political equality and social and economic inequality and about the need to have one man one vote and one vote one value. The inequality trap thus created, as the Report of the Expert Group on Diversity Index put it in 2008, 'prevent the marginalised and work in favour of the dominant group in society'. As a result, it adds, 'unequal economic opportunities lead to unequal outcomes which in turn lead to unequal access to political power. This creates a vicious circle since unequal power structure determines the nature and functioning of the institutions and their policies. All these result in persistence of initial conditions.' Debate is also beginning to focus on the relationship between caste and class and between caste and minority; it has been argued that 'the politics of inclusion has to go beyond caste inequalities as deprivation and discrimination are widespread and not confined to a single community or group'. The situation is aggravated, in actual governance, by the fraying of the rule of law norms.

On all three counts, therefore, practice has fallen short of promise. What has been its impact—physical and psychological—on the largest minority? What has been the direction of debate within? How, and to what extent, has it interacted with the larger citizen body and sought solutions?

Insecurity, frustration and uncertainty characterized the Indian Muslim mind in the immediate aftermath of the Partition. Evidence of the official attitude in earlier years, cited by Ramachandra Guha, leaves little room for doubt. Balraj Puri summed up the position succinctly in an essay written in 1993: 'Their expectations were low and fears high... Gradually, the mood of withdrawal and resignation gave way to consciousness of rights, assertion of identity and protests against perceived injustices...'[5] The grievances (with some important local variants) centred on five core concerns: security, employment and reservations, Urdu, the Aligarh Muslim University (AMU) and Muslim Personal Law. The community's internal discourse on these, as also in the wider Indian circle is, therefore, of relevance. It was articulated through the ulema, political leaders, intellectuals and the general public. In many cases, these categories overlapped; their responses varied. The record of six decades suggests an unduly defensive approach, sporadic and emotional rather than systematic and rational. The internal discourse repeated an old lament:

> *Ab woh altaf nahin, hum pe enayat nahin*
> *Baat ye kya hai ke pahle si madaraat nahin?*

Suggestions for possible corrections were few, unfocused and far between. On the other side, the wider community and the political class preferred to be in a state of denial. As a result, an inter-community dialogue to seek correctives did not emerge; this enhanced distances.

Security concerns and the inability of the state apparatus, from time to time, to ensure physical security, still tend to condition reactions across the board. It has affected visibility in public spaces and induced ghettoization with all its attendant consequences. The same holds good for livelihood concerns. The government's follow-up actions on the Sachar Committee Report made some impact but many of the grievances persist, as is evident from the thrust of testimonies given in the meeting that was organized in New Delhi by a civil society group. Some of the recommendations for corrective action emanating from the meeting need to be given a closer look.

The patterns of differentiation in the employment of Muslims in the public and private sectors, as well as deprivation from other forms of state largesse, identified by the Sachar Report and other studies, combined with low performance levels in education, has caused economic hardship and given a fresh impetus to the demand for reservations, notwithstanding its evident limitations. Some of the state governments have seen merit in it and responded in varying degrees. The Ranganath Mishra Commission, whose report is yet to be made public, is said to have recommended specific steps based on assessment of backwardness irrespective of religion. More is likely to be heard about this in the coming months and years.

In regard to Urdu, there is sufficient evidence to show that it suffered from deliberate official neglect in some of the states. Jawaharlal Nehru complained about it to the chief ministers as early as 1954. Half a century later and belying the requirement of Article 350A, large segments of a generation have grown up without knowing their mother tongue. Equally glaring is the failure of Urdu-knowing people to nurture the language, particularly among the youth. The general public, apart from occasional couplets and more frequent melodies in Mumbai movies, considers Urdu synonymous with Muslims, with its teaching confined to madrasas or universities but rarely undertaken in normal schools. An international conference on the Urdu language in 2003 recommended that 'in order to protect Urdu in its land of birth, while it flourishes abroad, a national movement for the revival of Urdu commanding strong political will is the need of the hour'. There is little evidence of this taking shape. What was said many years back still holds good: *Sad salah jalse huai, magar is se zubaan ki yaad to qaim rahti hai, taraqqi nahin hoti.* Thus, the onus for salvaging Urdu rests primarily with those who claim it as their mother tongue and those who value its inherent strength and beauty and its substantial contribution to Indian literature and culture.

The demand for the acknowledgement of the distinctive, minority character of the Aligarh Muslim University (to rectify a Supreme Court ruling of 1965) has been a persistent one, but seems to have lost its centrality in community perceptions with the emergence of good-quality minority-run institutions of higher and professional education in several states and the resultant erosion of AMU's all-India identity and character. It remains to be seen if the attempt now underway to reincarnate the AMU in different parts of the country and link it to the mother institution by an umbilical cord of uncertain quality and character would necessarily serve better either the purpose of minority education in specific minority-concentration areas or do away with the demand to restore the minority character of the university.

The concern over the protection of Muslim Personal Law from parliamentary legislation is of later vintage and surfaced only in 1972 in the wake of a suggestion that an effort be made to move towards a uniform civil code. The debate has thrown up polarized positions and generated more heat than light. More relevant is the argument that the provision of Article 44 does not demand a 'mechanical application of a single family law to the entire nation by one stroke of legislation' since it goes against its rationale and ignores ground realities. This is supported by the Supreme Court's observation that 'a uniform law, though it is highly desirable, enactment thereof in one go may be counter-productive to the unity and integrity of the nation' and that 'the mischief or defect most acute may be remedied by process of law in stages'. This notwithstanding, the need for segregating harmful social customs from religious law per se does stare the community in the face and seeks a response; so does the precedent set by a number of Muslim countries to codify the law relating to marriage, divorce and succession. 'Voluntary surrender of intellectual independence', to use Allama Iqbal's phrase, does not signify a vibrant community; nor is self-imposed isolation an answer.

Do these readings become an imperative for course correction? Do they provide sufficient social and political momentum for change? Our national objective is inclusive growth. The state has to ensure this in its policy formulation and, more importantly, in its implementation. Public support thus becomes an essential ingredient. It is here that the citizen body in its entirety has to shoulder its responsibility and try to dilute, if not undo, the binary construction of the social universe. By the same token, Muslim citizens need to acknowledge the insufficiency of their interface with the rest of the citizen body and the limitations of their initiatives on self-help in social and educational matters needed to bring about a qualitative change in approach. Egalitarian pluralism, in other words, propels counterpart obligations for both the self and the other.

Many readers would know that the corrective was prescribed a long time back:

> *Khuda ne aaj tak uss qaum ki haalat nahin badli*
> *Na ho jisko khayaal aap apni haalat ke badalne ka*

There is, specifically, a requirement to address three challenges:

- Sustained, candid and uninterrupted interaction with fellow citizens without a syndrome of superiority or inferiority.
- Involvement of all segments of the community, particularly women who constitute half the population and are to be empowered in social responsibilities as equal partners with Muslim men.

- Self-empowerment in areas where competence already exists, making the best use of government assistance that is available, and creating capability to benefit from the opportunities being offered by an expanding economy.

A careful observer has summed up the requirement in blunt terms: '*Fiza aap ke haq main bhale badal rahi ho magar jab tak aap aage barh kar us se faaida nahin uthaenge, kuch nahin hone wala.*'

The failure of communication with the wider community has tended to freeze the boundaries of diversities that characterize the Indian society. People have tended to live together separately. As a result, stereotypes have been developed and nurtured. Many years ago Edward Said had portrayed Western perceptions of Islam and Muslims: 'For the right, Islam represents barbarism;[6] for the left, medieval theocracy; for the center, a kind of distasteful exoticism.' In our country, mercifully, perceptions were less stark, thanks to the cultural interaction of a thousand years. However, the politics of history textbooks has left its imprint on the mind of a good section of the public. Media images add to this. The past, however rosy or gory, will neither sustain the present nor help create a better future. There is, therefore, an urgent need to correct the image, go beyond identity issues, project a more holistic view of Muslims as normal human beings and fellow citizens with the same rights and responsibilities as other citizens. The requirement is of an authentic dialogue among equals about the universality of values. Its objective should be Gandhiji's 'union of hearts'. Islam's emphasis on observance of ethical principles in interaction with all human beings should help Muslims to propel a positive image.

In regard to the status of women the dead weight of tradition, poverty and communal politics has resulted in three deficits: (a) literacy, (b) economic power resulting from work and income and (c) autonomy of decision-making. This has produced a pattern of structured disempowerment. It is most visible amongst the poor. It is, therefore, imperative to seek correctives through social awakening; in this effort, religious texts are not an impediment, rather, social custom is. The endeavour should be inclusive; the traditionalists, who have a wider social reach, have to be included and reminded of Islam's teachings on the status of women, as also of the imperative of our times. What is needed is a virtual revolution in our approach to this question. The examples of education of women in Muslim societies like Indonesia, Malaysia, Iran and Turkey, and its eventual impact on the status of women in society, can be emulated with benefit. Given the ground situation, a beginning can be made by a time-bound programme of opening primary and secondary schools for girls in Muslim-concentration localities. This, and the scholarship schemes being implemented by the government, should show some results over a five-year period.

The third challenge is of empowerment and self-empowerment. The state can assist as it must, and is committed to do so; by the same logic, however, this only initiates the process and cannot be the end of it. The syndrome of victimhood does not help and there are lessons to be learnt from the experience of other minorities. An expanding economy like ours needs active participation in emerging opportunities and in equipping the youth with skills to improve employability. In today's India, time is of critical importance; so is the need to remember that mediocrity means marginalization. There are a great many success stories in small and medium businesses, educational institutions and in professions. These need to be studied, publicized and internalized. The process, admittedly, is unevenly spread and a much greater community and governmental effort is needed in the northern and eastern states. It can, nevertheless, be said that a new Muslim identity is emerging in different regions, language areas, professional groups and social classes. It exudes confidence in varying degrees, refuses to shoulder the burden of the past and is assertive about the rights due to it as citizen. They thus become partners in the promotion of inclusive development.

Let us look again at the characteristic of uniqueness. This has three dimensions: of India being a plural, secular and democratic state; of its Muslim minority being the third-largest community of Muslims in the world; and of this minority's distinctive experience in terms of cultural contributions and dialogue. Indian Muslims constitute 10 per cent of the total Muslim population of the world. Other countries where Muslims live as significant minorities (Ethiopia, China, Russia and Tanzania) do not have the democratic framework or the record of cultural interaction; on the other hand, the Muslim numbers in individual Western countries are a miniscule percentage of their populations. The Indian experience and the Indian Muslim experience, therefore, could be of relevance to others also, particularly in the context of globalization that has induced much greater mobility of people. More and more countries in the world, therefore, will be called upon to accommodate diversity within a framework of equality; many of them are encountering conceptual and practical difficulties. India thus offers an alternate working model of pluralism in thought and action.

Despite our credible record of accommodation of diversity, it would be a folly to consider it a finished product. A living society evolves continuously in terms of its perceptions and practices, including those pertaining to equality, plurality, secularism, human rights and minority rights. The deepening of the democratic process in the country, and heightened consciousness of egalitarian diversity, would unavoidably propel all segments of the population to exercise the moral muscle, explore the normative potential and question some of the traditional symbols, customs and prejudices. The social and economic rejuvenation of Indian Muslims is important for its internal dimension, as also for revitalizing India's traditional engagement with, and contribution to, the Muslim world beyond our borders.

While the Indian Constitution was well ahead of its time in recognizing diversities and in providing for representation of and affirmative action for identified collectivities in our formal democratic structures, there would come a time when we would need to revert to focus on redressing the deprivations of individual citizens, irrespective of their group affiliations.

Eternal vigilance, it is said, is the price of liberty. There is, therefore, a need to be vigilant, keep the process on a progressive track and prevent regressions. The key seems to lie in a sincere, unconditional and uninterrupted dialogue and requisite corrective action within the framework of the Constitution. All segments of society, majority and minority, have a national duty to do so:

Mere ahl-e-watan yeh aadmiyat ka taqaaza hai
Muhabbat ka, sharaafat ka, hameeyat ka taqaaza hai

15
THE ART AND CULTURE OF ISLAM IN INDIA

LET ME BEGIN WITH TWO couplets that have remained a sound preamble down the ages:

> *Ba naam-e-Khudawand jaan aafarein*
> *Hakim-e-sukhan dar zubaan aafarein*
>
> *Khudawand bakhshanda-e-dastgeer*
> *Karim-e-khata bakhsh pozish pazeer*

> In the name of the Lord, soul-creating
>
> Wise One, speech-creating in the tongue
>
> Lord forgiving, apt to help
>
> Generous, fault-forgiving, excuse-accepting

The subject is vast, almost nebulous. The best that can be attempted is to touch upon some overarching themes. Islam has been a part of the Indian landscape for well over a millennium and has impacted on, and been impacted upon, in very many layers. A very good reason for it is the unique nature of Indian culture. The doyen of historians of an earlier era, Dr Tara Chand of revered memory, delineated it with some precision:

> Indian culture is synthetic in character. It comprehends ideas of different orders. It embraces in its orbit beliefs, customs, rites,

---

Note: Speech delivered at the International Seminar on 'Islamic Art', 30 December 2011, Hyderabad.

institutions, arts, religions and philosophies belonging to strata of society in varying stages of development. It eternally seeks to find a unity for the heterogeneous elements which make up its totality. At worst its attempts end in mechanical juxtaposition, at best they succeed in evolving an organic system.[1]

Historical record makes evident the absence of mechanical juxtaposition. Islam as a faith, as a body of ideas and practices, came to India through human interaction in different ways in different parts of the subcontinent. This took place over time, and 'in a manner that was beyond social and political control'. The unifying factor for the adherents of the new faith was a common allegiance to Islam. Beyond it, variations in doctrine and observances and diversity in regional terms remained; nor were the differences in rural–urban practices erased. Each left its imprint on art and culture.

A discourse on culture necessarily confronts definitional impediments. How do we define culture? One study compiled 164 definitions! We could accept the anthropologist Edward Taylor's definition and consider culture to be 'that complex whole which includes knowledge, belief, art, law, morals, custom, and any other capabilities and habits acquired by man as a member of society'. Emanating from this, the art and culture of Islam in India could be taken to mean such contributions inspired, made or caused to be made, by persons or groups living here and professing to belong to the Islamic faith.

It is known that within a few centuries from its inception Islam became a world religion with its adherents living in different countries imbibing, and shaping, the local environment. The historian Ira Lapidus has neatly characterized this interaction as 'a dialogue between the realm of religious symbols and the world of everyday reality...of interaction between Islamic values and historical experiences of Muslim peoples that has shaped the formation of a number of different but interrelated Muslim societies'.[2]

The nature of this interaction also depended on the type of contacts and the cultural level of the societies concerned. In regard to the first, there is sufficient evidence to show that Indians, particularly those all along the west coast, were familiar with various communities in western Asia in the period before the advent of Islam. There were extensive trading ties with, and through, the lands of Arabia, Persia, the Red Sea, the Persian Gulf and beyond. Transient traders, as well as settled communities, were a frequent occurrence. The rise of a centralized state in the wake of the early Islamic expansion gave a considerable impetus to existing interaction.

India, therefore, was a known land, sought after for its prosperity and trading skills and respected for its attainments in different branches of knowledge. Baghdad became the seeker, and dispenser, of Indian numerals and sciences. The *Panchatantra* was translated and became *Kalila wa Dimna*. Long before the advent of Muslim conquerors, the works of Al-Jahiz, Ibn Khurdadbeh, Al-Kindi, Yaqubi and Al-Masudi testify to it in ample measure. Alberuni, who studied India and Indians more thoroughly than most, produced a virtual encyclopedia on religion, rituals, manners and customs, philosophy, mathematics and astronomy. He commenced his great work by highlighting differences, but was careful enough 'to relate, not criticize'.

For the purpose of this chapter, I shall opt for some selectivity in the choice of impact areas, and restrict my observations to the most noticeable ones: to architecture and painting in the realm of art proper and to history, literature, religious and philosophical speculation and Sufism in the wider area of culture.

This discourse took shape through rulers and the ruling class, scholars and intellectuals, and all those who interacted with and influenced the masses in general.

Historians have shed much light on the essential features of the Muslim rule and the ruling classes. In the first place, the state was not theocratic, notwithstanding the fact that throughout the medieval period the rulers in Delhi and in many other kingdoms were Muslim; they however 'paid scant attention to Islamic concepts of the State'. Kingship was absolute rather than conditional; governance was conducted through state-made regulations (zawabit) and not on the principles of Sharia. The nobility (with a few exceptions) was a hierarchy of salaried officials. Over time, the imprint of Indian social organization was clearly visible. Social interaction at different levels, and within those levels, diluted rigid norms and induced adaptability. Creativity followed.

One unavoidable consequence of the capture of authority anywhere is to reflect it physically. The mosque and the tomb in the religious domain and the palace, pavilions, town gates, gardens and landscape architecture in the secular domain, thus, became reflective of the new, changing reality. So, towards the close of the 12th century, India saw the arrival of a totally distinct tradition of architecture. Its major characteristics, in the words of Professor Irfan Habib, were:

...the use of arch, vault and dome, and the application of lime cement; it could achieve in consequence a lightness and grace that the earlier trabeate construction could not easily match. Its love of light and space and 'simple severity' seems to stand in sharp contrast to 'plastic exuberance' of the earlier Indian tradition.[3]

This tradition of distinctive style evolved over a period of four centuries and produced regional variants. Competent observers have noted that in the Moghul period 'the combination of scale, detail and good taste was sometimes breadth-taking and has seldom been surpassed'. The mosques and tombs of that era, as also the landscape architecture in the shape of ornamental gardens, are too well known to be mentioned individually; their grandeur immortalizes the architectural and building skills of the planners, engineers and craftsmen.

Provincial styles in architecture also blossomed. Ahmedabad and Mandu were distinctive. The Qutub Shahi forts, mosques and monuments in the vicinity of the city of Hyderabad, and the Charminar, are too well known to most readers to be dilated upon. Scholars like Percy Brown have dwelt in detail on the stylistic evolution in this period.

Painting was another area of excellence. The Ajanta frescos are reflective of the high technical and artistic quality attained in the pre-Muslim period. Humayun, during his exile in Persia, developed a taste for Persian paintings and was able to bring back masters like Abdus Samad. The Moghul style, in the words of Annemarie Schimmel, 'developed from the interaction of the refined Persian style and the strong, lively, vision of the Hindu artists'; its evolution is well reflected in the miniatures of the *Tutinama* and the *Hamzanama*, reaching its peak in the reigns of Jahangir and Shahjahan. They, like Akbar, regarded painting as a means of bringing historical and romantic texts vividly to life. Jahangir in particular used paintings as a guide to physiognomy, to enable him to recognize and assess nobles and as a scientific instrument to study flora and fauna. He mentions in his memoirs the names of Abul Hasan and Ustad Mansur; their respective titles, *Nadir-uz-zaman* and *Nadir-ul-Asr*, speak for themselves. He also dwells on his own expertise on the subject in words that need to be quoted without abridgement:

> As regards myself, my liking for painting and my practice in judging it have arrived at such a point that when any work is brought before me, either of deceased artists or of those of present day, without the name being told me, I say on the spur of the moment that

it is the work of such and such a man. And if there be a picture containing many portraits, and each face by the work of a different master, I can discover which face is the work of each of them. If any other person has put in the eye or the eyebrow of a face, I can perceive whose work the original face is, and who has painted the eyes and the eyebrows.

Yet another area of excellence was calligraphy. Suspicion of figurative art as idolatrous led to it; thus, abstract depictions became a major form of artistic expression in Islamic cultures, especially in religious contexts. Fine handwriting was also regarded as an essential accomplishment for a noble man and 'aesthetics was made an aspect of sovereignty'. The emperors were not merely admirers of calligraphy, they were also practitioners. The Moghul artists, like their Ottoman counterparts, developed new variations and formed pictures and figures out of words.

An impetus to the writing of history is particularly noticeable. In the period prior to the 12th century, there was, in the words of Narayanan Bandyopadhyaya, 'a lack of recorded history', an exception to it being Kalhana's history of Kashmir. In the subsequent five centuries historical writings flourished. The names are too many to be mentioned here. An early example is Ali bin Hamid Kufi's *Chachnama*. Much more followed, in the pre-Moghul and Moghul periods. The wealth of material compiled by Juzjani, Barani, Abul Fazl, Badauni, Qazwini, Khafi Khan and others have made possible comprehensive study of that period. Equally significant are the autobiographies of rulers; the most prominent of these were the *Babur Nama* and *Tuzk-i-Jahangiri*.[4] Gul Badan Begum's *Humayun Nama* could be counted in the proximate category.

Belief, consciousness and practice became a particularly rich area of interaction. On one side, high value was placed on orthodoxy 'because it maintained the identity of a community against other communities and prevented an assimilation that could lead to the community disintegrating and being absorbed by others'. On the other, and living in a non-homogenous social milieu, the pious often communicated values through personal practice. In this sense the values of faith, though not its theological content, reached a wider circle of the public. The popularity of different Sufi personalities is evidence enough of their reach. Thus, there is merit in Professor Mujeeb's observation that 'Sufism took Islam to the masses and in doing so it took over the enormous and delicate responsibility of dealing at a personal level with a baffling variety of problem'.

Scholars have analysed the socio-cultural role of the Sufi dargahs in the cultural integration of the religious communities. The Sufi trends sought commonalities in spiritual thinking. One example of it is *Dabistan-i-Mazahib*, a mid-17th century work believed to have been written in Srikakulam (present-day Andhra Pradesh) and described by an eminent scholar as 'the greatest book ever written in India on comparative religion'. Dara Shikoh went further in his *Majmu' al Bahrain*, gave a Vedantic view of universe and truth and concluded 'that the differences between Islam and Hinduism were merely verbal'.

Alongside, the influence of Islam can be discerned in the vocabulary of preachers and saints of other faiths and Bhakti traditions.

The pattern of convergence or parallelism has been traced with precision by many scholars; their judgement is that some Islamic precepts and many Muslim practices seeped into the interstices of the Indian society and gave expression to a broader and deeper unity of minds expressive of the Indian spiritual tradition.

This tradition was aptly summed up by Allama Iqbal in his poem '*Hindustani Bachon Ka Qaumi Geet.*'

To conclude, I can do no better than to go back to Dr Tara Chand's classic work *Influence of Islam on Indian Culture* written in 1922 and cite a telling passage:

> It is hardly possible to exaggerate the extent of Muslim influence over Indian life in all departments. But nowhere else is it shown so vividly and so picturesquely, as in customs, in intimate details of domestic life, in music, in the fashion of dress, in the ways of cooking, in the ceremonial of marriage, in the celebration of festivals and fairs, and in the courtly institutions and etiquette of Marathi, Rajput and Sikh princes. In the days of Babar the Hindu and Muslim lived and thought so much alike that he was forced to notice their peculiar 'Hindustani way'; his successors so gloriously adorned and so marvelously enriched his legacy that India might well be proud today of the heritage which they in turn left behind.[5]

16
CHALLENGES FOR A HOMELESS LANGUAGE: URDU IN PRESENT-DAY INDIA

Yeh maikhana hai, bazm-e-jum nahin hai
Yahaan koi kise se kam nahin hai

CLOSE TO FOUR DECADES OF my life was spent in the profession of diplomacy, trying to explain to foreign governments and audiences the Indian impulses and responses emanating from our heterogeneity and unique socio-cultural complexity. One aspect of this was the multiplicity of languages. My message was decisively understood whenever I asked them to examine an Indian rupee currency note to count the languages in which its monetary value was written!

Historians and political scientists have written about the intense debates on the language question in the Constituent Assembly. The outcome was reflected in Part XVII of the Constitution and in its Eighth Schedule. This did not settle the matter. Some years later we witnessed the emergence of the impulse for linguistic homogeneity, seeking expression in territorial identity. It was sought to be satisfied through the States Reorganization Commission whose report was tabled in the Parliament in 1955.

It is to be noted that most of the 22 languages now listed in the Eighth Schedule find territorial expression in a 'home state'. A notable exception to this is Urdu which, despite its spread across many states, finds itself to be in a condition of homelessness, with all its attendant consequences. Sindhi is in a similar position, except for the fact that the total number of Sindhi speakers is 2.57 million.

Note: Nizam Urdu Lecture delivered in Urdu, 6 January 2012, Delhi.

Besides being an officially recognized language, Urdu also has an official language status for some specified purposes (whose details vary and condition the impact substantively) in Andhra Pradesh, Bihar, Delhi, Jammu and Kashmir, Jharkhand, and Uttar Pradesh.

According to the Census of India 2001, there were a total of 51.5 million Urdu speakers in the country, amounting to 5.01 per cent of the population and constituting the sixth-largest language group. Five states (Uttar Pradesh, Bihar, Maharashtra, Andhra Pradesh and Karnataka) account for 41.5 million of the Urdu speakers. If you add Jharkhand, West Bengal, Madhya Pradesh, Tamil Nadu and Delhi to it, the figure reaches 48.55 million. Data also reveals that the percentage of Urdu speakers was 5.25 and 5.18 in the census of 1981 and 1991 respectively.

This decline, in a framework of overall increase of population and more specific demographic data, raises a question. Why is the number of Urdu speakers declining when the areas and groups generally associated with the language have registered normal increases in population?

Does this suggest a pattern of language abandonment?

An explanation in a wider context was given by Professor Abram de Swan in a paper published in the *European Review* in October 2004 (pp. 567–588):

> People who abandon their native tongue do so because they move elsewhere or take up something else and in this new existence they have higher expectations of a different language. Or they neglect it because another language is preferred at school, by public authorities, or in courts of law, and their own language is treated with disdain. Or they have to stop using it because they are ruled by another nation that imposes its language on them, and, having lost heart, they no longer take care to preserve their own language.

He went on to add that since 'every language is a product of the collective creativity of people expressed over hundreds or thousands of years, its disappearance is an irreversible loss of culture'.

Where, then, do we look for an explanation for the decline of Urdu speakers? Since language is principally a matter of affiliation and usage, giving it up is unlikely to be voluntary or an act of 'enlightenment' and must necessarily emanate from some form of compulsion or necessity. Hence, the key to our primary question has to be sought amidst the factors cited by Professor de Swan and, of the three possible situations visualized by him, the answer seems to be in the second—namely, language at school level and in use by public authorities.

Two sets of facts emerging from official data or pronouncements could be relevant here:

1. In a question answered in the Rajya Sabha on 12 August 2011, the Ministry of Human Resource Development stated that Urdu is not being taught in Kendriya Vidyalayas in various states since in none of them 20 or more students opted for the language, adding that for the same reason, no posts of Urdu teachers were sanctioned.

    The simple conclusion to be drawn is that Urdu-knowing students do not make it to Kendriya Vidyalayas in the minimum numbers prescribed. The data has other implications, since these schools are primarily for transferable central government employees.

2. In a study completed shortly before his death last year, the late Dr Omar Khalidi of the Massachusetts Institute of Technology had examined the state of Urdu literacy in India as gauged through school education and raised five questions:

    o   How many students in primary schools are having Urdu as the language of instruction?

    o   How many are learning Urdu as one of the subjects under the three-(or four-) language formula?

    o   Have the various levels of government—central, state and local—facilitated or obstructed learning of Urdu in various states?

    o   To what can we attribute the uneven levels of Urdu literacy in various states?

    o   What are the other institutions, besides schools run by the state, involved in promoting Urdu literacy?

Khalidi's conclusions on the first two questions, based on available official data, reveal that Urdu literacy in terms of Urdu-medium enrolment in primary–secondary schools is highest in Maharashtra and Bihar, less so in Karnataka and Andhra and least in Uttar Pradesh and Delhi. In terms of percentages of total enrolment for the year 2007–2008, it was 6.53 in Maharashtra, 5.2 in Bihar, 5.9 in Karnataka, 2.8 in Andhra, 1.0 in Delhi and 0.40 Uttar Pradesh.

The answers to the third and fourth questions require delving into recent history. Here I can do no better than to recall Jawaharlal Nehru's own assessment. In a confidential letter to chief ministers on 16 July 1953 he spoke of 'a pettiness in mind, a narrowness in outlook and an immaturity' that characterized 'a deliberate attempt to push out Urdu which is spoken and written by a large number of people'. This was repeated two weeks later, and in a wider framework, in the letter of 1 August:

> We encourage the smallest tribal language in its own area, but many of us resent even the mention of Urdu, and yet Urdu is very much a child of India and is a vital and graceful aspect of our many-sided culture. I am deeply grieved at this narrowness of outlook which so frequently comes in our way...[1]

Nehru repeated his views in the matter in the Hyderabad session of the All India Congress Committee in October the same year. A Union Home Ministry circular of July 1958 mentioned the need to provide Urdu language teaching at the primary stage to children having it as mother tongue, and some other related facilities. It did not refer to Article 350A of the Constitution nor did it invoke Article 347.

The American scholar Paul Brass, in his 1974 book *Language, Religion and Politics in North India,* shed much light on the policy and procedural methodology by which some states succeeded 'in diverting large number of Urdu speakers' from the path of education in their mother tongue.

Narrow political perceptions and mistaken identification of language with a community thus led to a unilingual approach and prevailed over the linguistic diversity of a plural society and the ethos of the Constitution.

In 1972, the Government of India Resolution, that set up the Gujral Committee to ascertain ways for the promotion and development of Urdu, stated that 'Urdu is not the concern of any one State Government or of any community. The responsibility for its development has also to be shared by the Central Government'. Its recommendations received in 1975, as also of the Ali Sardar Jaafri Committee in 1990, to the extent they have been implemented, have not altered the picture meaningfully. Nor has the National Council for Promotion of Urdu Language, established in 1990, registered a significant success in its primary objective. The pashemani remained formal rather than corrective.

> *Meri zuban pe shikwae ahl-e-sitam nahin*
> *Mujh ko jaga diya yahi ehsaan kum nahin*

Lamentation about the past is relevant only to draw lessons from it. Our concern today should be with the present, and the future. Where does Urdu stand now on the basis of the data cited above? What is its place in our social and cultural life, our political and economic life? How can its attributed affiliation to a specific community, with all its unstated suggestions, be overcome to recapture its rightful place in the kaleidoscope of languages and cultural patterns of India? How can it be rejuvenated, its future be made livelier?

On one plane, official acknowledgement of Urdu is extended with unfailing regularly. Anniversaries are observed, patronage given to 'mushairas'. Its limitations are obvious: *Is se zubaan ki yaad to qaim rahi hai, taraqqi nahin hoti.*

This dichotomous approach was commented upon many years back by Sahir Ludhianavi:

> *Ghalib jise kahte hain Urdu ka hi shair tha*
> *Urdu pe sitam kar ke Ghalib pe karam kyon ho*

A commentator observed in a newspaper last year that 'Urdu has been kept alive by the Hindi cinema, FM radio, madrassas and occasional recitation of couplets in Parliament'. He drew attention to Professor Gopi Chand Narang's remark that 'Urdu is like a patient on oxygen at the fag end of his life. This is the last generation of Urdu'.[2]

'Bollywood' films have unquestionably played a major role in keeping alive the usage of Urdu. The historian Ramachandra Guha has referred to its rationale in a perceptive chapter in *India after Gandhi* (2007). From a different angle, Ira Bhaskar and Richard Allen have shed much light in their book *Islamicate Cultures of Bombay Cinema* (2009), to highlight the points of intersection between history, culture, language, community and contemporary tensions and to demonstrate, as they put it, its 'cultural and political value… in the plural and multicultural imagination of India'.

The role of Madaris is noteworthy. They have sustained Urdu in difficult times in the context of their curricula of studies and have helped take it to a segment of the younger generation. By the same token, however, the effort has been community-specific and confined to those of its members who preferred a madrasa, generally for economic reasons, to normal, state-run, schools. At the same time, confining Urdu to the Madaris also impacts on what is historically an essentially secular, occasionally libertarian, temper of the language:

> *Dharkanen sadyion ki jismain, kaif be-bakana hai.*

Languages are learnt, and sustained, for a variety of reasons. They are, in the first place, imbibed at home as mother tongue and supplemented through primary (and secondary) schooling in it. This necessitates availability of schools, textbooks and teachers provided either by the state or local authority or through community efforts. Second, languages are learnt through economic compulsions and in quest of economic opportunities. It implies participation in wider and prevalent community patterns of education and employability and the requisite effort by society to make available educational institutions and teachers. In the third place, a language may be learnt as a preferred elective for social or religious prestige or academic excellence.

Thus, the challenge for a declining language is at two levels. The child's inherited awareness of the mother tongue is part of his/her personal, social and cultural identity and has to be shaped and consolidated by structured instruction to enable him or her to proceed from illiteracy to basic literacy. Thereafter, the instrumental motivation and contours of language revival must necessarily be shaped by economic factors. In most multilingual societies (including India), the latter is a function of dominant language for administration, business and interregional and international communications. The picture here is evident, and fully accepted.

The situation is different with regard to the mother tongue. It is a fundamental right of citizens, under Article 29, to conserve their distinct language and script. The objective of Article 350A—'for every State and every local authority within the State to provide adequate facilities for instruction in the mother tongue at the primary stage of education to children belonging to linguistic minority groups'—however remains unachieved for a great number of Urdu-speaking children. In some cases, their linguistic identity is overlooked or ignored; in others, primary school arrangements remain non-functional by the absence of Urdu language teachers and textbooks. The persistence of these defaults raises doubts about the sincerity of the effort.

The conclusion is inescapable—that this is a case of multiple failures: on the part of the state in its constitutional obligations, of the Urdu-speaking communities in their cultural duty to be assertive in seeking to learn and sustain the language, and of individual families for not making the additional effort required for doing so.

What, then is to be done? An observation by a Senegalese poet is of some relevance to this discussion: 'In the end we will conserve only what we love; we will love only what we understand; and we will understand only what we are taught.'

The imperative need is to find ways of teaching Urdu to those who declare it to be their mother tongue. The task has to begin with the primary school and should continue at least in part of the secondary school. The problem would be resolved if, in the 'Three-language formula', evolved and accepted under the National Language Policy, Urdu is assigned the same status as its sister Indian languages. This, regrettably, is not forthcoming in government schools in some states and in others through tardiness in recruitment of teachers and publication of textbooks, etc. The deficiencies in the implementation of safeguards for linguistic minorities in different states are recorded with some precision in the Forty-fifth Report of the Commissioner for Linguistic Minorities for the period ending June 2007. It asserts that 'the constitutional safeguards provided for the linguistic minorities can only become real when there is necessary supportive legislation'.

Until more assertive state action is taken, the only alternative, therefore, is organized effort at the family and Urdu-speaking community level. The experience of declining-language communities elsewhere in the world would be relevant in this context. A good example is the practice of the Jewish community in the United States of undertaking weekend instruction in Hebrew. Other examples of successful language revival are Catalan in Spain and French in Canada.

Alongside, the need to keep alive the effort to make the state honour constitutional obligations in regard to those who claim Urdu as their mother tongue has to be galvanized. Public opinion and electoral pressures do produce results, as has happened in several states of the Indian Union. We have, at all times, to remember that justice is the first of the four principles enshrined in the Preamble of our Constitution and, as the philosopher John Rawls put it, 'the rights secured by justice are not subject to political bargaining or to the calculus of social interests'.[3]

There are, nevertheless, some silver linings on the horizon. Urdu newspapers and magazines have survived the decline and have shown signs of a revival. Corporate media has shown interest in the Urdu press. Books in Urdu continue to be published and are inexpensively priced. Several Urdu television channels (apart from Doordarshan-Urdu) have come into existence and seem to survive commercially. The music industry continues to prosper on Urdu ghazals, songs and qawwalis.

One other factor of relevance needs mention. Urdu is now an

international language and is being studied and promoted beyond the Indian subcontinent. The Internet is assisting the effort in good measure. It would indeed be a tragedy of profound dimensions if the language would regress and disappear in the land of its birth.

The question, in the final analysis, also pertains to our perception of Indian pluralism and of the ambit of Indian culture. Is it to be inclusive or exclusive? Has it to be characterized by catholicity of approach or otherwise? Do we retain what has enriched it in the past and continues to do so today, or discard for considerations emanating from illiberal outlook?

Kisi bhi shama se be-zaar ho kyon koi parvana
Yeh kya is daur ka diwanapun hai hum nahin samjhe

17
PHYSICAL INTEGRATION AND EMOTIONAL INCONSONANCE

SARDAR VALLABHBHAI PATEL WAS AN iconic personality, a close associate of Gandhiji, a leader in the freedom struggle, a person who, along with Jawaharlal Nehru, was at the helm of affairs in the early years of our existence as a free country. His contributions were manifold; above all, history and generations of Indians remembers him as the man who presided over the process that resulted in the integration of the Indian states, following the end of British rule and the termination of the 'vague and undefined' relationship that princely states (together constituting 40 per cent of the Indian landmass) had with the United Kingdom as the paramount power.

The process of integrating 554 large and miniscule states was complex. It involved intricate negotiations on political, administrative and financial matters as also those relating to the armed forces of these units. It was almost completed by the time the Constitution of India came into force on 26 January 1950. Nevertheless, a passage in V.P. Menon's classic and first-hand account highlights what was not accomplished at that point:

> We had demolished the artificial barriers between the States inter se and the rest of India and had indeed laid the foundations for an integrated administrative and financial structure. But the real integration had to take place in the minds of the people. This could not be accomplished overnight. It would take some time for the people of erstwhile States to outgrow their regional loyalties and to develop a wider outlook and a broader vision.[1]

Note: Annual Sardar Patel Memorial Lecture, 7 November 2012, New Delhi.

Menon goes on to quote Sardar Patel's apprehension in the matter:

Almost overnight we have introduced in these States the superstructure of modern system of government. The inspiration and stimulus has come from above rather than from below and unless the transplanted growth takes a healthy root in the soil, there will be a danger of collapse and chaos.[2]

Passage of time was to show that this integration of the minds, not only by the residents of the erstwhile princely states, but by citizens on the national scale was to be a longer process, at times torturous, and covered all regions and all segments of population in our vast land.

Nor was this unanticipated; as early as 1902, Rabindranath Tagore had observed that 'unity cannot be brought about by enacting a law that all shall be one'.

The Constitution-making process reflected the concern for national unity. One aspect of it, legal and structural, put into place a parliamentary democracy; the other pertained to sociological and emotional dimensions. Emerging from the inherited pattern of centralized governance, the concern was to prevent Balkanization as well as to accommodate what Sunil Khilnani has called 'layered Indianness' that specifically recognized linguistic and cultural identities. This was reflected in the end product—a Union of States, described by Ivor Jennings as 'a federation with strong centralizing tendencies'.

The imperatives of democracy were spelt out with great insight, and foresight, by Babasaheb Ambedkar in the closing days of the work of the Constituent Assembly. Effective functioning of democracy, he said, required focus on three aspects: first, holding fast to constitutional methods and abandoning 'the method of civil disobedience, non-cooperation and satyagraha'; second, not allowing anyone, however mighty, to subvert the institutions; and third, not resting content with political democracy only and recognizing the twin principles of equality (through one man one vote and one vote one value) and fraternity (through common brotherhood of all Indians). 'The sooner we realize', he added, 'that we are as yet not a nation in the social and psychological sense of the word, the better for us.'[3]

Some years later, and speaking on national integration, Jawaharlal Nehru stressed the same point. 'I lay stress on the unity of India,' he said, 'not merely the political unity which we have achieved but something far deeper, the emotional unity, the integration of our minds and hearts, the suppression of feelings of separatism.'

The working of the Constitution in terms of the arrangements between the Union and the states in the context of 'a changing social, economic and political environment' has been examined on a number of occasions, the most recent being the Punchi Commission. Its report submitted in March 2010, built on earlier works, particularly of the Sarkaria Commission (1988), took note of the failure of expectations generated by it, and concluded with the observation that 'cooperative federalism will be the key for sustaining India's unity, integrity and social and economic development in future'.

In one of the questionnaires circulated by the Punchi Commission to stakeholders it was enquired if, given the pluralistic identity of India, political and social developments and increased socio-political mobilization around sectarian identities would pose a threat to the unity and integrity of the country? Furthermore, what could be done to ensure that the national vision and wider collective purpose are always paramount and do not get distorted? The answers received are not yet in the public domain.

In this context, another set of questions come to mind. While the debate on the functioning of the federal system is very much a part of the national political discourse, can the same be said for the realization of fraternity? How far, and how well, have we as a people travelled on the path of social and emotional integration?

Record shows that in September 1961, Prime Minister Nehru convened a National Integration Conference to find ways and means to combat the evils of communalism, casteism, regionalism, linguism and narrow-mindedness that were becoming hurdles to maintenance of national unity and integrity. The Conference decided to set up a National Integration Council to address these matters and make recommendations thereon. The first meeting of the Council was held in June 1962. To date, 15 meetings have been held in 50 years, with glaring gaps of over 10 years between some of these meetings.

Could the frequency be suggestive of priorities? Perhaps the answer is to be found in a propensity to evade troubling questions until they begin to dent the certitudes or the major premises that envelop public discourse.

In 2005, Rajni Kothari had written about 'a need to think beyond the merely political and tap the psycho-spiritual dimensions of Indian reality'; he concluded that 'the Indian model of development is characterized by the politicization of social structure, through a wide dispersal and permeation of political forms, values and ideologies'.[4] Other competent observers have noted democracy in India advancing 'through the competitive negotiations between groups, each competing for their interests, rather than the diffusion of democratic norms'.

A natural consequence of this is 'the politics of identity', perhaps even a Balkanization of the Indian mind.

It is in the backdrop of these ground realities that the question of national integration is to be viewed. How do we bring about 'the integration of minds and hearts'?

Many years back a political scientist had sought to delineate the contours of the desirable on this count:

> In the semantics of functional politics the term national integration means, and ought to mean, *cohesion* and *not fusion, unity* and *not uniformity, reconciliation* and *not merger, accommodation not annihilation, synthesis* and *not dissolution, solidarity* and *not regimentation* of the several discrete segments of the people constituting the larger political community…Obviously, then, Integration is not a process of conversion of diversities into a uniformity but a congruence of diversities leading to a unity in which both the varieties and similarities are maintained.[5]

A conceptual framework of this degree of sophistication would obviously require a comprehensive endeavour by the state and the society to ensure its implementation on an ongoing basis. It has to become part of the social discourse and of the educational curricula aimed at making the citizens imbibe the virtues of integration and eschew the vices emanating from its absence. Such an effort has to be to move beyond the presumed Indianness in cultural terms or its spirited display on special occasions on which national integration and national solidarity are most obvious—in the face of an external enemy (1961, 1965, 1971 and 1998), a celebratory occasion like success in an international sporting event, an achievement of note by an Indian citizen or person of Indian origin, or a social or religious festival; above all, and on a fairly continuous basis, success stories in the film industry.

It is, therefore, essential to have a re-look at the basics of our methodology and of the contours within which it has worked. Our ground reality is a plural society; our operating radius is a democratic polity and a secular state structure, both based on a Constitution aimed at seeking justice, liberty, equality and fraternity for all citizens within a single political and juridical entity whose federal structure provides for separate legislative and executive powers for states, but stipulates uniformity in civil and criminal jurisprudence;

a single judiciary; a common All India Civil Service; a common armed forces; a common market; and a constitutional provision on sharing of financial resources between the centre and the states. The assumption was that political and administrative integration of the state would lead to an integration of hearts and minds of those who may speak a different language or follow a different faith or come from a different region, but would subscribe to and believe in a common Indian identity in which all other identities would be subsumed and also flourish at the same time.

This however has turned out to be insufficient. Hard issues agitating the public mind in different regions have come to the fore and seek acceptable solutions. B.G.Verghese has rightly observed that 'as India's multitudinous but hitherto dormant diversities come to life, identities are asserted and jostle for a place in the sun'. He lists among these issues of majority and minority, centre and periphery, great and little traditions, rural and urban values, tradition and modernity and concludes that 'this management of diversity within multiple transitions is a delicate and complex process aggravated by inexorable population growth'.[6]

One obvious reason for this is the ripening and deepening of the democratic process in the country, the awareness generated by it and the terms and shape of the dialogue propelled by it. Another is the failure of the state to comprehend the dimensions of change and the resultant failure to respond appropriately, without undue procrastination, and adapt existing mechanisms to newer requirements. As a result, the immediate has taken precedence over the remote; the obvious over the less obvious. There has been a shift of focus, perhaps a narrowing of the vision, with the national receding behind the regional or local. This is also evident in the domain of foreign policy where complex questions of national interest are involved and should not be impinged upon by transitory considerations.

The size and diversity of the Indian landscape adds to the difficulty of finding solutions. A population of 1.25 billion dispersed over 4,635 communities, 78 per cent of whom are not only linguistic and cultural but social categories—the human diversities are both hierarchical and spatial. 'The de jure WE, the sovereign people is in reality a fragmented "we", divided by yawning gaps that remain to be bridged.'[7] Around 30 per cent of our people live below the official poverty line and the health and education indicators, for the population as a whole, despite recent correctives, leave much to be desired. There are, in addition, problems arising out of Naxalism and insurgency in some areas where the writ of the state runs in name only, demands for a better deal for the states of the union, as also for tribes, Dalits and most of the minorities within them. Each of these also relates to the requirements of fraternity and the achievement of national integration.

A sense of urgency is thus imperative. How should we proceed? What institutional and policy devices can be availed of?

A beginning can, and must, be made with the lodestar of our national destiny, the Constitution. Experience shows that its provisions have been used creatively to expand the area of rights, to redress grievances, to allow greater space for federal units in specific areas. The need of the hour is to reinvigorate this process, to explore and make better use of existing constitutional provisions; above all, to ensure better delivery. Prescriptions of despair, unwise or impracticable, do not help the process.

A case in point is the working of our federal system. The underlying major premise is the rule of law. Without it, the carefully calibrated framework of power-sharing, and the jurisdictional allocation spelt out in the Seventh Schedule, become irrelevant. And yet, this does appear to be happening. To quote a knowledgeable scholar's analysis of the resulting situation:

> That coalition politics makes effective governance a challenge is not surprising... The more important question is what state politics and political parties are doing to the Indian federation. For federalism is not only about giving more powers to the states; it is also about preserving the integrity of those areas that lie within the exclusive preserve of the centre. Undermining the centre's governance over its own jurisdiction does not do any service to the federal idea. Today the Indian federalism is gravely endangered by populist imperatives originating in the states which encroach so far into the Union's as to enervate Parliament and the Union Executive.[8]

This is not to say that genuine disagreements of perception and functioning do not, or would not, arise; the question is the presence or absence of a will to seek fair and equitable solutions within the ambit of the law. The only way to do so is through dialogue and adequate flexibility within the framework of the Constitution. The obvious platform for such a dialogue, besides the Parliament, is the Interstate Council, belatedly established in 1990 under Article 263 on the recommendation of the Sarkaria Commission. Its meetings have been infrequent, except in 1997, and the political will to explore its full potential has clearly not been forthcoming. At the same time, the Council must desist from efforts to expand its ambit into matters unambiguously in the Union List of the Seventh Schedule, or to convert itself into a super federal executive, since both would be destructive of the delicate balance envisaged in the Constitution, a balance integral to the preservation of the union itself.

The same holds good for constitutional safeguards for tribal areas where the potential of Schedules V and VI of the Constitution could have been realized in fuller measure and could have retarded, if not prevented, resort to violence in tribal areas, arising out of their marginalization. Nor is the situation any better with regard to the actual implementation of various programmes for uplifting some of the most backward minorities, both educationally and economically.

More instances can be cited. These relate to ethnic or communal violence in different parts of the country, the efforts to differentiate between resident and 'outsiders' when both are citizens, to differentiate between Indian and Indian on specious and malicious considerations. Each is a manifestation of parochialism that has crept into our body politic. Each derogates from the requirement of fraternity and thereby affects national integration. The responsibility for failures is shared by all.

The conclusion is unavoidable that the process of emotional integration has faltered and is in dire need of reinvigoration. A corrective is imperative and would lie in reaffirmation of the democratic process bequeathed to us by the founding fathers, adherence to the letter and spirit of the Constitution, rejuvenation of the institutions beginning with the Parliament and state legislatures, and reaffirmation of the sanctity of dialogue. These principles need to be imbibed and implemented at all levels of the polity and particularly in educational policy, in the workshops of the mind that mould the thought process of the citizens of tomorrow.

18
IDENTITY AND CITIZENSHIP: AN INDIAN PERSPECTIVE

A FEW YEARS BACK, WHEN I was in the vicinity of Oxford, in a group dabbling in the unfathomable mysteries of the Iraq quagmire, Dr Nizami provided a welcome distraction by inviting me to see the site, and the plans, for the new building of the Oxford Centre for Islamic Studies. He also mentioned the debate on the proposed architectural design, and of the view in some quarters that it would change the inherited landscape of a hallowed community.

The change, as I understood it, implied an assertion of identity. It is now conceded, I am told, that the new structure did no aesthetic or spiritual damage to the skyline of Oxford. Perhaps the injection of diversity has enriched it.

Speculating on the 'ifs' of history, Edward Gibbon had visualized a course of events that might have resulted in the teaching of the interpretations of the Holy Qur'an at Oxford. He could not foresee a happier, intellectually more rewarding happening that the concluding decades of the 20th century would bring forth. Among its manifestations is the establishment of this Centre.

This is a tribute to Oxford's capacity to accommodate the unusual.

Encouraged by this accommodative approach, let me share some thoughts on the twin concepts of identity and citizenship and the manner of their impact on the building blocks of modern states.

Needless to say, it is an Indian perspective and draws in good measure on the Indian experience. It may be of relevance to some of the objectives

---

Note: Speech delivered at the Oxford Centre for Islamic Studies, 1 November 2013, Oxford.

of this Centre, since India counts amongst its citizens the third-largest Muslim population in the world and the largest Muslim minority anywhere.

It is a truism that the human being is a social creature and societies consist of individuals who come together for a set of common purposes, for whose achievement they agree to abide by a set of rules and, to that extent and for those purposes, give their tacit or explicit consent to the abridgment of individual free will or action. They, in other words, do not get subsumed totally in a larger whole and retain their individual identity. This identity, as pointed out by William James and sustained by more recent social-psychological research, is a compound of the material, social and spiritual self. Furthermore, and when acting together in smaller groups, they develop group identities and these too are retained. Thus, in every society we have identities at three or four levels, namely individual, group, regional and national. We can also, in this age of globalization, add an international dimension to it. The challenge in all societies, therefore, is to accommodate these layered identities in a framework that is harmonious and optimally conducive to social purpose.

Much has been written about identity, its theoretical framework and practical manifestations. An eminent sociologist has defined it as 'the process of construction of meaning on the basis of a cultural attribute, or a related set of cultural attributes, that is given priority over other sources of meaning. For a given individual, or a collective of actors, there may be a plurality of identities.'[1] The question is to determine how this identification is expressed in the everyday life of individuals who are members of such specific groups?

Conceptually and legally, citizenship of a modern state provides this framework and encapsulates the totality of rights and duties emanating from the membership of the citizen body, inclusive of the right of representation and the right to hold office under the state. By the same logic, a certain tension is built into the relationship, even if the society happens to be relatively homogenous, in itself a rarity in modern times. Rabindranath Tagore described his family background as a 'confluence of three cultures, Hindu, Mohammedan and British'.[2] Away from India but in our own neighbourhood, Abdolkarim Soroush depicted the Iranian Muslim as 'the carrier of three cultures at once' having national, religious and Western origins.[3]

Thus, instead of a narrow concept of a singular identity implied by the classical concept of citizenship, the need is to recognize and accommodate the existence of a plurality of social identities. The contours of this were explored earlier by Thomas Marshall, and more recently by Will Kymlicka,

Manuel Castells, Charles Taylor, Gurpreet Mahajan and others. Put simply, it has been argued that identity encapsulates the notion of authenticity, the demand for recognition, the idea of difference and the principle of equal dignity.[4]

What then has been the Indian approach to, and experience of, the concepts of identity and of citizenship in a modern state? What is the accommodative framework for identities in modern India?

A distinctive feature of Indian society is its heterogeneity. The historian Ramachandra Guha depicts our recent history as 'a series of conflict maps' involving caste, language, religion and class, and opines that conflicts relating to these 'operate both singly and in tandem'.[5] Each of these also brings forth an identity of varying intensity; together, they constitute what the opening line of the Preamble of our Constitution depicts as 'We, the People of India'.

In other words, the superstructure of a democratic polity and a secular state structure put in place after Independence on 15 August 1947 is anchored in the existential reality of a plural society. It is reflective of India's cultural past. Our culture is synthetic in character and, as a historian of another generation put it, 'embraces in its orbit beliefs, customs, rites, institutions, arts, religions and philosophies belonging to different strata of societies in varying stages of development. It eternally seeks to find a unity for the heterogeneous elements which make up its totality.' It is a veritable human laboratory where the cross-breeding of ideas, beliefs and cultural traditions has been in progress for a few thousand years. The national movement recognized this cultural plurality and sought to base a national identity on it. The size and diversity of the Indian landscape makes it essential. A population of 1.27 billion comprising over 4,635 communities, 78 per cent of whom are not only linguistic and cultural but social categories. Religious minorities constitute 19.4 per cent of the population; of these, Muslims account for 13.4 per cent amounting in absolute terms to around 160 million. The human diversities are both hierarchical and spatial. 'The de jure WE, the sovereign people is in reality a fragmented "we", divided by yawning gaps that remain to be bridged.' Around 22 per cent of our people live below the official poverty line and the health and education indicators for the population as a whole, despite recent correctives, leave much to be desired.

The contestation over citizenship surfaced early and was evident in the debates of the Constituent Assembly. The notion of citizenship was historically alien to Indian experience, since throughout our long history (barring a few exceptions in the earliest period), the operative framework was that of ruler and subject. There was, of course, no dearth of prescriptions about the duties of rulers towards their subjects and about the dispensation of justice but none of these went beyond Kautilya's pious dictum that 'a king who observes his duty of protecting his people justly and according to the law will go to heaven, whereas one who does not protect them or inflict[s] unjust punishment will not'.[6] The Constitution-makers, therefore, had to address three dimensions of the question relating to status, rights and identity, to determine who is to be a citizen, what rights are to be bestowed on the citizen and the manner in which the multiplicity of claimed identities is to be accommodated. This involved addressing three aspects of the question: legal, political and psychological. The outcome was the notion of national-civic rather than national-ethnic, emphasizing that the individual was the basic unit of citizenship whose inclusion in polity was on terms of equality with every other citizen. At the same time and taking societal realities into account, the concept of group-differentiated citizenship was grafted to assure the minorities and other identity-based groups that 'the application of difference-blind principles of equality will not be allowed to operate in a way that is unmindful of their special needs, and that these needs arising out of cultural difference or minority status will receive due attention in policy, and that the polity will be truly inclusive in its embrace'.[7]

The crafting of the Constitution was diligent and its contents reflective of the high ideals that motivated its authors. The Preamble moved Sir Ernest Barker to reproduce it at the beginning of his last book because, as he put it, it seemed 'to state in a brief and pithy form the argument of much of the book and it may accordingly serve as a keynote'.[8] The Constitution's chapter on Fundamental Rights addresses inter alia the protection of identities and accommodation of diversities. These identities could be regional, religious, linguistic, tribal, caste-based and gender-based. The right to equality and equal protection of the laws and prohibition of discrimination on grounds only of religion, race, caste, sex, or place of birth is guaranteed. Affirmative action is mandated by law in favour of those historically discriminated against on grounds of caste or tribal origin, as well as all those who are identified as socially and educationally backward. Also guaranteed is freedom of conscience and the right to freely profess, practise and propagate religion. Yet another section safeguards the right to have and conserve language, script or culture and the right of religious or linguistic minorities to establish and administer educational institutions of their choice. The purpose of these, taken together, is to bestow recognition, acknowledge the difference and thereby confer dignity that is an essential concomitant of equality.

Nevertheless, an inherent problem was evident to the Constitution-makers, or at least to some of them. This was expressed candidly, almost prophetically, by Ambedkar in words that need to be cited in full:

> On the 26th of January 1950, we are going to enter into a life of contradictions. In politics we will have equality and in social and economic life we will have inequality. In politics we will be recognizing the principle of one man one vote and one vote one value. In our social and economic life, we shall, by reason of our social and economic structure, continue to deny the principle of one man one value. How long shall we continue to live this life of contradictions? How long shall we continue to deny equality in our social and economic life? If we continue to deny it for long, we will do so only by putting our political democracy in peril. We must remove this contradiction at the earliest possible moment or else those who suffer from inequality will blow up the structure of political democracy which this Assembly has so laboriously built up.[9]

Thus, the objective of securing civic, political, economic, social and cultural rights as essential ingredients of citizenship was clearly delineated and the challenge squarely posed to the beneficiaries of the new dispensation. The dire prognosis of the last sentence, however, has not come to pass! The very complexity of the landscape impedes linear and drastic happenings. One serious student of Indian polity has noted that 'the Indian model of development is characterized by the politicization of a fragmented social structure, through a wide dispersal and permeation of political forms, values and ideologies'.[10] As a result, and in a segmented society and unequal economy, the quest for substantive equality and justice remains a work in progress. Nevertheless, the slowing down of the egalitarian social revolution that was envisaged by the Constitution-makers and the implicit social contract inherent in it does give rise to wider concerns about its implications.[11]

Two questions arise out of this and need to be explored. First, what has been the impact of this on the perception of identity? And second, how has the challenge been addressed?

Identity assertion in any society has three sets of impulses: civic equality, liberty and opportunity. Identity groups are a by-product of the right of freedom of association. They can be cultural, voluntary, ascriptive and religious.

They are neither good nor bad in themselves but do present challenges to democratic justice.[12] This is also true of India. The functioning of democratic institutions and the deepening of the democratic process along with the efforts to implement constitutional mandates for affirmative action induced higher levels of political mobilization. These manifested themselves, most visibly, in demand groups, each with its own identity. A multiplication of identities seeking social status and economic well-being through the route of politics thus emerged as a logical consequence.

It has been argued that 'casteism in politics is no more and no less than politicisation of caste which, in turn, leads to a transformation of the caste system'.[13] The same holds for religious and tribal minorities. In an evolving quasi-federal state structure, yet another imperative emanates from the requirements of regional or state identity. 'The new politics of caste has also reinforced old, upper caste solidarities. Brahmin, Kshatriya, Bramharishi Sabhas have reemerged and the logic of electoral politics has forced the forces of social justice to strike strategic alliances with them.'[14] These, together, have induced political actors to develop narrower foci on their electoral management methodologies; these have been reinforced by the shortcomings of the FPTP electoral system and the ability of a high percentage of candidates to win on a plurality rather than the majority of votes cast in an election.

A society so diverse inevitably faced the challenge of integration. It was twofold, physical and emotional. The former, involving the merger of 554 large and minuscule princely states with those parts of the former British India that became the Indian republic, was attended to with commendable speed and was almost completed by the end of 1949. Emotional integration, on the other hand, was a more complex process. As early as 1902, Tagore had cautioned that unity cannot be brought about by enacting a law and in 1949 Sardar Patel, the architect of integration of states, had laid emphasis on the process taking 'healthy roots' and bringing forth 'a wider outlook and a broader vision'. The challenges posed by it were aptly summed up by a political scientist:[15]

> In the semantics of functional politics the term national integration means, and ought to mean, cohesion and not fusion, unity and not uniformity, reconciliation and not merger, accommodation and not annihilation, synthesis and not dissolution, solidarity and not regimentation of the several discrete segments of the people constituting the larger political community.

Obviously, then, Integration is not a process of conversion of diversities into a uniformity but a congruence of diversities leading to a unity in which both the varieties and similarities are maintained.[16]

Thus, the Indian approach steers clear of notions of assimilation and adaptation, philosophically and in practice. Instead, the management of diversity to ensure (in Nehru's words) the integration of minds and hearts is accepted as an ongoing national priority. Some have described it as the 'salad-bowl' approach, with each ingredient identifiable and yet together, bringing forth an appetizing product.

The question of minority rights as a marker of identity, and their accommodation within the ambit of citizenship rights, remains a live one. It is not so much on the principle of minority rights (which is unambiguously recognized in the Constitution) as to the extent of their realization in actual practice. A government-commissioned report on Diversity Index some years back concluded that 'unequal economic opportunities lead to unequal outcomes which in turn lead to unequal access to political power. This creates a vicious circle since unequal power structure determines the nature and functioning of the institutions and their policies.'[17] This, and other official reports, delineate areas that need to be visited more purposefully.

How far can this to be taken? A Constitutional Amendment in 1977, adding a section on Fundamental Duties of citizens as part of the Directive Principles of State Policy, carries a clause stipulating promotion of harmony and spirit of brotherhood 'transcending religious, linguistic and regional or sectional diversities'. It is at this point that the rights of identity and the duties of citizenship intersect. The identification of this point, with any degree of precision, is another matter. The litmus test, eventually, must be the maintenance of social cohesiveness through a sense of citizenship premised on equality of status and opportunity so essential for the maintenance of democracy. The need for sustaining and reinvigoration of this sentiment is thus essential.

The Constitution of India was promulgated in 1950. The past six decades have witnessed immense changes in social and political perceptions in societies the world over. Theories and practices of 'assimilation', 'one-national mould' and the 'melting pot' have been discredited and generally abandoned; instead, evolving perceptions and practical compulsions led individual societies to accept diversity and cultural pluralism. In many places, on the other hand, a process of reversal induced by xenophobia, Islamophobia and migrant-related anxieties, is also underway. The concept of multiculturalism, pioneered to address accommodation of diversity within the framework of democracy, is being openly or tacitly challenged. An ardent advocate of multiculturalism concedes that 'not all attempts to adopt new models of multicultural citizenship have taken root or succeeded in achieving their intended effects' because 'multiculturalism works best if relations between the state and minorities are seen as an issue of social policy, not as an issue of state security'.[18]

There is an Indian segment to the debate on multiculturalism. It has been argued that 'while a multicultural polity was designed, the principles of multiculturalism were not systematically enunciated'. It is asserted that multiculturalism goes beyond tolerance and probes areas of cultural discrimination that may exist even after legal equality has been established; it therefore

> ...needs to explore ways by which the sense of alienation and disadvantage that comes with being a minority is visibly diminished, but in a way that does not replace the power of the homogenising state with that of the community. It should therefore aspire towards a form of citizenship that is marked neither by a universalism generated by complete homogenisation, nor by particularism of self-identical and closed communities.[19]

These debates and practices vindicate in good measure the vision and foresight displayed by the founding fathers of the Republic of India. The vindication is greater when considered in the context of the size and diversity of India and the stresses and strains it has withstood in this period. And yet, we cannot rest on our laurels since impulses tilting towards 'assimilationist' and homogenizing approaches do exist, suggestive of imagined otherness and seeking uniformity at the expense of diversity. Indian pluralism, as a careful observer puts it, 'continues to be hard won'.[20] Hence the persisting need of reinforcing and improving present practices and the principles underlying them. Such an endeavour would continue to be fruitful as long as 'the glue of solidarity' around the civic ideal remains sufficiently cohesive, reinforced by the existential reality of market unity and the imperative of national security. There is no reason to be sceptical about the stability of the tripod.

19

PATRIOTISM, NATIONALISM AND SOCIAL PEACE: SOME ASPECTS OF LALA LAJPAT RAI'S IDEAS

IT HAS BEEN SAID, WITH justice, that Lala Lajpat Rai ranked among the first three leaders of our nationalist movement prior to the advent of Gandhiji in the twenties, the other two being Bal Gangadhar Tilak and Bipin Chandra Pal. He was a prolific writer and, as the late Krishan Kantji put it, 'reform of the Hindu society remained his abiding mission'.

Many years back, and in another context, I had read the October 1923 'Appeal for Inter- Communal Harmony' signed by 100 public figures of all faiths. Lala Lajpat Rai's name is the first on this list. The text is given in Volume 10, p. 404 of Lalaji's *Collected Works* and the names of all signatories is available in Volume 4, pp. 496–503, of the *Selected Works of Motilal Nehru*.

The Appeal's approach to the question was unique: that indulging in communal misdeeds is a sin in religious terms and it is 'the duty of co-religionists of such offenders' to resist it.

Since the question of social harmony regrettably continues to remain on our national agenda, it is time to have a closer look at Lala Lajpat Rai's perceptions on these and related matters. My purpose is to discern the manner in which an earlier generation, principally of eminent freedom fighters, sought to address it and to benefit from their successes and shortcomings. The latter, in hindsight, were many and have been written about by scholars.

The history of the early decades of the last century is, in places,

---

Note: Speech delivered at the inauguration of the 150th Birth Anniversary Celebrations of Lala Lajpat Rai organized by Servants of the People Society, 6 May 2015, New Delhi.

characterized by competing narratives. Different elements in the national movement, in agreement on the final objective, did not always converge in terms of methodology and tactics. There were varying perceptions about how 'the constitutional space offered by the existing structure could be used without being co-opted by it'. The Non-Cooperation Movement, while it lasted, brought about a unity of ranks. Its demise, and other happenings in that period, aggravated communitarian tensions with resultant impact on leaders of opinion.

It is common knowledge that tracing the evolution of national movements in contemporary history is a complex endeavour. In our own case, and given the societal and historical complexity of the Indian landscape, the impulses emanating from patriotism, nationalism and social peace or harmony need to be carefully assessed to determine the positive energy and negative vibes emanating from their collective impact on a fast-evolving situation. The role of individual actors on the scene thus assumed a role in the shaping of public perceptions. At times, their own perceptions underwent changes of a far-reaching nature.

On 8 December 1923, Lala Lajpat Rai gave the Presidential Address to the Punjab Provincial Political Conference at Jarawala. He devoted this to the problem of communal harmony and surveyed the benefits and shortfalls of the Non-Cooperation Movement. He referred, in that context, to the Draft National Pact then under discussion and said, in words that bear repetition in full:

> The first article of our future constitution of India must provide absolute religious liberty to all religious denominations, subject only to such restrictions as are inevitable for the general maintenance of law and order. To this must be added the absolute religious neutrality of the future state…According to our idea, the future Swarajya government should not be at liberty to use public funds for any religious or denominational purpose whatsoever. In a land of many religions and many cults this, in my view, is the best safeguard against religious or denominational partisanship. With this provision the risks of the majority rule are very much lessened.

No progress however was made in this endeavour. Instead, and as the ground situation worsened, different perceptions crystallized. A case in point is the series of 13 articles written by Lala Lajpat Rai in the *Tribune* in November–December 1924. They were reflective of his dismay over the communal situation and the deterioration that came about after the unity displayed in the 1919–1922 period. The 12th article gives a summary of his conclusions and 13 points of advice, including a suggestion for proportional representation in legislature but not separate electorates, as also a suggestion to 'divide the Punjab into two Provinces to make majority rule effective.' The series ended with 'A plea for mutual co-operation' and an anguished cry to do away with distrust:

> Let us live and struggle for freedom as brothers whose interests are one and indivisible. Let us live and die for each other, so that India may live and prosper as a Nation. India is neither Hindu nor Muslim. It is not even both. It is one. It is India.

Lala Lajpat Rai was an activist in the discourse on Indian nationalism and lent to it his version and understanding of it. This discourse was multidimensional, reflective of the diversity of Indian society, sought empowerment from a variety of sources considered legitimate by its adherents and endeavoured to accommodate it in a convergence of interests, objectives and tactics. This also brought forth communitarian perceptions and ideas of strident Hindu and Muslim nationalisms subversive of secular values. They, to use a phrase used by Gandhiji, 'encircled the nationalist dream like coils of a snake.'

The situational imperatives also had theoretical moorings. Influence of thinkers like Mazzini and his ideas on cultural nationalism were evident in the writings of some Indian activists, including Lalaji. He presided over the annual session of the Hindu Mahasabha at Calcutta in April 1925 and the programme of action adopted there has been called by a credible scholar as 'the single document that had the most enduring influence on subsequent programmes and strategies' of some of the successor organizations of that persuasion.

This change of direction, or absence of consistency in the thought process and practical commitment, brings to the fore competing versions of nationalism that characterized the Indian scene in that period, versions that underlay the strong sentiments of patriotism that were evident at all stages. Were these versions liberal and inclusive, or restrictive and exclusive? This had practical implications in the shape of a direct impact on strategies of attaining social peace.

Record shows that leaders of the freedom movement having varying or conflicting viewpoints struggled with competing impulses on political and societal challenges that surfaced in the '20s and '30s of the last century when so many of these perception crystallized. Closer scrutiny also shows that a lesser dose of cultural bias and a greater element of cultural accommodation may have brought forth greater harmony. Since conflicting ideologies were embedded in, or attributed to, identities of faith, it is a moot point whether a different approach may have produced less painful outcomes. In this context, the October 1923 *Appeal for Inter-Communal Harmony* that pegged better conduct to the imperatives of the individual faiths themselves may just have had a more lasting impact and caused lesser trauma.

This, I concede, is now a hypothetical preposition. The thought nevertheless lingers that the journalist, novelist and film-maker Khwaja Ahmad Abbas may have had a different answer to his question about 1947: 'Who killed India?'

20
HISTORY AND HISTORIANS

MY OWN ACADEMIC DISCIPLINE IN the distant past was political science and I can still recall Professor John Seeley's jingle, well known in my time and presumably not forgotten today, that 'History without Political Science has no fruit and Political Science without History has no roots'.

In more recent times, and for professional reasons, I came to value Winston Churchill's aphorism: 'Study history, study history; in history lies all the secrets of statecraft.'

Historians at all times have endeavoured, as Herodotus put it, 'to preserve from decay the remembrance of what men have done'. Historians have dwelt on the facts of the past and sought to make implicit or explicit judgements about those facts. Not to be ignored is a mid-19th century caution that historians 'have been seduced from truth not by their imagination but by their reason' pursuant to the impulse of 'distorting facts to suit general principles'.[1]

Equally hazardous is the propensity to read the past into the present or the present into the past; so is the temptation to ignore the distinction between memory and history. Memory is based on identification with the past and is unavoidably egocentric while history is based on its treatment as an external object and not a part of the self.

History also cannot be faith-based. The domains of the two exist separately and conflation does not further the cause of either.

To a layperson, a number of questions are unavoidable. What then is history, and with what does it deal? What is the task of the historian? Is

Note: Speech delivered at the inauguration of the 75th session of the Indian History Congress, 28 December 2014, New Delhi.

history a science, or an art, or a bit of both? Does it really deal with the past, or does so in the context of contemporary knowledge and imagination?

A simple answer is that it is a method of inquiry which deals with what has reportedly happened and not exactly as it happened. It is a narrative of change. It has been suggested that historical objectivity is seen to be not a single idea but rather sprawling sets of assumptions, attitudes, aspirations and antipathies. It is evident that on most, if not all, occasions, the narrative is contested. Nevertheless, such contestations need to have a basis in facts, demonstrable and logically sustainable. As E.H. Carr put it, 'The historian without facts is rootless and futile; facts without their historian are dead and meaningless.' He added that 'the study of history is inescapably the study of causes.'[2] This would exclude what has been called 'counterfactuals' or the 'what if' category and its simplistic assumptions and premises.

It is thus evident that methodology is critical to the study of history. Efforts to curb 'intellectual efflorescence' through official dicta can only be viewed as undesirable. Furthermore, contestations over the historical past need civility of discourse to ensure that it does not cross the imperatives of ensuring social peace and societal cohesion.

Carr also dwelt on history's wider relevance: 'An individual stripped of memory finds the world a confusing place: a society with no sense of history is unaware of where it has come from or where it is going.'

Is there a more practical relevance of history? To my mind, it helps us know and, hopefully, learn from the mistakes of the past. Those mistakes relate to frailties in judgement, leading to mistakes in statecraft and governance. As one historian has put it, these could be due to tyranny or oppression, excessive ambition, incompetence or decadence, and folly or perversity. In each, the inability or the unwillingness of society or its ruling establishment to pay heed to reason and realism, to dissenting opinion and to alternative courses of policy or action, led to unfounded certitude, resulting in mistakes.

It is for this reason that in every period of the past, beginning perhaps with the 30th century BC Egyptian King Menes, codes for dispensing justice were enunciated. Alongside, manuals were penned for the guidance of rulers. Departures from these and the resulting consequences are what historians have dwelt upon.

History writing, and history teaching, have a contemporary relevance in a more evident sense. We live in a world of nation-states but the idea of a homogenous nation state is clearly problematic. Diversity is identifiable even in the most homogeneous of societies today. The global scene in modern times has been replete with complexities and tensions of what has been called the national question. 'Domestic hostilities and licentiousness of private wars in violation of laws', to recapitulate a phrase used by Edward Gibbon in the concluding section of his monumental *Decline and Fall of the Roman Empire*, 'are the most potent and forcible cause of destruction.' Instances can be found in 20th-century history.

In our own country the sheer diversity of identities—4,635 communities according to the Anthropological Survey of India—is a terse reminder about the care that needs to be taken while putting together the profile of a national identity. It has of necessity to be liberal and accommodative; marked, to quote an eminent scholar, neither by complete homogenization, nor by the particularism of closed communities. Instead, it is a balance struck by 'the mutual gravitational pull of disparate sections that make the whole'. Our sagacity in building pluralist structures that have stood the test for over six decades, stands in contrast to many straitjacket edifices in other societies that came to grief. By the same token, these structures need constant nurturing.

It is no longer a matter of debate that history has to be more than narrowly political or economic. The imperative is to make it comprehensive and inclusive of neglected groups in society. These subaltern classes, as Gramsi had pointed out, are not unified and their history therefore has to be intertwined with that of civil society. It has challenged what has been called 'the univocality of statist discourse'. It has sought to focus on Dalit and gender issues. The methodology of studying these opened up new and enriching vistas of study for historians.

The pasture of stupidity, said the great medieval historian Ibn Khaldun, is unwholesome for mankind. He warned historians not to succumb to the 'temptation of sensationalism', adding that 'a hidden pitfall of historiography is disregard for the fact that conditions within nations and regions change with the change of period and the passage of time'.[3]

This congress of historians has the traditional six sections, and section IV focuses on countries other than India. I wonder if this could read 'countries and regions other than India'. This will help explore the fascinating maritime history that unavoidably emanates from the 7,517 kilometres of coastline and the Exclusive Economic Zone that we have on the Arabian Sea and the Bay of Bengal and in relation to the Indian Ocean as a whole.

People living in coastal regions have traditionally depended on the sea for their livelihood. They are one with the sea and the sea is an integral ingredient of their world view. The maritime people of India are no exception to this and trading activities of Indians in coastal areas in ancient and medieval periods testify to this. 'Our culture,' wrote a Katchi scholar some years back, 'is wet with the sea.'

Prior to the arrival of the Portuguese in the 16th century in the seas around India, trade in the Indian Ocean region was characterized by a group of ports (sometimes in virtual independence of land powers in the hinterland). Surat and Calicut on the west coast and Masulipatnam and a number of ports on the Coromandel coast in the east stand out in historical and commercial records. The Portuguese, followed by the Dutch and the British, intruded on this autonomous regional activity and began to change its character and its multiple human faces. In subsequent centuries, European colonial empires effectively put an end to it.

Apart from the earlier work of Radha Kumud Mookerji, the studies conducted by S. Arasaratnam and Ashin Das Gupta in the second half of the last century and some excellent monographs by European and Australian scholars, sufficient research work on these aspects of our history has yet to be done. A corrective is necessary, more so in the context of the changed regional requirements in the 21st century that necessitate trading and economic cooperation that will come in the wake of the announced 'Look East and Act East' policy of the government. There is also the expectation that a similar approach would be formulated in the foreseeable future, for the region to the west covering the Arabian Sea, the Persian Gulf, the Red Sea and the East African regions.

Another region deserving attention is beyond the subcontinent in the north and northwest. The situation of historical scholarship relating to Afghanistan and Central Asian republics is no better. The extant works worthy of mention relate to the period before 1947. Each of these societies is relevant to us in economic, strategic and social terms; each necessitates much greater scholarly attention.

To conclude, it needs to be said that history cannot be studied in isolation. I draw the attention of this learned gathering to what a contemporary French historian, Emmanuel Le Roy Ladurie, has observed: 'History is the synthesis of all social sciences turned towards the past.'

Therein lies the majesty of one of the noblest of disciplines.

21
INDIAN MUSLIMS: QUEST FOR JUSTICE

THE ALL INDIA MAJLIS-E-MUSHAWARAT WAS formed in response to a perceived need to defend and protect the identity and dignity of the Muslim community in India in terms of the rights bestowed by the Constitution of India on the citizens of this land. This objective remains relevant, though some of its ingredients may stand amplified or modified today.

The Muslims of India constitute a community of about 180 million, amounting to a little over 14 per cent of the population of the country. They are, after Indonesia, the second-largest national grouping of followers of Islam in the world. Their contribution to the civilization and culture of Islam is in no need of commentary. They were an integral part of the freedom struggle against the British rule. They are dispersed all over the country, are not homogenous in linguistic and socio-economic terms and reflect in good measure the diversities that characterize the people of India as a whole.

The Independence of India in August 1947, and the events preceding and following it, cast a shadow of physical and psychological insecurity on Indian Muslims. Unfairly, they were made to carry the burden of political events and compromises that resulted in the Partition. The process of recovery from that trauma has been gradual and uneven, and at times painful. They have hesitatingly sought to tend to their wounds, face the challenges and seek to develop response patterns. Success has been achieved in some measure; however, much more still needs to be done.

In the past decade, work has also been done to delineate the contours of the problem. The Sachar Committee Report of 2006 did this officially. It

---

Note: Speech delivered at the Inauguration of the All India Majlis-E-Mushawarat Golden Jubilee, 31 August 2015, New Delhi.

laid to rest the political untruth in some quarters about the Muslim condition and demonstrated that on most socio-economic indicators, they were on the margins of structures of political, economic and social relevance and their average condition was comparable to, or even worse than, the country's historically most acknowledged backward communities, the Scheduled Castes and Scheduled Tribes. It specified the development deficits of majority of Muslims in regard to education, livelihood and access to public services and the employment market across the states.

In the same vein, Expert Group Reports were prepared in 2008 on the need to develop a Diversity Index and establish an Equal Opportunity Commission.

When clubbed together, these and other studies brought forth sufficient evidence to substantiate the view that 'inequality traps prevent the marginalised and work in favour of the dominant groups in society'.

More recently, the Kundu Report of September 2014, commissioned to evaluate the implementation of decisions taken pursuant to Sachar recommendations, has concluded that though 'a start has been made, yet serious bottlenecks remain'. It makes specific recommendations to remedy these. It asserts that 'development for the Muslim minority must be built on a bed-rock of a sense of security'.[1]

It is evident from this compendium of official reports that the principal problems confronting India's Muslims relate to:

- identity and security;
- education and empowerment;
- equitable share in the largesse of the state; and
- fair share in decision-making.

Each of these is a right of the citizen. The shortcomings in regard to each have been analysed threadbare. The challenge before us today is to develop strategies and methodologies to address them.

The default by the state or its agents in terms of deprivation, exclusion and discrimination (including failure to provide security) is to be corrected by the state; this needs to be done at the earliest and appropriate instruments must be developed for it. Political sagacity, the imperative of social peace, and public opinion play an important role in it. Experience shows that the corrective has to be both at the policy and the implementation levels; the latter, in particular, necessitates mechanisms to ensure active cooperation of the state governments.

The official objective of '*Sab ka sath sab ka vikas*' is commendable; a prerequisite for this is affirmative action (where necessary) to ensure a common starting point and an ability in all to walk at the required pace. This ability has to be developed through individual, social and governmental initiatives that fructify on the ground. Programmes have been made in abundance; the need of the hour is their implementation.

The foregoing pertains principally to governmental action or lack thereof. Equally relevant is the autonomous effort by the community itself in regard to its identified shortcomings. What has it done to redress the backwardness and poverty arising out of socio-economic and educational underdevelopment? How adequate is the response in relation to the challenge?

A century back the lament was emotive:

Firqa-bandi hai kahein aur kahein zaatain hain
Kya zamaane main panaph-ne ki yahi baatain hain?

Today, we have to admit that both 'firqa bandi' and 'zaat' identity is a ground reality. The imagery of Mahmood and Ayaz standing shoulder-to-shoulder in the same line is confined to the mosque; so are the injunctions on punctuality, cleanliness and discipline. Each of these is violated beyond the confines of the congregational prayer. Corrective strategies, therefore, have to be sought on category-differentiation admissible in Indian state practice and hitherto denied to Muslims (Scheduled Caste status) or inadequately admitted (segments of OBC status). Available data makes it clear that a high percentage of Muslims falls into these two broad categories.

It is evident that significant sections of the community remain trapped in a vicious circle and in a culturally defensive posture that hinders self-advancement. Tradition is made sacrosanct but the rationale of tradition is all but forgotten. Jadeediyat or modernity has become a tainted expression. Such a mindset constrains critical thinking necessary both for the affirmation of faith and for the wellbeing of the community. The instrumentality of adaptation to change—Ijtihad—is frowned upon or glossed over. Forgotten is its purpose, defined by the late Sheikh Abul Hasan Ali Nadwi as 'the ability to cope with the ever-changing pattern of life's requirements'. Equally relevant is Imam Al-Ghazali's delineation of the ambit of Maslaha—protection of religion, life, intellect, lineage and property. Both provide ample theoretical space for focused thinking on social change without impinging on the fundamentals of faith.

It is here that the role of Mushawarat becomes critical. As a grouping of leading and most respected minds of the community, it should go beyond looking at questions of identity and dignity in a defensive mode and explore how both can be furthered in a changing India and a changing world. It should widen its ambit to hitherto unexplored or inadequately explored requirements of all segments of the community, particularly women, youth, and non-elite sections who together constitute the overwhelming majority.

This effort has to be made in the context of Indian conditions and the uniqueness of its three dimensions: plural, secular and democratic. Some years back a close observer had posed the problem:

> To deny discrimination and pretend all is well is to fly in the face of facts. But agitation against discrimination can arouse the very emotions that foster discrimination. The solution of the Muslim problem lies in a resolution of this dilemma by devising a form and content of agitation which heals old wounds and inflicts no new ones. This resolution can be achieved by regarding discrimination as what it is; a problem of Indian democracy to be resolved within the framework of national integration.[2]

This would necessitate sustained and candid interaction with fellow citizens without a syndrome of superiority or inferiority, and can be fruitful only in the actual implementation of the principles of justice, equality and fraternity inscribed in the Preamble to the Constitution and the totality of Fundamental Rights. The failure to communicate with the wider community in sufficient measure has tended to freeze the boundaries of diversities that characterize the Indian society. Efforts may be made to isolate the community; such an approach should be resisted.

The Indian experience of a large Muslim minority living in secular polity, however imperfect, could even be a model for others to emulate.

The world of Islam extends beyond the borders of India, and Muslims here, as in other lands, can benefit from the best that may be available in the realm of thought and practice. A few years ago I had occasion to read the Algerian-French philosopher Mohammed Arkoun and was impressed by his view that our times compel us to rethink modernity so that, as he put it, 'critical thought, anchored in modernity but criticising modernity itself and contributing to its enrichment through recourse to the Islamic example'[3] could open up a new era in social movements.

Would Future Generations Forgive us for Failing to Explore these Options?

'Verily never will God change the condition of a people until they change it themselves with their own souls.'[4]

And so the task before Mushawarat in the foreseeable future should remain a threefold one: to sustain the struggle for the actualization in full measure of legal and constitutional rights, to do so without being isolated from the wider community, and to endeavour at the same time to adapt thinking and practices to a fast-changing world.

22
MOHAMMAD MUJEEB: AN INTELLECTUAL'S LOCUTION OF DISSENT

'AT THE AGE OF SIXTY man's folly knows no limits.' So runs a Lebanese proverb. The condition, presumably, gets worse at seventy! The task of talking about Mohammad Mujeeb and his achievements is a daunting one, for he was no ordinary mortal. Enough is known about his life and his dedication to scholarship and to Jamia Millia Islamia. But little is known about the sheer range of his interests: history, theology, mysticism, literature, poetry, drama, painting, wood carving, carpentry, gardening and much else. His was, in every sense, an encyclopaedic personality. Even in history, his chosen discipline, the sweep of his knowledge was staggering to the laymen and challenging to the specialists. There were, nevertheless, areas that attracted him more than others, the history of ideas, the debates between orthodoxy and dissent being one of them, and he explored these with some relish in his writings.

Yet, nowhere through all his historical and literary writings do we find a cohesive theory of dissent. The glimpses of his own thinking are mostly revealed in his treatment of individual historical figures. His personality contributed to this approach in no small measure. A certain diffidence, combined with acceptance and scepticism, produced an unusual mix. He made a confession, overtly modest, in an essay that was autobiographical in nature:

> This is just a preface to my confession of an utter failure to understand life or anything about it. I have not, however, allowed my intellectual

---

Note: Mujeeb Memorial Lecture, 30 November 2006, New Delhi.

curiosity or my sense of freedom to be smothered beneath the weight of a borrowed philosophy or of plain despair...I do not know what success is and I have not tried to find out. I do not know what is the right thing or the good thing to do. The question is just too complicated. So why not say that we cannot measure success with any confidence, that we cannot know what is the right thing to do; we can only hope that we shall have the good sense not to do the wrong thing and the courage to examine what we have done without partiality towards ourselves.[1]

A strong moral sense defined his approach. This was expressed unambiguously:

Conscience, being the moral sense of right and wrong, has been commonly associated with religion. But religion, like politics, can have its own interest. There are reasons of religion, as there are reasons of state; religion is no more absolutely subject to moral law than the state. Conscience stands above both, helping, guiding admonishing. This may sound like a heresy, and I suppose it is. But the heretic, though he may completely misrepresent himself by being aggressive, foolish and fanatical, stands out as the symbol of the human conscience, of the human mind demanding its freedom to express the moral laws in its own way in word and deed.[2]

This approach led him to address a question close to his heart:

Every Muslim who talks or writes about Islam has the feeling of being a reformer...I have no intention of becoming a reformer. My purpose is merely to attempt a re-examination of our approach to Islam, and I am doing this because re-examination has to be a continuous process if we are to prevent belief and practice from becoming habits, and for that reason, sterile if not lifeless.[3]

The question of critical interest to him, therefore, was the debate between the advocates of Taqlid on the one hand and of Ijtihaad on the other. He explored this with diligence in different periods of medieval and recent history. This is evident from the scheme of chapters of his major work, *The Indian Muslims*. The debate between orthodoxy and dissent, as Mujeeb saw it, was between 'Shariah as Law' and 'Shariah as a System of Living'.

Orthodoxy is defined as 'the principle and system of maintaining uniformity in belief and practice by determining what is true or desirable, by discouraging deviations, and applying social and religious sanctions to enforce uniformity'. As against this, 'The history of human thought is the record of conflict between the desire for stability and the need for change, between orthodoxy and innovation. Stability and change are both essential for survival, and an innovation that is accepted becomes a part of orthodoxy'.[4]

The unstated major premise in the legal arguments in the medieval period in India (and elsewhere) was the injunction on a Muslim ruler to supervise the application of Sharia on his Muslim subjects. This required correct legal advice. Such advice emanated from the ulema, qualified to state and interpret the law as scholars, and administer it as judges. Differences and nuances in the interpretation of the law were inevitable. Practical necessity, therefore, compelled the ruler to opt for scholars whose opinions and rulings met to the requirements of the state. Other, no less qualified, remained outside this charmed circle. Their views covered a wide spectrum; many were Sufis who interpreted the commands of religion in spiritual rather than the legal context. Many others questioned, in 'Islamic terms, the legitimacy of a hereditary ruler or one who has captured power through the use of force'. Their line of argument tended to reopen an older, wider debate. Muslim political consciousness, while refusing to accept a king as a sovereign de jure, conceded a de facto status for reasons that were stated much earlier by Al Ghazali:

> There are those who hold the Imamate is dead, lacking as it does the required qualifications. But no substitute can be found for it. What then? Are we to give up obeying the laws? Shall we dismiss the *qadis*, declare all authority to be valueless, cease marrying and pronounce the acts of those in high places to be invalid at all points, leaving the population to live in 'sinfulness'? Or shall we continue as we are, recognising that the Imamate really exists and that all acts of the administration are valid, given the circumstances of the case and the necessities of the actual moment? The concessions made by us are not spontaneous, but necessity makes lawful what is forbidden…we should like to ask: which is to be preferred, anarchy and the stoppage of social life for lack of a properly constituted authority, or acknowledgement of the existing power, whatever it be? Of these two alternatives, the jurist cannot but choose the latter.[5]

The independent scholar-theologian, and the Sufi did not subscribe to this line of reasoning. They sought the inner message of faith, beyond ritualistic conformity. Mujeeb sought to explore the resulting tensions while surveying the early period of the Muslim rule in northern India that set the pattern for subsequent periods. He conceded the relevance of orthodoxy and its professed role in maintaining identity and stability but was trenchant in his criticism of its application:

> Orthodoxy maintained the identity of the Indian Muslim community by condemning the unbelievers in the inherited theological phrases, but demanded from the Muslims little beyond conformity at the lowest religious and ethical levels. Its concept of integration in matters of doctrine was confined to the assertion of the principle of *taqlid*. Anyone who challenged this principle was an enemy; anyone who expressed an independent opinion in matters of doctrinal or ritual detail was a still greater enemy. But rulers and those in power were not criticised. No protests were made against the infliction of punishments severe than those laid down by the *Shariah*, or against the levy of taxes not permitted by it. The pattern of the good life remained a sacred hypothesis. Answers were given only if questions were asked. The duty of maintaining the *Shariah* was a part of the ruler's functions, and the responsibility of any contravention of the *Shariah* also lay on his shoulders. The orthodox *ulema* did not consider it an obligation to insist on the right thing being done. Even those who followed practices contrary to the *Shariah* were left alone, so long as they did not attempt to justify these practices on theological grounds...
>
> That orthodoxy had not succeeded in any degree of stability was evident whenever the government was shaken by a revolution. The *ulema* never gave the lead to the Muslims as a political community. They waited till something decisive occurred, and then came out to confirm the decision... An orthodoxy that permitted everything to depend on the chances of war could not claim to have achieved or even systematically worked for stability. It could not establish the *Shariah* as the normative principle; instead, it made religion a poor dependent of politics, and converted a source of moral nourishment into a parasite...
>
> The Muslim community was not integrated by orthodoxy; it was taught to maintain its identity not through the spiritual and

social values which it represented but through the cultivation of prejudices and claims to inherent superiority. Laying such foundations was worse than laying no foundations at all.'[6]

Mujeeb contends that the religious thinkers of the age were opposed to the official *ulema* because the latter 'served not God but the state, and they (the religious thinkers) were opposed to the state because its structure and policy was a negation of the *Shariah*'.[7] At times this led to open dissent, as happened in the case of Sayyad Mohammad of Jaunpur whose 'movement for moral and social reform is the first expression of religious thought as an assertive social force in Indian Muslim society'.[8] He called himself 'the Mahdi' (the guided one), collected many followers, incurred the wrath of the authorities and said he had been sent by God because faith has been nullified by social custom, personal habit and innovations. His followers (Ma/Mantis) indulged in collective action. Mujeeb calls their doctrine 'militant sufism' but concedes that the claim to being the Mahdi resulted in 'a theological pandemonium in which the real teachings of Syed Mohammad became of secondary importance even for his own followers, and no change came about in Muslim society and its way of life'.[9]

Mujeeb's interest in Sufism and Sufis is evident in his writings. He admired their broad outlook, their conscious detachment from the state apparatus and their assertion of 'the possibility of there being many paths to God'. The emergence of the hereditary principle in Sufi orders was not to his liking. He acknowledged that 'subtle change' that took place in the outlook of Sufis in their outlook on matters worldly. Because of their individualistic approach, the Sufis could not become an integrating force for the community. Sufism may have lost spiritual intensity but became 'more missionary in character'. The teaching of some 'seem no more than a reshuffling of concepts, at manipulation of terms that creates the illusion of reality'.[10] He found an explanation for it: 'Political authority, orthodoxy and Sufism established themselves at about the same time, and an adjustment had to be made that would allow each of the three adequate freedom and room for expansion. The Chishti *Sufis* rejected the religious and moral claims of both the state and of orthodoxy, and had to fight for their position.'[11]

In the Moghul period of Indian history the figure of Jalal ud-din Akbar looms large as much for the duration and stability of the reign as for the vigour of intellectual activity. Mujeeb examined at some length the controversies relating to Akbar's religious views:

Intellectually and to some extent politically Akbar rejected the religious orthodoxy of his day. In practice he did not go beyond refusing to be a partisan of the *ulema* of the court and the few decrees that we have mentioned above (relating to the abolition of *Jaziya,* forbidding of inter-marriage between people of different faiths, prescribing minimum age of marriage for Muslim boys and girls). He could not go beyond this because of the identification of Muslim orthodoxy and Muslim political power was too close and too real, and they would stand or fall together. Akbar would have found no support whatsoever if he had attempted to establish a secular state based on the equality of all religions, and until the state became secular there was no alternative to orthodoxy.

Despite this, Mujeeb considered Akbar's efforts 'towards the harmonisation of religious law with political realities and social ideals' as being 'of fundamental significance'. This, while anathema to the traditional *ulema,* 'was in fact the principle and the practice of the majority of thoughtful public men'.[12]

Mujeeb's critique of the religious thought of that period, and of subsequent periods, begins with a succinct statement of the orthodox position in the opening paragraph in Chapter XIII of *The Indian Muslims:*

> It is necessary to distinguish between *shari'ah* as a system of law and the *shari'ah* as an ideal code of ethics. In theory no difference existed; that the *shari'ah* comprehended all situations and circumstances was accepted without question...We have in fact to distinguish between those who looked upon Islam as divinely instituted, operative and binding law, and those who regard it primarily as a set of moral commands. In the one case it was enough to know that the law was operative, in the other an attempt was made to give the law a moral and spiritual basis, and emphasis was laid on conduct rather than relationships.

Having stated the principle, he proceeded to amplify its practical implications:

> For this purpose it is not enough to know the interpretations, opinions and judgements of the founders and outstanding exponents of the *fiqh* of the four orthodox schools; a study of the *Qur'an* and *hadith* was also necessary. It was unfortunate that those who made

this study considered themselves bound by the principle of *taqlid,* and did not claim the right to independent thinking. Their intellectual effort was directed towards the amplification of the *shari'ah* as a system of law and ethics. The emphasis on conduct, however, did give their effort a distinct and characteristic religious significance by introducing a powerful element of idealism. Every Muslim had to obey the operative law; but that was not enough. He had also to realise, and. as far as possible express in his own life, the moral ideals of Islam as revealed in the acts and sayings of the Prophet and his Pious Companions.

Mujeeb considered this to be an improvement on current practice, but not sufficient. The dissident in him showed up at this stage:

The risk of giving a personal formulation to accepted beliefs was not taken up by the religious thinkers—they gave at best, a new and higher meaning to *taqlid.* The *shari'ah,* as they understood it, was an exalted way of life but did not allow of experiment and adventure. Even their scholarship was not a search for new ideas, a means for discovering new answers to questions.'[13]

The indictment is near total. A partial exception is Shah Waliullah whose critique of *taqlid* evokes support.[14] In more recent times, his assessment of Syed Ahmad Khan and of Iqbal Lahori is of relevance. He considered the former 'a secular mind, or rather one dominated by common sense, and he sought to achieve essentially secular values'. His interpretation of the basic doctrines of Islam amounted to '*Ijtihad* with a vengeance'. He 'went far beyond any religious thinker before him in giving a concrete form to the concept of *amal-i-salih,* good work'.[15] In the case of Iqbal, and despite the sweep of his ideas, 'the challenge thrown out to the Muslims to reconstruct their life in accordance with the ideals of Islam is reduced to a hesitant and formal admission that some change might be made somewhere, but caution is more necessary than courage. This is all the more surprising in view of Dr Iqbal's ideals of social justice and personal self-realisation and the exalted expression he has given to them'. The people whom he addressed 'did not possess the faculty of self-criticism', identified themselves with his poetry and 'lost the chance he offered them of shedding their narrowness and their fears and becoming the true believers', the 'men of God whose work endures for all times'.[16]

Mujeeb's total admiration is reserved for Maulana Azad whose *Tarjuman al Qur'an* 'is, perhaps, the finest example of constructive thinking enjoined on the Muslim' in his discovery of 'a new world of religious thought to redress the balance of the old'.[17]

The articulation of dissent is complex business. The historian is constrained by the ritual of his discipline. The dramatist has greater freedom of creative expression. Mujeeb resorted to the latter to communicate the views of the dissident par excellence, Sheikh Mohammad Saeed 'Sarmad'. He was an Armenian Jew from Kashan who converted to Islam, found his way to Sindh where he fell in love with a Hindu boy, came to Delhi and received the patronage of Dara Shikoh. When the latter lost the battle for succession, a tribunal of religious scholars was asked to ascertain if Sarmad's views and bohemian ways of living amounted to apostasy. The verdict was a foregone conclusion.

Mujeeb tells the story and conveys the message in a play of five acts, *Khana Jangi* (Civil War). The principal characters are Prince Dara Shikoh, Sheikh Sarmad, a well-known teacher Mulla Abul Qasim, Chief Inspector and Chief Justice Aitamad Khan Abdul Qawi and Emperor Aurangzeb.

Mulla Abul Qasim is orthodox but does not share official perceptions. The focus of his teaching is on morals and ethics. He considers civil dissention particularly harmful to the community and a sign of impending destruction. He has high regard for Sarmad and his Sufi teachings. He turns down the emperor's request to join the tribunal but was nevertheless summoned.

Act Four pertains to the proceedings of the tribunal. Aitamad Khan reads the charges: two on moral grounds (being in love with an idol worshipper and going around naked) and three on theological grounds (denial of mairaj—the Prophet's physical journey to heaven, not reciting the full kalima— profession of faith—and thereby denying God and his Prophet). The official ulema reacted predictably; Abul Qasim dissented vigorously. The emperor witnessed the proceedings from behind a curtain and later engaged Abul Qasim in a conversation in which he sought to explain the gap between theory (as preached by Abul Qasim) and the imperatives of statecraft. He invites the mulla to join him: 'Truth is to be found in political power also, not only in books.' Receiving no response, he accuses scholars of indecisiveness: 'Life could wait for your decisions earlier, but not any longer.'

In the last act, Abul Qasim returns to his madrasa, crestfallen. He articulates his helplessness: 'I could not save Sheikh Sarmad from the sword of bigotry nor could I confront the sword of politics that was offered to me. I have become lifeless.' He urges his students to be steadfast: 'This life is a tussle between truth and falsehood; there is another life in which truth seeks truth.'

The passion is reflective of the dilemma. Is it also suggestive of Mohammad Mujeeb's personal position?

Mujeeb's essays and historical writings are similarly peppered with his views on the orthodox Muslim positions on matters of faith and conscience, freedom and obligation. They reveal a pattern of dissent. The primary impulse is provided by his understanding of what it means to be a Muslim:

> In one sense a Muslim has no freedom at all: he has been created that he might serve God (Qu'ran 51:56), and God has acquired him body and soul, with all else that he possesses (Qu'ran 9:112). In another sense he enjoys the greatest freedom, for belonging as he does to God, it releases him from every other form of bondage. This is the interpretation that has been put on these verses by the Sufis generally. In practice every Muslim who believes that he must live according to the *shari'a,* which comprises the creed as well as the law, follows the *shari's* as defined by his sect or by one of the four schools of jurisprudence (Hanafi, Shafi's, Maliki, and Hambali) which are recognised as orthodox. But the law has curious anomalies. The ruler is not bound by the short 'a in the sense that he is not answerable to the community, the *millat,* or the divines, but only to God and he must be obeyed unless he forbids the religious practices enjoined by Islam and upholds *kufr,* or unbelief. The officers of the ruler who have to carry out his command are answerable only to the ruler. A Muslim who holds, but does not propagate heretical beliefs commits no cognisable offence. A Muslim who disregards traditional practices or taboos, is answerable only if he claims that he possesses theological status and maintains that his own views or practices are more correct than those prescribed by tradition.[18]

Mujeeb's critique of religious conformity is based on a close examination of Muslim history, principally in India. The historian in him, focusing on the gap between Islam's principles and the actual practice of Muslim rulers, has a sense of revulsion over what has been done in the name of religion. His articulation of dissent, and dissociation, takes the form of a basic contention that a Muslim should be guided by his conscience and not by tradition. This, while taking care of the individual, says nothing about the group or the community. Mujeeb would argue that the answer lies in moving away from blind taqlid and reinforcing the thinking Muslim's capacity for Ijtihad. How is this to be converted into group action? He does not offer a practical framework in which this could be undertaken.

Human beings live in groups and need rules to regulate their social intercourse. For this reason, group impulse may be as necessary as the individual one and the question of striking a balance between the demands of individual conscience and of group interest must at all times remain in flux, to be determined empirically.

Mohammad Mujeeb asked questions of great relevance. He answered some of them, and left some unanswered. But either way, he made his audience think. In conclusion, I can only subscribe to what was said by a distinguished historian while delivering the first Mujeeb Memorial Lecture: 'Mujeeb had no predecessors and no followers. He was a class by himself.'[19]

23
LITERATURE, ART AND SOCIAL AWARENESS

KHWAJA AHMAD ABBAS WAS A low-profile yet iconic personality of an early independent India. Abbas lived and worked at a critical period in the history of modern India. His ideas relating to the evolution of consciousness on societal matters, as it emerged in the Independence struggle and in the early decades after 1947, remain of relevance to all those who care about the less fortunate segments of society and who attach value to the concepts of creativity and artistic freedom.

Some initial questions would be in order. Who was Khwaja Ahmad Abbas? Why was he what he was? What social and ideological impulses motivated him? Why is his vision of continuing relevance?

Instead of emphasizing on his lineage, it would suffice to say that Khwaja Ahmad Abbas's genes exhibited scholarly traditions worthy of citation in any company. He has recorded, for posterity, his efforts as a student in Aligarh to board a train just to talk to Jawaharlal Nehru in his railway compartment; the conversation—somewhat halting—ended with a request to sign his autograph book. A hurried inscription followed: 'Live dangerously. Jawaharlal Nehru.' Abbas took this to heart and described his relationship with Nehru as 'a long love affair'.

Abbas, in his own words, was 'a communicator of ideas'. He did this as a journalist, short-story writer, a novelist, a film critic and a scriptwriter. He is considered one of the pioneers of Indian parallel or neo-realistic cinema, having penned films like *Neecha Nagar, Jagte Raho, Dharti Ke Lal, Awara, Shri 420, Mera Naam Joker, Bobby* and *Henna*.

Note: Khwaja Ahmad Abbas Centenary Lecture, 7 June 2014, New Delhi.

As a journalist, his columns 'Last Page' and 'Azad Qalam' commenced in 1935 in *Bombay Chronicle* and continued in *Blitz* till his death in 1987. Each was a pithy commentary on contemporary happenings and had a wide following. His retort in early 1963 to US Senator Richard Russell's uncharitable criticism of India was characteristic of his passion for causes Indian.

A 16-minute documentary film made by Khwaja Ahmad Abbas in 1968 added a footnote to our legal history. Titled *A Tale of Four Cities*, it contrasted the life of luxury of the rich in Calcutta, Bombay, Madras and Delhi with the squalor and poverty of the poor, particularly the life of those whose hands and labour helped to build beautiful cities, factories and other industrial complexes. The documentary was silent, except for a song which the labourers sang while at work. One minute of the film gave a fleeting glimpse of the red-light district of Bombay and this was required by the Censor Board to be deleted for a 'U' certificate.

In the first case of its kind, it was argued in the Supreme Court of India on behalf of Abbas that pre-censorship of films is offensive to freedom of speech and expression and that the rules relating to it were vague, arbitrary and indefinite. The bench, headed by Chief Justice M. Hidayatullah, allowed the petition on the ground that treatment of motion pictures must be different from other forms of art and expression. He held that the clarifications and assurances given in the hearings by the solicitor general and procedural safeguards accepted by the government 'will make censorship accord with our fundamental law'. This, in effect, curtailed government's arbitrary exercise of censorship powers.

Interestingly enough, Abbas had written a letter to Gandhiji in 1939 requesting him to reconsider his views on cinema being included amongst other evils like gambling, sutta and horse racing: 'You are a great soul, Bapu. In your heart there is no room for prejudice. Give this little toy of ours, the cinema, which is not so useless as it looks, a little of your attention and bless it with a smile.'

Some of the short stories of Khwaja Ahmad Abbas, written in Urdu, and published in English translation a few years back, allow the present generation to appreciate the depth and diversity of his talent as a story writer. They are reflective of his social awareness. A reviewer has observed that reading them is a sobering exercise and remind one of another India 'when idealism of nation-building was more in evidence though often found bleeding on the jagged edges of poverty and deprivation, resistant feudalism, inequalities and the divides of caste and religion'.

Khwaja sahib attached particular importance to his literary work. This was summed up in his will: 'If you wish to meet me after I am gone just pick up one of the seventy odd books I wrote or view the films I have produced or written the scripts for. If you are not allergic to yellowing news-print then go to library and read any of the hundreds of columns I have written. I WILL BE THERE with you.'

In an age when being 'progressive' was considered almost synonymous with being dubbed 'communist', Abbas consciously drew a line. This is summed up in a passage in his autobiography: 'One of the persistent legends in Indian politics is that I am a communist, or at least a hidden communist, a fellow traveller or a stooge of the communists. All kinds of people seem to believe it—except the communists who think I am an un-regenerated "petite bourgeoise".' He recalls Nehru's amusement at his distinction between communists, ex-communists and anti-communists in ascending order of undesirability and goes on relate his expulsion (rescinded nine years later) from the Progressive Writers' Association and the Indian People's Theatre Association, and the ideological debate relating to conformity and dissent.

It is evident that Abbas was a passionate advocate of causes, not an adherent to ideological conformity. He summed up the social responsibilities of an intellectual succinctly: 'To mirror life, realistically but also critically, so that things can improve. The improvement of man, I think, is the greatest mission of a writer, or an intellectual or a creative artist. If he disregards the mission, he cannot be a good writer.'

An appreciation of Abbas the story writer was done by Mulk Raj Anand in a very long letter to him in 1947. Its concluding section was definitive and bears citation in full:

> The strength of your short stories, my dear Abbas, lies in the fact that you have grasped the weaknesses of your characters and strengths. You seem to have an uncanny, instinctive awareness of the dark side of the 'moon' coupled with a passion for the light. And if the moon may in this context stand for the land of our heart's desire, our India, then surely you have brought to it the only kind of love which can redeem its present wretchedness and stretch out to its unexplored future. So that if there is a message in your stories it seems to me this: 'you cannot love India merely for its strengths but you also have to love it for its weaknesses.

It is his qualities as a writer that propelled Abbas to the world of films, initially as a critic and subsequently as a script writer and film-maker. In each of these fields, his contribution was seminal. His work reflected his deep commitment to the ideals of socialism, secularism and nationalism. Through the medium of cinema, he highlighted relevant social and political issues of the day, such as poverty, communalism, casteism and the rural–urban divide.

His work remains one amongst the most impressive pieces of realism and social commentary. He could be rightly described as one of the pioneers of what was later called 'art films' or 'parallel cinema'. He was perhaps the most prominent progressive voice in Indian commercial films. As social activist John Dayal put it, 'He identified social relevance and critical realism as the mainstays of any cinema, particularly of cinema of an emerging tradition like India's.'

As a director, producer and script writer, Khwaja sahib was acclaimed by the public and critics alike. The older generation recalls his partnership with the legendary Raj Kapoor. Some of his films won the Nargis Dutt Award for National Integration. Another won the prestigious Palme d'Or at Cannes. *Shehar Aur Sapna*, depicting the struggle for survival in the brutalized environment of an urban slum, won the National Film Award for Best Feature Film. Yet another, *Saat Hindustani*, propagating patriotism and an aggressive secularism, will be best remembered for introducing the future superstar, Amitabh Bachchan, to the Indian public.

The list of some of his epoch-making, socially sensitive films is long and diverse. This promotion of social awareness is what distinguishes him as a writer and film-maker. He would have subscribed, but without being doctrinaire, to what Munshi Premchand said in 1936:

> We shall consider only that literature as progressive which is thoughtful, which awakens in us the spirit of freedom and of beauty, which is creative, which is luminous with the realities of life; which moves us; which leads us to action and which does not act like a narcotic; which does not produce in us a state of intellectual somnolence—for if we continue to remain in that state it can only mean that we are no longer alive.

Khwaja Ahmad Abbas subscribed in his life and work to an approach that was catholic rather than sectarian, and modernist rather than obscurantist. He revelled in India's cultural heterogeneity and celebrated it in his life and work. We find in his autobiography a delectable description of his film crew's journey in a freight train and singing three songs: '*Jana gana mana*', '*Saare jahan se achcha*' and '*Dekhna hai zore kitna baazu-e-qaatil main hai*'.

24

FAITH AND INTERFAITH: AN IMPERATIVE OF OUR TIMES

A CELEBRATION IS A MULTI-DIMENSIONAL occurrence. It is a happy occasion; it is also an occasion for introspection. Some questions do come to mind. Why bestow an honour upon someone? What is its relevance in individual and societal terms?

Here, as on many other occasions, semantics could be a starting point. The dictionary defines 'faith' as complete trust or confidence in someone or something; a second meaning is a strong belief in the doctrines of a religion, based on spiritual conviction rather than proof. 'Interfaith' is thus understood as interaction between faiths or belief systems professed by individuals or groups. Our definition would need to include agnostics and atheists since they too have a role in society.

Exceptions apart, the human being is a social creature and, throughout known history, has lived in groups or societies that had their own unique experiences and, in the process, developed ideas and beliefs as well as a set of desirable, less desirable and undesirable norms of behaviour. Some of these are also related to belief systems or perceptions on matters beyond the physical world. Interactions between these social groups therefore also necessitated interactions between these belief systems. Over time, and driven by the realization that concord is preferable to discord and harmony to disharmony, humankind in different societies sought an understanding of other thought patterns and faiths.

Note: Speech delivered at the event to mark the Silver Jubilee function and Presentation of Karan Singh Interfaith Harmony Award, 19 February 2016, New Delhi.

This was, and remains, the impulse for interfaith dialogue. From time to time and in varying measures, it is also reflected in the approach of governments or rulers in individual societies. Record shows that it could be accommodative or exclusionary.

An excellent example of high-minded approach to the question is to be found in Emperor Ashoka's Girnar Rock Edict near Junagarh in Gujarat around the year 260 BC:

> The King honours all religions and sects. His Sacred Majesty does not value gifts and honours as he values the growth of the essential elements of all religious sects. But the root of it is restraint of speech, that is, there should not be honour only of one's own religion and condemnation of other religions. On the other hand, other religions should be honoured too. By doing this, one helps his own religion to grow and benefits the religion of others also. By doing otherwise, one harms his own religion and injures the other religions too. For whoever honours only his own religion and condemns other religions injures more gravely his own religion. Hence concord alone is commendable and all should listen, and be willing to listen, to the beliefs professed by others.[1]

The historian Edward Gibbon made a succinct comment on the pragmatic approach to religious diversity in the Roman Empire:

> The various modes of worship which prevailed in the Roman world were all considered by the people as equally true; by the philosopher as equally false; and by the magistrate as equally useful. And thus tolerance produced not only mutual indulgence, but even religious concord.[2]

Either way, principled or pragmatic, societies have developed responses to respond to diversity of faiths within them. This has been particularly marked in the case of India where a plural society, reflective of a multiplicity of faiths, reinforced by teachings of Bhakti and Sufi saints, has been a ground reality for centuries.

It was this historical backdrop that propelled the makers of the Constitution of India to put in place a secular state structure premised on equality and fraternity. It also brought us face to face with what Dr Ambedkar called the 'life of contradictions' and tardiness in the recognition of 'evils that lie across our path'.

Societies are living entities that respond to challenges of changing times. India is no exception to it. In the globalizing world of the 21st century, spaces have shrunk, traditional practices are being eschewed and new means of communications, apart from the good they bring, are also facilitating the communication of prejudices and mischief. Each of these impedes the effort to understand the 'other' who may be a neighbour, a fellow citizen, a fellow human being.

What then is the choice before us? One option is to remain embedded in our prejudices and take them to their logical conclusion through promotion of strife to overcome the 'other'. The other is to seek understanding in the expectation that disagreements would be narrowed, perhaps even eliminated. The first option is becoming increasingly impractical since strife would disrupt social peace, impede development and thus obstruct the achievement of national objectives in any modern society.

The quest for understanding is a complex process. It proceeds from impressions and vivid mental phenomena to reasoned ideas based on factual information or conclusions derived from them. The first step in this process is tolerance, an acceptance that the *other*, though different, may not be harmful or undesirable; its apogee would be acceptance, that the other though different is not harmful or undesirable.

Given the cultural and spiritual legacy, we in India can assert that such an ideal is achievable and has, in fact, been advocated by rulers from time to time. One instance of it is Ashoka's Edict cited earlier; another is Akbar's institution of Ibadatkhana at Fatehpur Sikri, as also his assertion in his letter to Shah Abbas of Persia that 'we must be kind to all people who are the treasures of God and have mercy for everybody no matter what their religion or ideas are'.[3] Much more has been said by mystics and saints. Well known is Khwaja Nizamuddin Auliya's remark that *'har quam raast rahe, deen-e-wa qiblagahe'*; equally meaningful on this theme are the teachings of Sant Kabir and Khwaja Moinuddin Chishti. So is Swami Vivekananda's observation that we 'must not only tolerate other religions but positively embrace them as the truth is the basis of all religions'.[4]

In November 1995, and pursuant to earlier UN General Assembly Resolutions, the General Conference of UNESCO (United Nations Educational, Scientific and Cultural Organization) adopted a Declaration of Principles on Tolerance that defined as 'respect, acceptance and appreciation of the rich diversity of our world's cultures, our forms of expression and ways of being human,' adding that 'tolerance is harmony in difference' and 'is not concession, condescendence or indulgence' and that it is not only a moral duty but a political and legal requirement for the 'replacement of the culture of war by a culture of peace'. It emphasized that this is to be achieved by action at state, social and educational levels.

Tolerance is thus a virtue to be cultivated. Acceptance, however, goes a step beyond tolerance. It is a person's assent to the reality of a situation, recognizing a process or condition without attempting to change it, protest or exit. You can tolerate something without accepting it, but you cannot accept something without tolerating it. Moving from tolerance to acceptance is a journey that starts within ourselves; within our own understanding and compassion for people who are different to us. We need to challenge ourselves to see beyond the stereotypes and preconceptions that prevent us from accepting others.

Principles, however lofty and relevant, will remain in the realm of the ideal unless they are accompanied by an implementing methodology. It is here that dialogue becomes an imperative necessity. It is only through dialogue that misunderstandings are removed and understanding promoted. How then should the dialogue be initiated, and conducted?

Dialogue partners the world over have developed modalities to facilitate the process. The late Dr Asghar Ali Engineer had written an essay suggesting a set of rules for such dialogues. They were:

1. Those who enter into dialogue should be firmly rooted in the tradition of their faith and have inner conviction;
2. There should not be any feeling of superiority in their respective traditions;
3. Dialogue should not be polemical in style, should not be focused on right or wrong, and should be conducted to understand the other's viewpoint, and its integrity and uniqueness;
4. Its purpose should be to explain the viewpoint, not to convert the other to it;
5. The dialogue partners should recognize that diversity is the very basis of life;
6. Its purpose should be to promote the spirit of accommodation and adjustment to minimize conflict in society;
7. The difference between dialogue and monologue should at all times be borne in mind; and

8. An effective dialogue is possible when the partner not only listens but also makes the effort to understand and appreciate it.[5]

I commend the effort on the part of all, individuals and groups, who indulge in this noble venture.

SECURITY

25
INSECURITY AND THE STATE: EMERGING CHALLENGES

THE FIRST INDIAN CHIEF OF the armed forces of modern India, Field Marshal K.M. Cariappa, was a legend in his own lifetime and will undoubtedly remain so in the annals of history. Cariappa's greatest contribution, said Field Marshal Manekshaw, 'was that he taught the Indian Army to be apolitical'.[1] By doing so, as General Raghavan put it in an earlier lecture, he 'set the foundations of civil military relations in India'.[2]

There's a personal connection for me here too. The Field Marshal was, several decades earlier, a very distinguished predecessor of mine as High Commissioner to Australia. I called on him prior to my departure and he offered a valuable piece of advice. 'Do not waste your time in Canberra, young man,' he said, 'go out and meet the real Australians.'

I heard more about his work in Australia from his, and my, neighbour on Mugga Way in Canberra, the late Sir Harold White who was Australia's first national librarian. Cariappa is remembered to this day for his impromptu action in personally cleaning the brass plate at a war memorial; he was the founder-president of the Commonwealth Club at Canberra. Record also shows that he maintained a high public profile on some issues and was openly critical of the White Australia policy that characterized the official approach in that period to immigration from 'new' Commonwealth countries. An Australian historian has noted that 'his critics notwithstanding, Cariappa had a significant impact on progressive opinion in Australia'.[3]

Field Marshal Cariappa was a soldier of World War II, part of an imperial

---

Note: 14th Field Marshal K.M. Cariappa Memorial Lecture at DRDO Auditorium, 7 October 2009, New Delhi.

army in a global contest that produced a victor and a vanquished but, in Henry Kissinger's words, 'ended with a geopolitical vacuum'. The responsibilities entrusted to him in 1948 by a newly independent India were, however, of a different nature. The challenges were immediate, even if the security paradigm in that early period was considerably simpler.

So much for history and recollection! Let me return to the world of harsh reality. I intend to probe the concept of insecurity. I would argue that unless we understand it clearly in all its dimensions, our endeavour to craft comprehensive national security for the world of tomorrow would remain elusive.

The historian Eric Hobsbawm concluded his 1994 work *Age of Extremes: The Short History of the Twentieth Century* (pp. 584–585) with a prognosis:

> The future cannot be a continuation of the past, and there are signs, both externally, and, as it were, internally, that we have reached a point of historic crisis. The forces generated by the techno-scientific economy are now great enough to destroy the environment, that is to say, the material foundations of human life… Our world risks both explosion and implosion. It must change… If humanity is to have a recognisable future, it cannot be by prolonging the past or the present. If we try to build the third millennium on that basis, we shall fail. And the price of failure, that is to say, the alternative to a changed society, is darkness.

A number of questions arise. Is perception of this change reflected in current thinking on national security and strategies pertaining to it? Is national security synonymous with, or apart from, the security of citizens? Do we comprehend insecurity not merely in state-centric and military terms but also to cover insecurity pertaining to food, water, energy, other resources, pandemics, environment and, as Walter Lippman put it a long time back, 'core values'? How would they impact on national strategy in the world of tomorrow? Would it restrict or expand our choices in seeking security?

The traditional approach to security is state-centric, and for good reason. The raison d'etre of statehood is provision of security for its citizens, and to a lesser extent its residents, in both its internal and external dimensions. The post-World War II global order is premised on states acting as net security generators and providers and thereby contributing to systemic stability. The experience of the last six decades, and especially since the end of the Cold War, shows that real life veers quite significantly away from textbook assumptions. Many of the states have radiated insecurity towards their citizens and residents and thus destabilized their own societies and polities. This has led to state failures and implosions in the internal dimension and to regional and even global crises in the external dimension. One cannot escape the harsh conclusion that states have, quite often, been significant contributors to individual and systemic insecurity.

A good recent instance of it is the study on Global Trends 2025 published by the National Security Council of the United States in November 2008. It is based on a wide-ranging interaction with think tanks in America, Europe and China. Allow me to cite its conclusion on the likely shape of the international system:

> By 2025, the international system will be a global multipolar one with gaps in national power continuing to narrow between developed and developing countries. Concurrent with the shift in power among nation-states, the relative power of various non-state actors—including businesses, tribes, religious organisations, and criminal networks is increasing. The players are changing, but so too are the scope and breadth of transnational issues important for continued global prosperity... The next 20 years of transition to a new system are fraught with risks. Strategic rivalries are most likely to revolve around trade, investments, and technological innovation and acquisitions, but we cannot rule out a 19th century-like scenario of arms races, territorial expansion, and military rivalries... This is a story with no clear outcome...(These) trends suggest major discontinuities, shocks, and surprises.

Assessments emanating from credible studies elsewhere are on somewhat parallel lines. They focus on multipolarity, interdependence and changing nature of conflicts. Concepts like interpolarity and hybrid wars have acquired relevance. Other matters having security implications like governance, drugs, money laundering and immigration have been added to the framework. Each seeks a strategy to respond to a new situation; each compels a review of the security paradigm, and our response to it.

The Barcelona Report in 2004 focused on the capabilities needed by the European Union for dealing with situations of severe insecurity and for achieving 'freedom from fear'. It proposed a Human Security Doctrine for Europe in a set of seven principles. These were listed as the primacy of human rights, clear political authority, multilateralism, a bottom-up approach, regional focus, the use of legal instruments and the appropriate use of force. The report was selective in its approach to human security.

A more holistic view was taken in 2001 by the UN Secretary General Kofi Annan. 'We must,' he said, 'broaden our view of what is meant by peace and security. Peace means much more than the absence of war. Human security can no longer be understood in purely military terms. Rather, it must encompass economic development, social justice, environmental protection, democratization, disarmament, and respect for human rights and the rule of law.'

In such a framework the inescapable conclusion would be that absence of any of these would signal an element of insecurity.

In an interesting book on new perspectives of security, Professor T.K. Oommen argues that security is the conjoint concern of three pillars—state, market and civil society; as a result, only 'a society free from genocide, culturocide and ecocide may be conceptualized as a secure society'.[4] The sources of insecurity, he holds, tend to feed on one another and aggravate it. In more specific terms, the India Social Development Report 2005 used six indices—namely demography, healthcare, basic amenities, education, unemployment and poverty, and social deprivation—to assess the security perception of citizens in states of the Indian Union.

The substantive point that emerges is the felt need to assess security in a wider perspective. This is easier said than done. The human mind is not a tabula rasa; the response patterns of the past do condition its reactions. The challenge for the strategist is to overcome these and think beyond the obvious. Even in military terms, Donald Rumsfeld chose the expression 'known unknowns and unknown unknowns' to highlight the predicament. While developing response patterns, it would be relevant to recall Sun Tzu's dictum that the acme of skill is to subdue the enemy without fighting; hence the need to 'attack the enemy's strategy'. For the world of tomorrow, however, the 'enemy' has to be defined in wider terms. In one of Arthur Clarke's stories there is a fascinating portrayal of a situation in which 'the ancient battle between man and insect' is decisively settled in favour of the latter. The same may hold for other contestations with nature. The human strategist would need to visualize the improbable, perhaps even the impossible. He should have the ability to combine innovative, perceptive and holistic insights and yet be realistic enough to be comprehensible. The challenge is real; it is also bewildering.

It is essential, in the first place, to comprehend insecurity. The dictionary meaning is fear or anxiety stemming from a concrete or alleged lack of protection. It could relate to individual or collective insecurity, could be self-centred, state-centric or society-centric. Its manifestations and sources could be multifarious. It could emanate from natural or human causes. For purposes of today's analysis, our focus would be on collective insecurity that affects particular segments of the population or even society as a whole. A typology of insecurities, present and anticipated, thus needs to be developed. This takes us to the very purpose of being in a society.

Hobbes depicted the pre-society stage as one in which the life of a person was 'nasty, brutish and short'. Others dwelt on an essential implication of being in society. 'The strongest man,' said Rousseau, 'is never strong enough to be always master, unless he transforms his power into right, and obedience into duty.'[5] Hence, the need for an association which takes upon itself the obligation to, in Rousseau's words, 'defend and protect with the whole force of the community the person and property of every associate'. Furthermore, fear is not a correlate of underdevelopment and, to use Ashis Nandy's felicitous phrase, is to be found 'in the interstices of anxiety' even in the most developed societies.

Consequently the community encapsulated in a territorial state seeks collective and, by implication, comprehensive security and, in today's world, does so without wishing to be homogenized and deprived of identities within its fold. The same would hold for the global community.

An observation made in the Report of the 6th ARF Security Policy Conference held in May 2009 is indicative of some new thinking. Noting that as a result of globalization the international community has become more vulnerable to non-traditional security threats, it underlined the importance of 'a whole-of-society approach' to respond to these questions. It observed that 'both traditional and non-traditional security threats need to be balanced in terms of setting priorities and policy planning'.

What then should be the priorities for the world of tomorrow in terms of elements of insecurity and the imperative to address them?

It is evident that given the structure of the international system, traditional and more recent norms of state security would remain in place in the foreseeable future and make ever-increasing demands on resources of individual states. The sustainability of the effort, however, would be a debatable question and there are some lessons to be derived from the last decade of the Cold

War that demonstrated the inability of one of the contestants to cope with the burden. Equally relevant would be George Washington's caution about the impact on free societies of 'overgrown military establishments'. These apart, the right to wage war, a traditionally accepted attribute of state sovereignty, stands circumscribed by the Charter of the United Nations in 1945. It enjoined member states to refrain from 'the threat or use of force' in their dealings, except for Purposes of the UN and in self-defence as defined in Article 51. This, of course, has not prevented interstate wars; it has, nevertheless, put into place the constraint of legitimacy of state action. Introspection by some of those involved in decision-making has now brought forth new categorization: wars of necessity and wars of choice. Terminological refinement, however, has its own problems. Gradually but surely the concept of wrong, of illicit action, is beginning to seep into the discourse; it ventures into the 'unexplored normative potential' and would constitute a major advance in conceptual terms. Despite it, interstate wars remain an option, even though the easier availability of the weapons of mass destruction and the demonstrated futility of their use does seem to act as a deterrent on major conflagrations.

Going beyond the traditional security paradigm, the ambit of discussion does not remain confined to maintenance of state sovereignty and territorial integrity. Once we begin to address other threats, two characteristics rapidly emerge. We find, in the first place, that the initiating actors and eventual recipients are states as well as individuals and groups; secondly, because the latter do not always fall within the ambit of a single state, it necessitates departures from the traditional structure of command and compliance. The latter, in effect, would often depend upon demonstrated good rather than its a priori acceptance. Both, together, necessitate a paradigm shift.

Another aspect is the nature, and diversity, of challenges. Together they demonstrate the inefficacy of unilateral action and the imperative of a comprehensive and cooperative approach. The terms of this cooperation, and their equity, remain a work in progress. Since paucity of time does not permit a detailed scrutiny, I shall endeavour to illustrate the point by referring to a few obvious but relevant aspects.

A case in point is terrorism. It has domestic and external dimensions that are not mutually exclusive. Some states indulge in it as an act of policy to conduct, what Kautilya called, 'secret war'. The Security Council has described terrorism as any act 'intended to cause death or serious bodily harm to civilians or non-combatants with the purpose of intimidating a population or compelling a government or an international organization to do or abstain from doing any act'. Globalization and technology has made it transnational in organization and reach and devastating in its impact; hence the approach, mechanisms and commitments developed through various Security Council resolutions, as also the innumerable bilateral and regional arrangements that are unevenly implemented. These are essentially focused on preventive or punitive steps, on the dismantling of the infrastructure of terrorism, and do not deal sufficiently with the mental orientation that leads to terrorist acts. The latter emanate from a radicalization of the mind induced by an ideological or faith-based impulse and propelled by a perceived grievance. Combating terrorism thus becomes a sociological and political effort as much as a security one.

Another threat of transnational dimensions is pandemics. Their impact on societies is, and would be, devastating, apart from the havoc they bring about in terms of loss of human lives. A Princeton University Project in 2006 visualized the scenario in the wake of an apocalyptic pandemic. It is worthy of being cited in some detail:

> The global economy could grind to a halt, if not collapse entirely. Stock markets would fall, travel would cease, trade would be inhibited, and productivity would decline precipitously. In addition, the costs associated with directly tackling the crisis would be astronomical. Worse still would be the consequences of differential dying...we can plan on huge global disparities in the nationality and socio-economic status of victims. The repercussions of a catastrophe with such disparities would likely linger, fester, and cause rage for generations. Even in the industrialized world, trust might be obliterated as individual states hoard and nationalize vaccines that can be produced within their borders. In a post-pandemic world... dangerous patterns of interstate behavior might emerge that resemble those prevalent before World War II.[6]

The report recommended that 'we must broaden our understanding of national security so that health and development experts are included at every stage of the threat assessment and decision-making processes and not just consulted after the outbreak of a crisis'.

Despite these suggestions, an acknowledged expert wrote in the *Wall Street Journal* on 2 May 2009 that the United States remains 'under-prepared for any pandemic or major outbreak, whether it comes from newly emerging infectious diseases, bio-terror attack or laboratory accident'. Visualizing the consequences can be, at best, a matter of conjecture; a worst-case apocalyptic vision of the future was portrayed, in 2008 in the film *Doomsday* in which a whole country, quarantined for decades to contain a deadly virus, reverted to lethally primitive form of existence.

As for our own capabilities, a sober assessment would show that these are modest and the experience in regard to H1N1 was instructive. Given the global health trends there is a good case for creating, nationally or multilaterally, one primary facility and one backup facility for the production of vaccines and therapeutics expressly for emerging and re-emerging infections.

Similar arguments hold for environment and climate change. These too are not coterminous with political units. At the national level, and despite the good work done by a number of dedicated environmentalists, public awareness is still in its infancy and there is merit in Vandana Shiva's observation that 'the environmental movement can only survive if it becomes a movement for justice'. Official efforts, on the other hand, have often sought to strike an uneasy balance between competing pressures.

Awareness at the international level of the need for conservation and management of resources for sustainable development was initiated in the UN General Assembly as early as 1988, was highlighted by the Rio Summit of 1992 and thereafter allowed to linger while governments negotiated from narrow national perspectives. An acknowledgement that changing climate poses a threat to stability and human security has been slow to emerge. In his Nobel Lecture in December 2007, Dr R.K. Pachauri drew attention to some instances in recorded history of the link between climate and security. He laid stress on 'the equity implications of the changes that are occurring and are likely to occur in the future'. He defined peace as 'security and the secure access to resources that are essential for living. A disruption in such access could prove disruptive of peace'. He listed these essentials as: (a) access to water, (b) access to sufficient food, and impact on (c) public health, (d) biodiversity and (e) security of settlements particularly in Asian and African mega-deltas and small islands.

Despite frequent articulation of principles, especially at Kyoto and Bali, the harsh reality is that individual nations and particularly those in the developed world are dragging their feet on implementing their commitments.

Two conclusions emanate from these examples of dimensions of insecurity, transcending national frontiers and beyond solutions in the traditional security paradigm. They suggest that solutions have to be sought in a multilateral framework of equals; they also have to be equitable. The process would be tortuous and slow and would depend on the speed with which the gravity of the emerging threats sinks into public perceptions and governmental action.

Let me return to the question of the ambit of insecurity posed in the earlier part of this chapter. It clearly goes beyond challenges to state sovereignty and its territorial integrity. It is also evident that comprehensive security needs to focus on citizens and their right for a dignified existence. This does not limit the role of the state; instead, it changes it. The responsibility of the citizen and of the civil society is to keep the state glued to its purpose. This, in our case, is inscribed in the Preamble of the Constitution. From this emanates the imperative, at the conceptual level, to redefine the social purpose: to ensure that each citizen is assured freedom from fear and from want so that he/she is able to partake of all other activities open to a citizen. Such an endeavour at the national and global levels would help bring forth a new world, more in consonance with a sustainable existence in tune with human rights and the environment. Its rationale would be practical necessity and the imperative of survival, rather than utopian idealism. It would require adding new dimensions to the concept of threat assessment.

The need for a new approach to comprehensive security is underlined by a survey of both the traditional and non-traditional threats faced by us in the past three decades. The data is in the public domain. It presents a complex picture; it is also indicative of a certain imbalance in our allocation of resources and in the efficacy of their utilization. This suggests a need for correctives directed at capacity-building in societal structures and, in the security framework, a rationalization based on qualitative upgradation and quantitative resizing.

No venture into futurology can altogether rule out less-optimistic scenarios. There is always the possibility that evolution in thought and practice may not happen along the lines visualized in the foregoing. The result would be an optimization of insecurity. Insanity, goes a Lebanese proverb, has 70 gates. Reaching any of these would be entry into the capital of hell, aptly called Pandemonium by the poet John Milton.

Avoiding such an outcome would require collective community effort, based on sober reasoning, grounded in a set of agreed values and objectives. This is achievable since, as a 14th century historian said, 'The pasture of stupidity is unwholesome to mankind.'[7]

26
INTELLIGENCE FOR THE WORLD OF TOMORROW

IN ANOTHER AGE OR ANOTHER system of governance, Rameshwar Nath Kao, who dedicated his life to the service of the republic and created structures deemed essential for the security of the state and the promotion of its essential interests, would be honoured suitably in a pantheon of immortals. We as a people, however, are diffident in matters relating to some aspects of the functioning of the state and prefer a discreet veil to a public acclaim. It tantalizes imagination but does not add to the compendium of knowledge for succeeding generations.

We remember Rameshwar Nath Kao today for his work and for his engaging personality. In regard to the former, I cannot help recalling a couplet by an Arab poet of the 10th century:

> *These are our works, these works our souls display*
> *Behold our works when we have passed away.*

I personally cannot claim to have known Kao sahib well but do recall an occasion, in early 1980, when I happened to sit next to him on a journey from Bombay to Delhi. He spoke in chaste Urdu, discussed the happening in Iran and was candid enough to acknowledge that like most other people he had not anticipated the revolutionary changes.

Ramjee Kao created an organization, negotiated rather than confronted inter-agency contentions and achieved historic success. He could also be indulgent to a fault. Those who worked closely with him have described

---

Note: Fourth R.N. Kao Memorial Lecture, 19 January 2010, New Delhi.

Kao as a complex mix of objectivity and subjectivity in matters concerning human relationships. A peer in a position to assess from a distance described him as a fascinating mix of physical and mental elegance, and one who was shy to talk about his accomplishments.

Kao's business in life was intelligence, more specifically external intelligence. Its relevance is in no need of commentary. We can go as far back as Kautilya, or even earlier, to perceive its importance. In fact, the methodological sophistication exhibited in Kautilya's chapters on the secret service and internal security can be read with benefit even today. The same holds good for Sun Tzu's chapter on secret agents. He highlights the relevance of 'foreknowledge' and concludes with the interesting observation that 'there is no place where espionage is not used'.[1] Over centuries the ambit of intelligence, and the craft itself, expanded and enriched itself in response to requirements. Techniques were refined and technology opened up qualitatively different vistas. In the 20th century, individual agents on specific assignments gave way to regular agencies. Fascination with the unknown also brought forth a vast amount of literary output that combined fact and fiction, working powerfully on public imagination and even lending respectability to questionable acts. There is merit in C.P. Snow's observation that 'the euphoria of secrecy does go to the head'.[2]

Intelligence, by definition, is primarily directed at anticipating happenings. Intelligence information, by its very nature, is a glimpse of reality. It is often inconclusive because the methods of acquisition are at times surreptitious. On the other hand, the probabilities of reality that can be established by intelligence information are necessary and sufficient to enable national decision-makers to make reasonable judgements about courses of action. While intelligence information is at times incomplete, good intelligence often has made the difference between victory and defeat, life and death. By the same token, faulty intelligence leads to failures of varying degrees. Over time, reasons for failure are analysed and classified. These range from overestimation to underestimation, lack of communication, unavailability of information, received opinion, mirror-imaging, overconfidence, complacency, failure to connect dots and subordination of intelligence to policy. Case studies on each of these abound; they are a sobering reminder of Karl Popper's observation that 'the more we learn about the world, and the deeper our learning, the more conscious, specific and articulate will be our knowledge of what we do not know'.[3]

The qualities that go to make a good intelligence operative have been defined in all systems of governance. A medieval classic called it a 'delicate business involving some unpleasantness' to be 'entrusted to the hands and tongues and pens of men who are completely above suspicion and without self-interest, for the weal or woe of the country depends on them'. In an interesting passage in his book, the formidable Mr Allen Dulles observed that 'a good intelligence officer must have an understanding of other points of view, other ways of thinking and behaving, even if they are quite foreign to his own'. Record shows that this is easier said than done even in normal circumstances. The ability to assess what Troksky called 'changes in mass consciousness in a revolutionary epoch' is rarely acquired by those who collect and analyse intelligence. The reason for this would seem to lie in insufficient comprehension of the nuances of a changing situation, inadequacy of coverage and inability to challenge working assumptions.

Other problems emerge as occupational hazards. Compulsive secrecy tends to become obsessive and impacts the personality of the individual. An intelligence organization, one observer has noted, tends to be a self-sufficient society to which 'the outside world becomes more and more remote and its realities less and less important'. Rob Johnston, who conducted an ethnographic study of the US intelligence community in 2005, observed that 'within the intelligence community, more organizational emphasis is placed on secrecy than on effectiveness'.[4] Making a judgement about open source versus secret information, a professional concluded that 90 per cent information comes from the former and only 10 per cent from the latter. 'The real intelligence hero,' he wrote, 'is Sherlock Holmes, not James Bond.'

The need to strike a balance between secrecy, openness and efficacy on a continuous basis is thus essential. Much greater coordination is required to maximize results in complex situations. The time-honoured formula of 'need to know' has to be modified by the requirement of the 'need to share'. The point was driven home by an eminent leader very recently: 'I'll never fault anybody for not having full intelligence, what I will fault is when we have full intelligence that's not shared.'

Beyond the confines of professional competence, the question of intelligence is intrinsically linked to the nature of challenge perceived by a society. It tends to be based on past experience and on assumptions that seem logical. This is essential, but not sufficient, and its relevance now is increasingly open to question. The resulting dilemma was aptly expressed a few years back by the historian and jurist Philip Bobbitt:

Now it happens that we are living in one of those relatively rare periods in which the future is unlikely to be very much like the past. Indeed the three certainties...about national security—that it is national (not international), that it is public (not private), and that it seeks victory (not stalemate)—these three lessons of the past are all about to be turned upside down by the new age of indeterminancy into which we are plunging.

Bobbitt went on to assert the need to appreciate 'the essential ambiguity' of attacks to which societies may be subjected to and as a result of which strategies of retaliation and deterrence, may become less useful. In such a world, he added:

We must move our thinking from threat-based strategies that rely on knowing precisely who our enemy is and where he lives, to vulnerability-based strategies that try to make our infrastructure more slippery, more redundant, more versatile, more difficult to attack.[5]

This conceptual shift, from threat-based to vulnerability-based strategies, would necessitate a comprehensive reorientation of the work of the state and, therefore, of its intelligence apparatus, its objectives and its work methods. Some of this is already underway in the light of the experience of the first decade of the 21st century; this, however, has been pragmatic and halting since the requisite paradigm shift in thinking is yet to be put in place. The extent and speed with which it is done may well determine success or failure in the foreseeable future.

To develop the argument further, I would like to borrow the definition of the term 'vulnerability' from the meaning given to it in the terminology of computer security. There, it is referred to as a weakness which allows an attacker to reduce a system's information assurance. This happens at the intersection of three elements: a system susceptibility or flaw, an attacker's access to the flaw and an attacker's capability to exploit the flaw. In societal terms, this would read as: (a) flaw or susceptibility, (b) existence of an enemy or a threat, (c) ability of the threat to exploit the flaw. Such a framework would necessitate going beyond the traditional approach to a comprehensive assessment of both the susceptibility of the target and the capability of the opposing force.

A complicating factor of increasing relevance is the changing nature of the actors on the global stage. In addition to nation-states, it now includes a mix of non-state entities, benign and malignant. In the absence of effective multilateralism, the relative power of these non-state actors has increased to reflect the fragmentation of interests.

The conclusion is inescapable that in the world of tomorrow, the nature of intelligence required for comprehensive security would be qualitatively different. This would have implications for the methodology of acquiring and analysing it. As a first step, it would necessitate a wider understanding of target areas. Much too often, governmental intelligence efforts have focused on politico-military and economic intelligence. While its relevance cannot be questioned, its sufficiency can be. The reason is obvious. Most often, the standard checklist does not go beyond or behind the super-structure, does not look at societal realities, pays inadequate attention to other people's ways of thinking and behaving. Intelligence services, as David Kay of the Iraq Survey Group put it, 'don't do a very good job of trying to understand the soft side of societies'.

Nor does the checklist take a good look at the national security implications of non-traditional threats, including cyber-attacks, attacks on food and water security, bioterrorism, pandemics or worst-case apocalyptic visions of the future. It has, for instance, been assessed that in a post-pandemic world dangerous patterns of interstate behaviour may emerge and seriously endanger security of states.

The ambit of intelligence, consequently, has to be comprehensive. It is to be assessed simultaneously on three planes: state-centric, society-centric and environment-centric. The dynamics of these may be different and may require different tools of analysis. The resulting conclusions may be fluid, complex and contradictory and thereby challenge the analytical skills of the operative to bring forth options that can be comprehended and acted upon. Access to these skills, if not available in-house, would necessitate review of security rules that generally govern the functioning of intelligence organizations.

A particularly serious problem relates to the misuse of intelligence. The classic instance in recent times is the process leading to the invasion of Iraq in March 2003. The July 2004 Report of the US Senate Select Committee on Pre-War Intelligence Assessment of Iraq revealed that 'group think dynamics' led the intelligence community to interpret ambiguous evidence as conclusive and ignore the process established mechanisms to challenge assumptions and group think. Closer to the mark was the secret 'Downing Street Memo' of 23 July 2002 in which the head of British intelligence reported after discussions in Washington that 'intelligence and facts were being fixed around policy' of regime change.

These instances can be multiplied. They are not the monopoly of one nation or set of nations. They are revealed earlier in open societies and less so in closed ones. They have led to follies and catastrophes. Failures propel thinking in the direction of correctives and reforms. They focus analysis on the political or economic pressures at work in individual societies. These, together, propel thinking in the direction of accountability and necessitate oversight. Both are considered unwanted and bothersome by intelligence communities for reasons that range from secrecy and operational efficiency to downright contempt for any individual, body or arrangement that endeavours to assess their functioning. The problem nevertheless exists and was posed by an expert in precise terms:

How shall a democracy ensure its secret intelligence apparatus becomes neither a vehicle for conspiracy nor a suppressor of the traditional liberties of democratic self-government?

It is hardly necessary to remind an Indian audience that ministerial responsibility to the legislature, and eventually to the electorate, is an essential element of democratic governance to which we are committed by the Constitution. The methodology of this is in place for most aspects of governmental activity; the exceptions to it pertain to the intelligence and security structure of the state.

How then is oversight and accountability ensured?

The traditional answer and prevailing practice, of oversight by the concerned minister and prime minister and general accountability of the latter to Parliament, was accepted as adequate in an earlier period but is now considered amorphous and does not meet the requirements of good governance in an open society. Concerns in the matter have primarily arisen on two counts: (a) the nature and extent of supervision over intelligence services exercised by the political executive, and (b) the possibility and scope of misuse of these services by the political executive. Both concerns emanate from the absence of specific accountability, on these matters, to the legislature.

The problem is not a new one and has been faced by other democratic societies. In late 1970s, opinion in the United States reached the conclusion that 'oversight of the Intelligence Community is essential because of the critical importance of ensuring the nation's security, as well as checking the potential for abuse of power'. As a result, two congressional committees were established in 1976 and 1977. Despite this, the 9/11 Commission Report of 2004 found the congressional oversight of intelligence 'dysfunctional' and recommended structural changes. A similar exercise was conducted in the United Kingdom through the Intelligence Services Act 1994 that established the Intelligence and Security Committee of Parliament to examine the expenditure, administration and policy of the intelligence services. Other countries like Canada, Australia, South Africa, Norway, Germany, Argentina, the Netherlands, Poland and Romania have also put in place similar mechanisms of public accountability.

It has been argued that the scope of the mandate of the Parliamentary Intelligence Oversight Committee is crucial for its success. Three models of the mandate can be identified: (a) comprehensive to include both policy and operations, as in the United States and Germany, (b) limited to matters of policy and finance, as in the UK, (c) focused on human rights and rule of law, as in Norway. The basic purpose of all three is to ensure that government policy in a given field is carried out effectively within the boundaries of the law. For this reason, it is felt that without access to some operational detail, an oversight body can have, or give, no assurance about the efficacy or the legality of the intelligence services.

Given these models of calibrated openness to ensure oversight and accountability, there is no reason why a democratic system like ours should not have a Standing Committee of Parliament on intelligence that could function at least on the pattern of other Standing Committees. Since internal and external intelligence do not report to the same minister in our system, the possibility of entrusting this work to the Standing Committee on Home Affairs may not meet the requirement.

In the same spirit, and keeping with the practice of other democracies such as the United States of America and the United Kingdom, the concerned agencies should make their mission statement public, outlining their strategic intent, vision, mission, core values and their goals periodically. Existing models range from periodic executive review of the mission statement to statutory definition of the function of these agencies. Furthermore, and in step with the globalized information architecture, there is a case for greater openness with regard to the history of intelligence institutions. We need to study initiatives taken elsewhere and determine the extent to which we can proceed in the matter.

The shortcomings of the traditional argument, of leaving intelligence to the oversight of the executive, became evident in the Report of the Kargil Review Committee and its sections on 'Intelligence in its Findings and Recommendations'. It identified flaws, acknowledged the absence of coordination and of 'checks and balances' and noted the absence of governmental correctives. The report referred to relevant systems in major countries but did not include in it their systems of oversight and accountability.

Some correctives were introduced pursuant to the establishment of the National Security System and the report of the Group of Ministers on the reform of the national security system in its entirety. These improvements enhanced internal accountability and coordination but did not go far enough and did not put in place a more open system of public accountability. In the discussions that followed the publication of the Kargil Review Committee Report, and apart from inter-agency spats and the blame game, one informed commentator described it as a 'substantive contribution in educating our Parliament and public opinion' aimed at 'introducing transparency in this sensitive sector'.

Arguments of this nature tend to be condescending. They ignore the time-honoured formula which is the bedrock of democracy: that 'instead of looking on discussion as a stumbling block in the way of action, we think it an indispensable preliminary to any wise action'. They belittle the capacity of elected representatives to be responsible in matters of national security. Also overlooked is the fact that depending on the fall of the electoral dice, these same representatives are transformed into the political executive entrusted with the responsibility of supervising the work of intelligence agencies.

The contention that openness and public discussion would compromise the secrecy essential for intelligence needs to be examined carefully. Operational secrecy is one aspect of the matter and has to be maintained. The legislature, nevertheless, is the organ of the state that allocates funds and is therefore entitled to insist on financial and performance accountability. The practice of subsuming allocations is not conducive to transparency; it may even encourage misuse. The proposed Standing Committee could fill this void; it could also function as a surrogate for public opinion and thus facilitate wider acceptance of the imperatives of a situation. Given the nature of emerging threats to human security, a wider sampling of opinion would, in fact, facilitate better comprehension of the issues and of possible remedies to attain total national power and comprehensive defence.

Let me conclude by saying that in a fast-changing world, the challenges facing intelligence practitioners are enormous. Can they adapt their organizations, policies and practices to a world in which there is a qualitative change in the notion of security and in the nature of threats? Both compel a paradigm shift in procedures and objectives; so does the imperative of accountability in terms of democratic norms of good governance. Each of these needs to be factored into the work patterns of the intelligence operative of tomorrow. A timely synthesis would pave the way for success.

27

INDIA AND THE GREAT WAR

THE FIRST WORLD WAR WAS a seminal event in modern history. It transformed the global political, economic and social order irreversibly. Its repercussions were felt across the world, including in our country. A century later and with fading memories, it is relevant to recall its military and the politico-diplomatic aspects, as also some wider consequences.

The war, which began as the third Balkan War, rapidly turned into a European war and eventually ensnared countries on almost all the continents of our planet, with battles fought in Europe, Asia, Africa and the Pacific.

In one of his books Henry Kissinger has penned a perceptive chapter on the events leading up to the war. His assessment has a wider relevance. Allow me to cite a passage from it:

> The statesmen of all the major countries had helped construct the diplomatic doomsday machine that made each succeeding crisis progressively more difficult to resolve. The military chiefs had vastly compounded the peril by adding strategic plans which compressed the time available for decision-making. Since the military plans depended on speed and the diplomatic machinery was geared to its traditional leisurely pace, it became impossible to disentangle the crisis under intense time pressure. To make matters worse, the military planners had not adequately explained the implications of their handiwork to their political colleagues. Military planning had, in effect, become autonomous.[1]

The damage caused by the Great War had no parallel in history. In

---

Note: Remarks at the inauguration of the international conference on India and the Great War organized by USI, 5 March 2014, New Delhi.

earlier wars, the civilian populations were generally spared. In World War I, the casualties suffered by the civilian population from bombing and the famines and epidemics caused by the war far exceeded those suffered by the armed forces.

The war was also unprecedented in terms of resource mobilization. According to some estimates, the conflict mobilized 65 million troops, claimed around 20 million military and civilian deaths and 21 million wounded. It imposed a heavy cost on the global economy and led to many serious social problems.

The First World War also set new standards in the capability and willingness of the human race to inflict extreme violence and pain on their own kind through use of modern weapons of destruction, such as poisonous chemical gas, aircrafts and airships, tanks, U-boats etc.

In political terms, the war brought to an end four great empires—German, Austro-Hungarian, Russian and Ottoman—and transformed the geopolitical landscape of Europe and other parts of the world. One immediate result was the Russian Revolution of 1917. Economically and militarily, Europe was surpassed by the United States, which emerged from the war as a world power.

The post-war Peace Conference held at Versailles and the ensuing treaties were not a result of negotiations between the defeated and the victorious powers but were imposed on the defeated by the victors. They took on, to quote Kissinger again, 'a nihilistic character'. These created fertile conditions for future conflicts.

In Asia, Europe and Africa, new states were created out of the former imperial territories of the defeated powers. Their geographical boundaries were at times arbitrary, drawn to serve the interests of dominant European powers. Colonies exchanged hands and areas of influence were mandated amongst the victors.

The unethical and arbitrary sharing of the spoils of war between the victorious powers prepared the ground for some of the most intractable international territorial disputes. These continue to haunt international peace and security to this day, particularly in West Asia and Africa.

The American historian, Fritz Stern aptly described the war as 'the first calamity of the twentieth century, the calamity from which all other calamities sprang'.[2]

The war germinated the idea of an international organization of all independent states aimed at the preservation of peace and security and peaceful settlement of international conflicts. The resultant 'League of Nations' bound its members 'not to resort to war'. Its eventual fate is another story but it did inspire the founding of the United Nations in 1945.

The post-war perpetuation of colonial rule and exploitation by the victorious powers, in spite of their professed principles of freedom and democracy, was a wake-up call for the nationalist movements in Asia and Africa. Some of the colonies, including India, had supported the war effort expecting to be rewarded with a major move towards independence or, at the least, self-government.

This betrayal transformed the nationalist movements from seeking a more representative self-rule within the colonial framework to demanding complete freedom and independence from colonial yoke. The trend was aggravated by the resentment generated due to forced recruitment of soldiers and labour for war, and the exploitation of resources of the colonies by the imperialist countries.

The Great War marked a watershed in the political history of the freedom movement in the Indian subcontinent.

When the war broke out in August 1914, many in our country supported the war effort in its bid to gain dominion status. The overwhelming majority of mainstream political opinion was united in the view that if India desired greater responsibility and political autonomy, it must also be willing to share in the burden of imperial defence. This was summed up in Gandhiji's observation that 'If we would improve our status through the help and cooperation of the British, it was our duty to win their help by standing by them in their hour of need.'

The major impact of the First World War, and its aftermath, was the realization by the Indian nationalist movement that the British were not going to live up to the promises of representative self-rule which they had made during the war. The Montagu–Chelmsford Reforms of 1919 disappointed the Indian people who longed for greater constitutional changes in the direction of self-rule. Repressive legislations like the Rowlatt Act rubbed salt to their wounds. A combination of these factors led to a shift in nationalist aspirations from home rule under the British Empire, to complete independence from Britain; an objective which was realized almost three decades later on 15 August 1947.

According to the Commonwealth War Graves Commission, around 1.1 million Indian personnel were sent overseas on war duties, including to France, Belgium, Mesopotamia, Egypt, Persia and Palestine. Smaller contingents were deployed in Aden, East Africa, Gallipoli and Salonika. Around 60,000 troops from undivided India sacrificed their lives in the war. Over 9,200 decorations were earned, including 11 Victoria Crosses.

Despite this, the story of the Indian army in the Great War has so far received no separate scrutiny. The Indian story—and it was a substantial one—must therefore be unravelled from amongst the larger official accounts of the war. There are almost no records that preserve the subaltern voice of the Indian rank and file, apart from the fortuitous collection of letters passed down by the Indian censors in France. The various narratives get a human touch by the accounts of a few British officers of the Indian army, who recount the doings of their men in passing.

I hope this chapter will serve as a good starting point for redressing this glaring gap in our understanding of that period of our history.

28
GOLDEN JUBILEE COMMEMORATION OF THE INDIA-PAKISTAN WAR OF 1965

THE GENESIS OF EVENTS WHICH led to war lay in Pakistan's obduracy and the fallacious belief in its establishment that it could use force to alter the geography and political realities of the subcontinent. No praise is enough to salute the gallantry and sacrifice of our soldiers and the resoluteness of our then political leadership in successfully defending India against invasion by a neighbour.

Much has been written about this conflict by Indian, Pakistani and third-country military and civilian experts. The objective of this chapter is to draw attention to some international aspects of the matter and the manner in which they influenced the course of events, as also to draw lessons from the experience undergone.

The chronology of the conflict is relevant. Pakistan set in motion its stratagem on 5 August 1965 under the name 'Operation Gibraltar'. It involved infiltration into Jammu and Kashmir by trained 'irregulars' assisted and guided by its armed forces. Its mission was to carry out widespread acts of sabotage and arson and also to garner local support leading to the proclamation of a war of liberation and a 'Revolutionary Council'. Its objective, according to a credible Pakistani account, was to 'defreeze the Kashmir problem, weaken Indian resolve, and bring her to the conference table without provoking a general war'.[1] The effort failed because the people of Kashmir chose to resist it; instead, they informed the local police and our security forces about their location, movement and intentions.

Note: Speech delivered at the Tri-Services, Seminar organized as part of the golden jubilee commemoration of the India–Pakistan War 1965, 1 September 2015, New Delhi.

The failure of Operation Gibraltar forced the enemy to activate the second phase of its plan. This consisted of a direct attack on 1 September 1965 by the Pakistani army on Indian forces along the Chamb–Akhnoor–Jurian salient with the aim of taking the strategic town of Akhnoor where the international border ran into the ceasefire line. The aim was to sever the main communication link between India and the Kashmir valley.

Even though our forces were taken by surprise by this menacing move, they fought back strongly and the Pakistan plans soon lay in ruins. The political leadership, led by Prime Minister Lal Bahadur Shastri, responded with vigour and determination. To relieve the pressure on Akhnoor, it was decided to expand both the ambit and the geography of the conflict. Pursuant to it, air power was deployed and a new front was opened by crossing the international border in Punjab, threatening Pakistan's primate city—Lahore.

The conflict continued till 22 September. The diplomatic efforts to respond to it shed useful light on the interests and assessments of the interested global powers, principally the United States, the Soviet Union, China and the United Nations.

The United States took the first diplomatic initiative as soon as the hostilities began. Given the alliance relationship, it was tilted towards Pakistan. It urged India and Pakistan to allow the UN Secretary General to resolve the issue. Secretary of Defence Dean Rusk informed the US Ambassador in India that 'the highest level decision taken here is not to engage in direct pressure on either Pakistan or India for the time being, but to place primary reliance on the UN'.

He noted, in a classic exercise of feigned impartiality, that 'India and Pakistan allowed the matter to escalate very fast on both sides, contrary to the advise that was being given to them by the US. So in effect we shrugged our shoulders and said, well, if you're going to fight, go ahead and fight, but we're not going to pay for it.'[2]

This approach saw the UN Security Council, with tacit support from the United States, trying to play an active role in the matter. Security Council Resolution 209 of 4 September 1965 called for immediate ceasefire and withdrawal of all armed personnel of the two sides to its side of the CFL. Two days later, on 6 September, Resolution 210 reiterated this, expressed its 'deep concern', decided to keep the matter 'under urgent and continuous review' and asked the UNSG (United Nations Secretary General) to strengthen UNMOGIP (United Nations Military Observer Group in India and Pakistan). Pursuant to this and on US prompting, Secretary General U.

Thant visited India and Pakistan but failed to evolve a consensus on the terms of a ceasefire.

Faced with this impasse, the Security Council's language underwent a change. Resolution 211 on 20 September *demanded* a ceasefire by 0700 hours GMT on 22 September and *decided* that once it is implemented the Council would consider what steps to take 'to assist towards a settlement of the political problem underlying the present conflict'.

Parallel to these developments, a provocative tenure, reflective of partisanship, if not overt intent to interfere, became evident in official communications from the Government of China to India in August–September 1965 period. A 'not very credible ultimatum' was delivered, but was subsequently watered down by unilaterally announcing an extension of the time limit.

More positive was the Soviet approach. Apart from its support to the Security Council resolutions, Prime Minister Alexei Kosygin sent several communications to Prime Minister Shastri and President Ayub Khan, offering good offices for settling the dispute. This move was supported by the United States and its rationale, spelt out by Secretary of State Dean Rusk, makes interesting reading:

> We encouraged the Russians to go ahead with the Tashkent idea because we felt that we had nothing to lose. If they succeeded in bringing about detente at Tashkent, there would be peace on the subcontinent and US would gain from the fact. If the Russians failed at Tashkent, then they would experience some of the frustrations that we have faced for 20 years in trying to sort out things between India and Pakistan.[3]

This effort culminated in the Tashkent Agreement of 10 January 1966. A view subsequently emerged that while the agreement brought the war to an end, it denied India the political advantage of its military successes because of pressure from the major powers and UN. Ironically, public reaction in Pakistan was similar, although for different considerations.

The 1965 war was a medium-scale, limited conflict. It was inflicted on India. The military and political assessments on our side, and the exercise of identifying shortfalls in strategy and tactics, are in the public domain and in no need of reiteration here.

According to his biographer, Prime Minister Shastri had briefed his service chiefs on 3 September on India's war objectives. These were threefold:

- To defeat Pakistani attempt to seize Kashmir by force and to make it abundantly clear that Pakistan would never be allowed to wrest Kashmir from India;
- To destroy the offensive power of Pakistan's armed forces; and
- To occupy only the minimum of Pakistani territory necessary to achieve these purposes, which would be vacated after satisfactory conclusion of the war.

The post-conflict picture on the other side was kept opaque. A secret air dash by the leadership to Beijing on the night of 19-20 September was not rewarding. The US ambassador reported that President Ayub Khan was 'disenchanted with Bhutto's reckless adventurism, grieved at Pak losses, strongly averse to entering Chicom association and open to a sensible compromise way out'.[4]

In the final analysis, the war was a costly military and political misadventure for Pakistan. The failure was camouflaged; even the announcement of ceasefire was described as 'fire bandi' rather than 'jang bandi'.

In a wider political perspective, some general conclusions that impact on decisions to initiate hostilities may be drawn. In the first place, purely bilateral wars are unlikely in our times. The decision to initiate hostilities may be an autonomous one; thereafter, however, all warlike conflicts tend to draw in concerned and interested players. The end of the conflict, therefore, can rarely be calculated with any degree of precision.

Secondly, the instrumentalities available to the global community or to a group of likeminded countries to influence decisively the war-waging capabilities of participants in conflicts can upset initial calculations and thus act as a disincentive.

Thirdly, due note of international opinion and of the balance of forces in the Security Council would need to be taken when considering conflict-like eventualities.

In conclusion, I recall a pertinent observation by the historian Paul Kennedy. He referred to the conundrum that has confronted strategists down the ages: 'To be a Great Power demands a flourishing economic base. Yet by going to war, or by devoting a large share of the nation's "manufacturing power" to expenditures upon "unproductive" armaments, one runs the risk of eroding the national economic base, especially vis-à-vis states which are concentrating a greater share of their income upon investment for long-term growth.'[5]

EMPOWERMENT

29
SCIENCE AND TECHNOLOGY

THE POSTAGE STAMPS THAT WERE released, to mark the centenary of the Indian Institute of Science (IISc), were a nation's tribute to an institution of rare eminence. The Institute stands tall amidst institutions of excellence in our country.

By the same token, the IISc has imposed on itself the duty of sustaining its work in a new century before whose challenges the ones of the last century recede into relative insignificance.

We, in India, have set for ourselves the goal of becoming a knowledge society. Beyond the slogan, however, is the realization that the long march towards the destination entails a great deal of work aimed at ensuring access to knowledge of more and more people so that they become its beneficiaries meaningfully and in turn contribute appropriately.

This enhanced level of access to knowledge also implies a heightened awareness of the criticality of fundamentals, of basic research. It is here that the IIS must remain the torch-bearer and I have no doubt that it would continue to be so.

The work of the scientist in relation to the priorities that individual societies set for them is of immense relevance. Let me illustrate this with reference to India. In the first decade of Independence, the government set forth their science policy with three objectives:

1. To secure for the public the benefits accruing from the acquisition and application of scientific knowledge.

Note: Golden Jubilee Memorial Lecture of the Indian Institute of Science, 14 December 2008, Bengaluru.

2. To promote the cultivation of science and scientific research—pure, applied and educational.
3. To ensure an adequate supply of research scientists and scientific personnel for the country's diverse requirements.

As is well known, much has been done in the past six decades to create an infrastructure of science and technology, and endow it with the potential for advancement. Many notable landmarks have been reached. At the same time, significant gaps remain and are hampering achievement of targets. An HRD (Human Resource Development) Taskforce in 2005 found that 'the quality and quantum of scientific research had been declining over the years' due to inadequate facilities, funds, declining enrolment and an acute shortage of qualified teachers in basic sciences, engineering, technology and medicine.

The first relates to the paucity of scientists. This may sound paradoxical but is nevertheless reflective of ground reality. The prime minister referred to it in his address to the 2005 session of the Indian Science Congress and this has been amplified in the report of the Steering Committee on Science and Technology and in the Eleventh Five-Year Plan.

The plan accepts that basic research in science, engineering and medicine is a critical input for development. It has stressed the need for making available equipment and facilities in colleges and universities, as also the need to create attractive career options talented young scientists.

The old debate about basic research, directed basic research, and applied research and product development surfaced in the Steering Committee report. The recommended solution attempts a balance: 'while basic research should be encouraged, self-directed basic research should also receive substantially increased support'.

The challenge now lies in converting these policy commitments into time-bound programmes.

Secondly, attracting young minds to the domain of science is often a matter of igniting interest. This is best done through inspiring teaching and creation of role models. There seems to be a disconnect here at two levels: between senior teachers and undergraduates, and between teaching and researchers. The net result is that the young science student is deprived of contact with sources of inspiration that may fire his/her imagination.

A few years back Jayant Narlikar had pointed out that a panel constituted for the decadal meeting of the Astronomical Society of India, had only one of its 37 members drawn from a university. The message, he said, was that universities had best confined themselves to teaching while research institutes will look after research! The Knowledge Commission has now drawn attention to the absence of interconnectivity between educational institutes and R&D (Research and Development) laboratories, and has suggested ways of bridging the gap.

My third point relates to the methodology of teaching, science. Nearly 50 per cent of school students fail in mathematics and science. What is needed is a culture of experiment-based learning. This would also involve re-training of teachers. How long would such an exercise take?

A related problem is the high level of vacancies in universities. A sample survey of 47 universities conducted by the UGC (University Grants Commission), for the academic year 2007–2008, shows an overall vacancy level of 51 per cent. The situation is particularly depressing in state universities where almost 90 per cent of students are enrolled. Some academic administrators attribute this, in part, to the poor quality of candidates; if so, it adds to the problem of quality that plagues many institutions of higher education.

My last point pertains to innovations and patents, in the light of the generally voiced complaint that our national performance on this count is inadequate. Is this due to the absence of adequate linkages between research institutions and industry? Does our industry itself spend enough on R&D? Our modest performance is certainly not due to a lack of inventive genius. A report published in the *IndUS Business Journal* in October last year cited a Harvard Law School study indicating that one in every 10 inventions patented in the United States had an owner or co-owner with an Indian name.

Given our requirements, therefore, capacity building in science is the need of the hour. Only then would we be able to sustain technological advancements imperative for national development. Let me recall what Sir Mokshagundam Visveswaraya, an engineering genius of yester-years, had said: 'To build a better nation, build better individuals,' adding that 'action, not sentiment, will be the determining factor.' This certainly holds good for the scientific community that, to use Thomas Kuhn's phrase, 'is an immensely efficient instrument for solving the problems or puzzles that its paradigm defines'.

Our aspiration to be a hub of knowledge has other implications. In a conceptual sense, it necessitates promotion of knowledge about knowledge, its nature and character, its social and ethical content and their implications.

The latter problem has been posed by many down the ages; let me cite a fairly recent formulation by a scholar from the University of Leuven in Belgium:

> Science is a mix of creativity and of goal oriented effort, on the basis of our natural urge to know. On the way to its goal, science obeys certain laws, the rules of logic and rational reasoning being the most important ones. By having an impact on reality, scientists automatically and inevitably acquire a responsibility. Our work will have consequences, which we are not to ignore. Reflecting on our activities is the main target of ethics. Therefore, ethical reflection is related to science and to scientific progress.

This view may be contested but is not altogether isolated. An eminent British scientist, Professor Lord May of Oxford, said in his valedictory address as president of the Royal Society in 2005 that 'the scientific community should be energetically engaging the societal process to dispel 'the darkness of fundamentalist unreason'.[1]

The matter has various dimensions. Two of these are relevant to our argument: the first pertains to rationality and logic, the second to the identity of scientists as moral creatures living in societies. Neither can be evaded and their connotations need to be probed.

The ancients considered humans as rational creatures. The process by which they reached this conclusion was somewhat complex. Aristotle divided the soul into three types: vegetable soul common to plants and animals, and concerned only with nourishment and growth; animal soul shared by man and lower animals, and concerned with locomotion; and the rational soul or intellect confined to humans.

At the same time, as Erasmus found, folly is perennial; hence the need to cultivate rationality since, as the historian Ibn Khaldun put it, the pasture of stupidity is unwholesome for mankind. Thus, the process by which unreason is replaced by reason has to be both deliberate and continuous.

The process is one aspect of the matter, content is another. Should the scientific method and temper be confined to the domain of science in the narrower sense, or should they be imbibed as part of consciousness? Jawaharlal Nehru wanted all Indians to cultivate a scientific temper through the application of reason and the avoidance of preconceived notions and Amartya Sen has shown that the dialogic tradition of India plays a part 'in supporting democracy, secularism and the pursuit of mathematics and science, and the use that can be made of dialectics in seeking social justice, against the barriers of class, caste, community and gender'.[2]

Most readers must be well aware of the role that heterodoxy has played in the emergence of new ideas and discoveries. The teasing question for the men and women of science is the application of this heterodoxy to the social realm. What should be questioned? To what extent should it be questioned? How is a balance to be struck between conformity and nonconformity?

One approach lies in state-centricity. The state is the keystone of the social arch and the final repository of the will of a society. In practical terms, however, the will of the state is the will of the government of the day and its claim to be obeyed, apart from narrow legality, lies in the content of that will and in the processes by which it is determined and communicated to the citizen-body.

The sceptic, on the other hand, draws attention to possible pitfalls. It was aptly stated by Bertrand Russell. Writing in the middle decades of the 20th century about the growth of dogmatism and the power of governments over men's belief, he expressed concern over 'the discovery that man can be scientifically manipulated, and that governments can turn masses this way or that as they choose, is one of the causes of our misfortunes'.[3]

Since historical record sustains both positions, an enquiring mind is lead to philosophical and practical questions about implications. This endeavour goes back to Arjuna's doubts in the debate in the Mahabharata. In our own times, the scientist qua scientist is driven by the logic and impulse of work underway. Its implications may or may not be immediately discernable. The dilemma was stated by Robert Oppenhiemer in 1954:

> When you see something that is technically sweet, you go ahead and do it and you argue about what to do about it only after you have had your technical success.[4]

The resulting choices tax the conscience. Should scientists work in a moral or ethical vacuum? Should they, instead, be what has been called citizen-scientists? Answers to these questions can only be sought in open debate and without a priori conclusions. Society facilitates scientific research and therefore has a right to know, perhaps also a right to judge; the latter right, however, has to be exercised with utmost care to ensure that such judgements do not stifle scientific research. At the other end of the spectrum, no free society can deny the right to dissent. The social responsibility of scientists has to be posited within such a framework.

To quote B.J. Marden, written as early as 1921:

> May I venture, as a citizen, to make an appeal to men of science and to urge that the time has come when they should no longer stand aside from the social and political questions that vex the world? ... Science has made civilisation possible for mankind. It must now provide civilisation with that authority the lack of which is causing such waste of human energy today. Men of science alone have the power; they alone are above suspicion.

30
HIGHER EDUCATION—CHALLENGES AND IMPERATIVES FOR CHANGE

INDIA'S OLDEST MODERN UNIVERSITY, THE University of Calcutta, a great and famous seat of learning, will always hold a special place in my heart, more so because of an ancient association of a few youthful years with this city. I also subscribe fully to what the Urdu poet, Ghalib, said about Kolkata, which he visited around the year 1830:

> *Kalkatte ka jo zikr kiya tune hum nasheen*
> *Ik teer mere sine main maara ki haye haye*

> Ah me, my friend! The mention of Calcutta's name
> Has loosed off a shaft that pierces into my very soul

Voltaire was perhaps unduly cynical when he described history as 'nothing more than a tableau of crimes and misfortunes'. This is certainly not true of the history of this great city which is, in a sense, also the history of modern India.

Most of us associate the year 1857 with the First War of Independence, with the heroic deeds of many, as also with the eventual failure of the effort to overthrow the foreign yoke and seek freedom from bondage. Few today would associate 1857 with another event of seminal significance. It was on 24 January 1857 that the Calcutta University Act was enacted. It was the culmination of a process initiated by Lord William Bentinck and energized by his successor Lord Auckland. The conceptual input and framework had come earlier from Sir Charles Wood. Its purpose, and ambit,

---

Note: Foundation Day Lecture 2010 of the University of Calcutta, 20 December 2010, Kolkata.

was unambiguously linked to a colonial purpose, namely 'to confine higher education to persons possessing leisure and natural influence' over the minds of their countrymen and who, by attaining a higher standard of modern education, 'would eventually produce a much greater and more beneficial change in the ideas and feelings of the community'.

The expectations from this endeavour were anticipated to be modest. The first vice chancellor, Sir James William Colvile, was candid about results. 'We must recollect,' he said in the first Convocation address, 'that we are not merely planting an exotic (tree), we are planting a tree of slow growth.' His successor went against the tide of opinion in the British Indian establishment in the aftermath of 1857 and said three years later: 'Educate your people from Cape Camorin to the Himalayas and a second mutiny of 1857 will be impossible.'

These worthy gentlemen evidently could not discern the thirst for new knowledge among segments of the public, nor could they anticipate the use that would eventually be made of it. The alumnae of this institution played a great role in the freedom struggle as also in the furtherance of knowledge in all fields. The record does speak for itself.

The proclaimed and principal purpose of the university was, and is, 'Advancement of Learning'. There was an element of idealism about it. In a celebrated work published in November 1858, Cardinal John Henry Newman spelt out the idea of a university in terms worthy of reiteration:

> A university is a place of concourse, wither students come from every quarter for every kind of knowledge… It is a place where inquiry is pushed forward, and discoveries verified and perfected, and rashness rendered innocuous, and error exposed, by the collusion of mind with mind, and knowledge with knowledge… It is a place which wins the admiration of the young by its celebrity, kindles the affections of the middle-aged by its beauty, and rivets the fidelity of the old by its associations. It is a seat of wisdom, a light of the world, a minister of the faith, an Alma Mater of the rising generation.[1]

Over the past century-and-a-half, the ideal has retained its relevance. What has changed in response to the evolving external environment is the content, some of the methodology and some of the end product. These were propelled by the enormity of change—political, economic, technological and cultural. A historian of our times noted at the turn of the century that 'we are entering a fearful time, a time that will call on all our resources, moral as well as intellectual and material'. In this endeavour, the intellectual inputs from seats of learning and research would impact decisively on the moral and material resources needed to respond to the emerging challenges.

The need to revisit the framework for higher education in the country has been felt in recent years. This was summed up in the 2008 report of the National Knowledge Commission:

> The emerging knowledge society and associated opportunities present a set of new imperatives and new challenges for our economy, polity and society. If we fail to capitalize on the opportunities now, our demographic dividend could well become a liability. The widening disparities in our country will translate into social unrest, if urgent steps are not taken to build an inclusive society. And our growth rate, which is faltering now, will stagnate soon, if a sustainable development paradigm is not created.

A look at the ground reality is relevant to this discourse. Today, we have 504 universities, with varying statutory bases and mandates. Of these, 40 are central universities, 243 are state universities, 130 are deemed universities, five institutions established under state legislation, 53 are state private universities, and 33 are institutions of national importance established by central legislation. We have a total teaching faculty of around 6 lakhs in higher education.

The structure and quality of these institutions, and their output, was the subject of critical scrutiny in the Yashpal Committee Report of 2009, tasked to suggest measures for the renovation and rejuvenation of higher education. One of its observations is telling:

> Over the years we have followed policies of fragmenting our educational enterprises into cubicles. We have overlooked that new knowledge and new insights have often originated at the boundaries of disciplines. We have tended to imprison disciplinary studies in opaque walls. This has restricted flights of imagination and limited our creativity. This character of our education has restrained and restricted our young right from the school age and continues that way into college and university stages. Most instrumentalities of our education harm the potential of human mind for constructing and creating new knowledge. We have emphasized delivery of information and rewarded capability of storing information. This does not help in creating a knowledge society. This is particularly

vile at the university level because one of the requirements of a good university should be to engage in knowledge creation—not just for the learner but also for society as a whole.

The report goes on to say that our universities remain one of the most under-managed and badly governed organizations in society, with constricted autonomy, internal subversion within academia and multiple and opaque regulatory systems. Furthermore, university education is no longer viewed as good in itself but as the stepping stone to a higher economic and social orbit.

The report dwells on the increasing demand for expansion of private college-and university-level institutions necessitating an understanding of its implications in terms of the system's enrolment capacity, programme focus, regional balance, ownership pattern, modes of delivery, degree of regulation, quality and credibility, as well as social concerns of inclusiveness. It points out that state universities and affiliated colleges represent the bulk of enrolment in higher education and remain the most neglected in terms of resources and governmental attention.

Targeted government interventions to enhance access to elementary education through the Sarva Shiksha Abhiyan have been successful in quantitative terms, even though problems remain with regard to content, quality and outcomes. The focal themes of the Eleventh Five-Year Plan was the expansion and enhancement of access to higher education.

Our Gross Enrolment Ratio in higher education is half of the world's average, two-thirds that of developing countries and around a fifth that of developed countries. Even though we have been able to achieve an economic growth rate of 9 per cent of GDP (Gross Domestic Product), despite low enrolment in higher education, it would not be possible for us to sustain such economic growth, maintain our competitiveness and enhance our productivity without at least doubling our higher education enrolment. Unless we can increase access and educational outcomes at secondary and tertiary levels, our demographic dividend might turn into a demographic liability.

Contrary to conventional wisdom, gross enrolment in higher education is not directly linked to economic growth and prosperity or to elementary school enrolment. Thus, for example, some of the economically and educationally backward states with respect to literacy rate and school enrolment, such as Orissa, Assam, Jharkhand and Andhra Pradesh have higher enrolments in higher education as compared to relatively better off states such as Tamil Nadu and Karnataka. It would seem that enrolment is a function of a variety of social, cultural, institutional and economic processes, and is significantly affected by the availability of educational infrastructure and facilities.

In addition to expansion, the other two central themes of the Eleventh Plan are inclusion and excellence. This is recognition of the fact that expansion does not necessarily ensure automatic access to the marginalized sections of the society and that quantitative expansion without maintaining quality would defeat the basic objective.

There are five questions pertaining to higher education that need to be addressed urgently:

First, we must ponder whether the existing means of instituting new universities is desirable and sustainable. Currently, universities can be established only through central or state legislation or through recognition as deemed universities on a selective basis. Legislation has been accorded to many private universities by some state governments, and both central and state governments have accorded statutory status to some institutions.

Second, higher education cannot improve in India unless state universities, which are the backbone and represent the bulk of enrolment, are able to obtain greater funds, create new infrastructure and enrich their existing academic programmes. Anecdotal evidence suggests that the budget of one central university is almost the same or more than the budget of all state universities in some states. Just like the central government has assumed the responsibility for elementary education through Sarva Shiksha Abhiyan, it should also vastly enhance its support to state universities as a shared national enterprise. The midterm appraisal of the Eleventh Five-Year Plan takes note of this option and has observed:

> Many state universities including the old and reputed universities of Kolkata, Mumbai, Chennai and Pune are starved of funds and this allocation could be used for improving the conditions of the existing State universities and colleges which faces severe paucity of resources, to help them retain their excellence and competitive edge... The Central funding of state institutions should be linked to the reforms and an MOU (memorandum of understanding) signed between MHRD (Ministry of Human Resource Development), UGC (University Grants Commission), states, universities and institutions for implementation of time-bound reforms and outcomes.

Third, a significant focus of reform should be the college system, numbering around 26,000 colleges, where most of the enrolment in higher education occurs. Sadly, undergraduate education does not get the attention it deserves in universities amidst paucity of funds for qualitative development and quantitative expansion of colleges. The government is planning to establish colleges in 374 educationally backward districts in the country, representing over 60 per cent of all districts, with shared funding between the state and central governments.

Fourth, we need to liberate education from the strict and fragmented disciplinary confines of our formal higher-education structures. This has become a significant impediment in the creation of new knowledge, especially in view of our stated objective of creating a knowledge society. We need to remind ourselves that the Indian Nobel Prize winners in the early part of the last century were a part of our higher education set-up. We had then allowed free interplay between science and engineering, languages and the humanities, performing and fine arts. It was at the fringes of such inter-disciplinary interaction that new knowledge was produced and existing knowledge flourished. I am aware of academic administrators who bemoan that those pursuing mathematics could not simultaneously study Sanskrit grammar in India despite sound academic and research logic of doing so, due to systemic rigidities of our university system.

Fifth, higher education in our country must be an arena of choice, not of elimination. Increasingly, one notices that entrance and admission criteria and procedures are designed to screen out and eliminate, due to the adverse ratio of demand and availability, especially in disciplines with job potential or where the college or university reputation is likely to be a determining factor in employment. We must create avenues for skills training and vocational education so that entering universities does not become a default choice for the sake of employment, particularly for those who might not have interest in the subject or desire for higher education.

In conclusion, let me point out that the entire gamut of issues dealing with the rejuvenation and restructuring of higher education in India is in the public domain for an open policy debate. In the near future, we would witness civil society, policy community, academia, the government and the legislatures debating issues ranging from regulatory and governance structures, academic and administrative reforms, capacity building and teacher training, and entry of individual and institutional foreign education providers. This is a positive development and must be pursued to its logical conclusion.

Each of us is an important stakeholder in the process and must be part of the ongoing debates on higher education, must contribute to it not only as members of the academic community, but more importantly as citizens of this Republic. It is only with active engagement that we can hope to mould higher education as an instrument to achieve the Constitutional vision propounded by our founding fathers.

31
HUMAN DEVELOPMENT AND INEQUALITY

'SUBLIMELY MILD, A SPIRIT WITHOUT a spot' is what can be said of Vaidyanathapura Ramakrishna Iyer, a man who made it his life's mission to resist injustice, secure justice and take up just and compassionate causes—within the realm of law and beyond it. Few would know of his passion for animal welfare or his early career in politics as a member of the Legislative Assembly.

It was indeed fortuitous that Justice Iyer came back to the Bar. He was a visionary in championing human rights jurisprudence with a focus on women, dalits and the marginalized, much before it emerged on the international or national scene. The vision and morality of our Constitution was his guide all through. His stint in the High Court and the Law Commission was focused on delivering of justice to the common citizen.

In a span of seven years as a Judge of the Supreme Court during 1973–1980, when the nation was in political and legal tumult, Justice Iyer put the citizens and the values of the Constitution at the centre of his focus. The guarantees given to us by our founding fathers through the Constitution were reinterpreted for a new age, and new instruments fashioned to deliver justice. Thus, judicial remedies were sought through the instrumentalities of Public Interest Litigation, broader concepts of locus standi, and the Constitution was seen for what it could deliver to people.

His activism continued after retirement with renewed vigour, and is visible to this day. Justice Krishna Iyer can justifiably lay claim to be a karma

---

Note: Speech delivered on the occasion of the 97th Birthday of Shri Justice V.R. Krishna Iyer, 12 November 2011, Ernakulam.

yogi all his life. In an opinion piece on 'justice, justices and justicing' a few years back, he made some pithy observations. Allow me to cite one of these:

> There are three great pathologies that alienate the judiciary from the people. The curative pharmacopoeia of fundamental judicial reform to counter these comprises forensic democratization, a process of social justice delivery and structural transformation of the judicial system through innovative facilities for the have-not humanity. This trinity of recipes demands institutional creativity, procedural humanism, and joint action by the executive, the legislature and the judiciary, inspired by the radical values inscribed in the Constitution.[1]

Professor Upendra Baxi has rightly observed that Justice Iyer is 'an embodiment of secular saintliness'. He deserves the nation's appreciation and gratitude for his contribution.[2]

Change, great change, has characterized the decades since Independence. The past two decades have accentuated the trend. The success of our polity is to be measured by the dexterity with which we have negotiated the rapids of this transformation.

As we survey the recent past, we notice a fundamental shift in the debate from development of economy and industry to human development. This has propelled the discourse with greater vigour to questions of sustainability and equity, to the quest for fairness and social justice, and for ensuring the right of every citizen to have equal access to opportunities for personal growth and development of one's capacities to the fullest, and for leading fulfilling and meaningful lives.

There is also recognition that there can be no sustainable improvement in public welfare without good and institutionalized processes of governance and unflinching commitment to democratic norms, constitutionally-anchored fundamental rights and universally-accepted human rights.

At the global level over the past few decades, a state of gross prosperity has been achieved; it remains unprecedented when looked at as an aggregate. The advances in terms of scientific and technological knowledge and applications far outstrip the combined achievement of humanity to date. We have produced ever more, consumed ever more and wasted ever more than in history. Yet, we also know that these are aggregates, and averages always hide the condition of those below the average.

All over the world one hears today the cry of the common man protesting against the exclusion of the majority from accessing the benefits of economic growth and prosperity engendered by globalization of financial markets, economies, investment flows and processes. Real incomes of the top percentile across developed and emerging countries have grown disproportionately higher, exacerbating income inequalities. It is now clear that the system that has worked so well for the top percentile has delivered far lesser returns to others.

It is even more surprising that income distribution has worsened despite the great strides in narrowing the gaps in health and educational achievement across population groups. It is now globally recognized that human development is adversely affected under conditions of inequality, and that this can be quantified across indicators of health, education and income.

The Human Development Report 2011 of the UNDP (United Nations Development Programme) published last week has demonstrated that around a quarter of the human development at the global level is lost due to inequality. The South Asian region suffers the second largest human development losses due to inequality, after Sub-Saharan Africa.

In the case of India, there is an overall human development loss of over 28 per cent due to inequality. The loss due to inequality of human development achievements in education are the highest in the case of India and amount to over 40 per cent. While the Report does not cover overlapping inequalities, we know from our experience that certain groups of the marginalized, such as women, scheduled castes and scheduled tribes, linguistic and religious minorities and those below the poverty line, experience multiple deprivations and exclusions.

Inequality is a problem in the long run, especially when it kills aspiration for personal and societal betterment. In India, the matrix of inequality spans gender, the rural-urban divide, class, caste, tribe, linguistic and cultural groups. While growth is a necessary condition for societal welfare, it is not sufficient and does not automatically lead to equality in accessing development and opportunities for growth.

Indeed, securing to all citizens equality of status and opportunity is a solemn resolve that finds mention in the Preamble to our Constitution. The state has a constitutional and moral duty to expand opportunities for those being left behind. Thus, the state has on the one hand focused on affirmative action and provision of a social safety net for those marginalized, while on the other moved to improving the capabilities of citizens to be more productive through skills and improved infrastructure.

Here, once again, I find of relevance what Justice Krishna Iyer has written:

If Indian democracy is to redeem its tryst with destiny, a creative protocol and code of ethics must become the vogue in public life. Consensus must be the rule of life, contentment of the lowliest the testament and participative process the habit of governance.³

As I conclude, I am reminded of the words of Dr Rajendra Prasad on his election as the first president of independent India. 'I have always held that the time for congratulation,' he had remarked, 'is not when a man is appointed to an office, but when he retires.'

32
SOCIO-ECONOMIC PARAMETERS

AMONGST THE LUMINARIES WHO MADE important contributions to the resurgence of Kerala between the second half of the 19th century and the first half of the 20th century, Vakkom Abdul Khader Moulavi, one of the doyens of Kerala's renaissance, stands tall. The leaders of this renaissance led a heroic struggle against two forms of bondage: one, against oppressive political institutions that deprived the people of their political rights; and the other, against repressive social customs that denied them of their social freedoms.

This struggle for basic political, economic and social rights was a hallmark of Kerala's revival and amongst the main reasons for its subsequent social and economic development in modern India.

Unlike most members of the Muslim community in Travancore of the time, who were engaged largely in trade or agriculture, Vakkom Moulavi emerged as a great scholar and linguist through his own efforts. He read the writings of leading authors from the West and corresponded with the leaders of the Islamic renaissance in Egypt. More importantly, he believed that knowledge was not meant to remain in the realm of theory, but was a stimulus for action.

The Vakkom Moulavi Foundation Trust was set up with a mission to contribute to building the character of the people, through knowledge and action, promote social harmony and address the problems of the underprivileged. Each of these pursuits is relevant to the contemporary Indian society.

It is said that introspection is an incentive for action. When we adopted

---

Note: Moulavi Memorial Lecture, 16 February 2013, Thiruvananthapuram.

our Constitution on 26 January 1950, we solemnly resolved to secure for all citizens: Justice, social, economic and political; Liberty, thought, expression, belief, faith and worship; Equality, of status and of opportunity; and Fraternity, assuring the dignity of the individual and the unity and integrity of the nation.

63 years later, we need to assess the extent to which this has been realized.

Allow me to recall Dr B.R. Ambedkar's words in the Constituent Assembly:

> On the 26th January 1950, we are going to enter into a life of contradictions. In politics we will have equality and in social and economic life we will have inequality. In politics we will be recognising the principle of one man one vote and one vote one value. In our social and economic life, we shall by reason of our social and economic structure, continue to deny the principle of one man one value. How long shall we continue to live this life of contradictions? How long shall we continue to deny equality in our social and economic life? If we continue to deny it for long, we will do so only by putting our political democracy in peril.

He added that,

> We must remove this contradiction at the earliest possible moment else those who suffer from inequality will blow up the structure of democracy which this Constituent Assembly has so laboriously built up.[1]

How far have we succeeded in resolving this contradiction?

Needless to say, we have made notable progress in political, economic and social spheres, more so in the context of the magnitude of challenges that confronted us at the time of Independence.

Despite its immense diversity, India has emerged as a vibrant and robust multi-party parliamentary democracy with a federal structure and an independent judiciary. Regular free and fair elections are held, wherein people exercise their free will to choose their governments. The efficiency of the Indian electoral process, with its scale and complexity, is globally looked at with awe.

The Indian political system includes mechanisms aimed at accommodating diversity and redressing historical injustices, including by recognizing and promoting the rights of various groups in our society. Democracy has taken root at the grassroots level with the Panchayati Raj system maturing and getting firmly entrenched in our body politic.

Our economy has emerged as the third or fourth largest in the world in purchasing power parity terms. We have transformed from being a low growth to a high growth rate economy; from a shortage economy of food and foreign exchange to a surplus one, and from agro-based to service-oriented one. We have even joined the aid givers club. We are now in the process of emerging as a knowledge-based economy.

Despite the global economic and financial crisis and the resultant slowdown in growth, India still remains amongst the fast-growing economies. Thanks to the green revolution and subsequent agricultural research and development, food shortages and famines are only a dark memory from the past.

Our trained human resources in areas of science and technology, including doctors and engineers, are a great asset. In frontline areas of research, such as space, nuclear, bio-technology, nano-technology and information technology, our progress is commendable.

In terms of socio-economic parameters, indicators of poverty, unemployment, inequality, illiteracy, health, malnutrition, shelter, etc., have improved considerably. From being termed as an 'area of darkness', we are now being counted amongst the top emerging economies in the world.

Affirmative action or positive discrimination has improved a lot of the traditionally deprived and marginalized sections of society, including scheduled castes, scheduled tribes and the minorities. Equality before law and equality of opportunity have been guaranteed as per the Constitution. Discrimination on the basis of gender, caste, religion, creed or language has been made illegal and punishable under law.

These steps have established the prerequisites of making our democracy and society more egalitarian: politically, economically and socially, as had been visualized by the founding fathers of our nation.

Despite these achievements, our nation-building agenda is yet to be completed and formidable challenges still confront us. We confront violence emanating from forces who challenge the writ of the constitutional framework of the state. There are others who exploit the fault lines in our society based on narrow identities derived from caste, religion, ethnicity, language and regionalism. Declining standards of probity in public life threaten the very foundations of our Republic.

Poverty, inequality and unemployment remain the major obstacles to our development aspirations. In spite of the gains of the last six decades, 29.8 per cent of the population or 354.60 million people were estimated to be living below the poverty line in 2009–2010. On the other hand, the top 10 per cent of the income groups earned 33 per cent of the income.

While official unemployment figures may appear to be low, the real challenge is of ameliorating rampant under-employment and low productivity, particularly in the informal sector of the economy where around 90 per cent of the workforce is employed.

The national figures on illiteracy, disease, malnutrition, infant mortality, declining child sex ratio, homelessness and many other socio-economic indicators are less than comforting. According to the 2011 population census, 26 per cent of our population is still illiterate, bestowing India with the dubious distinction of having the maximum number of illiterate people in the world. The quality of our school and university education is mostly below global standards.

In UNDP's Human Development Report for 2011, India ranks 134 out of a total of 187 countries. This reflects our shortfalls in terms of a composite index, which includes life expectancy, educational attainment and income, despite the growth rates in GDP in the past few decades.

Moreover, apart from the aggregate figures of the socio-economic parameters at the national level, the horizontal and vertical inequality in terms of gender, caste, religion, states, even the rural-urban divide, further compound the gravity of the situation.

Similarly the shortage of skilled manpower will remain a constraint on our high growth aspirations if the quality and quantity of general and technical educational is not enhanced through greater investment and quality control.

A pre-requisite for all this is improvement in the quality of governance and delivery. For this purpose, reforms in the vital areas such as judiciary, police, electoral system, anti-corruption laws, environmental laws, education system, etc. are imperative.

It is clear that what we set out to achieve in 1947 in terms of making India a strong, modern and prosperous state is still a work in progress and much more needs to be done.

Foremost amongst these would be the task of improving the functioning of our democracy through eradication of corruption, de-criminalization of politics and reform of the electoral system.

Further, to realize the principle of 'one man, one vote, one value in our social and economic life', as visualized by Dr Ambedkar, we will have to combat and eradicate the social and economic ills such as poverty, unemployment, illiteracy, hunger and discrimination based on birth, descent, faith, language or region.

While we pursue our primary goal of rapid and inclusive economic growth and development, we will also have to give equal importance to the sustainability of the development process, particularly the conservation of our national environment and natural resources, for the sake of our future generations.

The task is momentous given the size of our population and the complexity of issues. It cannot also be left to the government alone. It requires a consistent national endeavour involving all stakeholders—the governments, civil society, NGOs, corporate sector, and above all, every citizen.

The examples set by Vakkom Moulavi, Shri Rajagopal and the Vakkom Moulavi Foundation Trust shows us the way. The model can be replicated.

The message for all of us is that despondency is not an option, nor is resignation a way out. Citizenship bestows rights and imposes duties. We have to follow Gandhiji's advise, 'Be the change you want to see in the world,' as the mantra for civic action.

A philanthropist had once said, 'Every right implies a responsibility; every opportunity an obligation; every possession a duty.'

If we follow this in our daily lives, we shall succeed in realizing fully the resolve in the opening words of the Preamble to our Constitution in which 'We the people' committed ourselves to establish justice, liberty, equality and fraternity for all, in our great country.

33
CHALLENGES IN INDIAN AGRICULTURE

IT IS OFTEN SAID THAT India resides in its villages with around 69 per cent of our population living in rural areas. Around half of our population is either wholly or significantly dependent for their livelihoods on some form of farm activity—be it crop agriculture, horticulture, animal husbandry or fisheries.

That is why Chaudhary Ranbir Singh ji's role as the Irrigation Minister of Punjab in the development of the Bhakra Nangal Project, a testament of his vision, is so significant. His work for the upliftment of the marginalized and deprived sections of the society, especially peasants and workers, gave him a prominent place in the pantheon of leaders in the post-Independence era.

Chaudhary Ranbir Singh ji was a committed Gandhian, a freedom fighter, an eminent constitutionalist and parliamentarian, an able administrator, a prolific institution builder and a popular leader connected to the masses. He had the distinction of being member of seven different constitutional bodies during his illustrious public life.

It is a matter of pleasure that his distinguished son, Bhupinder Singh Hooda ji, and his grandson, inspired by the ideals and work of their father and grandfather respectively, have continued the family tradition of public service and made their own contributions to society.

In his maiden speech delivered in the Constituent Assembly on 6 November 1948, Chaudhary Ranbir Singh articulated his deep roots in rural India. He said:

Note: 4th Chaudhary Ranbir Singh Memorial Lecture, 26 December 2013, Rohtak.

I am a villager, born and bred in a farmer's house. Naturally I have imbibed its culture. I love it. All the problems connected with it fill my mind. I think that in building the country, the villagers should get their due share and villagers should have their influence in every sphere.

He went on to say,

We want to create a classless society. All backward people are either peasants or workers... We should protect working classes; those farmers and workers.[1]

Chaudhary ji's life and work are a testimony to his devotion to furtherance of these very causes.

Given Chaudhary Ranbir Singh's legacy in rural development and Haryana's role at the forefront of the green revolution which transformed our country from being a land cursed with famines, and what was referred to as 'ship-to-mouth' existence, into one of self-sufficiency in food grains, the importance of Indian agriculture in the inclusive development of our country is undeniable.

Though, agriculture now accounts for only 14 per cent of the GDP and 11 per cent of our total exports, it is an essential link in the supply chain of the manufacturing sector and at the same time constitutes a big market for the industrial products. Agriculture, obviously, plays an important role in rural development of the country.

Accelerating growth of agricultural production is therefore necessary not only to achieve an overall GDP growth rate and meet the rising demand for food, but also to increase incomes of those dependent on agriculture and thereby ensure inclusiveness in our society.

Given the low levels of infrastructure and human development indices, and in a context replete with inequalities and other socio-economic challenges, the future of rural India would largely depend on the positive transformation of Indian agriculture.

Global development experience, especially from the BRICS (Brazil, Russia, India, China and South Africa) countries, reveals that one percentage point growth in agriculture is at least two to three times more effective in reducing poverty than the same magnitude of growth emanating from the non-agricultural sector. Herein lies the importance of agriculture for a developing country like ours.

Since Independence, we have made notable progress in agriculture and allied activities. Due to the combined efforts of governments, scientists and the farming community, we have succeeded in achieving record production of around 259 million tonnes of food grains during 2011–2012 compared to 52 million tonnes in 1952–1953. India has emerged as a net exporter of rice, wheat, maize, etc. India ranks second in fruits and vegetables production in the world, after China. It is the largest producer of milk in the world, and the second largest producer of fish in the world.

Commencing in the mid-1960s, the Green Revolution was responsible for this makeover in Indian agriculture. It was achieved through effective transfer of latest crop production technologies, including high-yield variety seeds, fertilizers, irrigation and mechanization, to farmers under various crop development schemes, backed by remunerative prices for various crops through enhanced minimum support prices. In the 1980s and thereafter, wider geographical spread of these technologies contributed to further enhancing productivity and thereby increasing agricultural production.

While we acknowledge the achievements of our agricultural sector over the last six-and-a-half decades, we must remain alert to the fact that India's large population continues to grow, albeit slower than before. This, coupled with increases in general economic prosperity and rising per capita incomes, is contributing to an enhanced and diversified demand for agricultural products, including raw materials for the industrial sector. Thus, raising the farm output is a necessity, not just for food security but also to boost growth in secondary and tertiary sectors of the economy.

The average annual growth rate of agriculture and allied sectors during the 11th Five-year-Plan was 3.7 per cent, short of the targeted 4 per cent, though better than the 2.4 per cent achieved in the 10th plan.

It is a matter of concern that the recent growth revival in agriculture has been weak in areas with high land productivity, not only in relatively more irrigated states such as Punjab, Haryana, Uttar Pradesh and West Bengal that had Green Revolution success, but also in less irrigated states such as Kerala, Himachal Pradesh and Jammu & Kashmir where high productivity reflects a high-value cropping pattern based on horticulture. These states together contribute about 35 per cent of national agricultural output from 20 per cent of arable land, but none of them have been able to surpass growth rates achieved in the past.

A second green revolution to achieve and sustain the required agriculture-sector growth rate of 4 per cent and beyond, as targeted in the 12th plan period, is thus an imperative in order to achieve an overall GDP growth rate of 9–10 per cent in the years ahead.

What are the challenges confronting our agricultural sector?

India accounts for only about 2.4 per cent of the world's geographical area and 4 per cent of its water resources, but has to support about 17 per cent of the world's human population and 15 per cent of the livestock.

Progressive fragmentation of land holdings, degrading natural resource base and emerging concerns of climate change are escalating pressure on land and water. Land and water resources being finite, increased agricultural production and a diversified food basket to meet the requirement of the increasing population with higher per capita income, has to emanate from the same limited net sown area by increasing productivity with an optimal use of available water and land resources.

It is a fact that natural resources, viz. arable land, water, soil, biodiversity, are rapidly shrinking due to demographic and socio-economic pressures, monsoon disturbances, increasing frequencies of floods and droughts. Overuse of marginal lands, imbalanced fertigation, deteriorating soil health, diversion of agricultural land to nonagricultural uses, depleting aquifers and irrigation sources, salinization and water-logging are pressing challenges that require urgent attention.

For making agriculture sustainable to meet the country's food requirement, a prudent land use policy, water availability and soil health have to be maintained at levels that are conducive to pursue agricultural activities with higher level of productivity.

Evidence suggests that there is enough untapped potential for productivity improvements on Indian farms. What then needs to be done?

The 12th Five-Year Plan document has enlisted the main determinants of agriculture growth in the future. These include viability of farm enterprise and creation of productive infrastructure such as soil and water conservation and expansion, improvement of irrigation systems, market access, prices and risk, development of suitable technologies and crop varieties, particularly for rain-fed areas since 55 per cent of cropped area is rain-fed and home to the majority of our poor, better delivery of services like credit, quality inputs like seeds, fertilizers, pesticides and farm machinery, crop diversification, improved functioning of markets, more efficient use of natural resources, and crop diversification towards high-value crops like pulses, oil seeds, fruits and vegetables.

This will need to be a collective effort of central and state governments, private sector and the farmers. Universities and research institutions also have a vital role to play as agricultural research and extension has played a vital role in agricultural transformation.

Research in the past has tended to focus mostly on increasing yield potential by more intensive use of water and biochemical inputs; less attention has been paid to the long-term environmental impact of this approach, and to methods and practices for efficient use of inputs and natural resources. This stands in need of correction, perhaps by shifting the focus from a commodity-based approach to a farming systems approach through convergent efforts of R&D agencies within each agro-climatic region to address local problems identified by stakeholders, including development agencies. Others call for an increase in public outlay for research in this area to 1 per cent of the GDP from the current 0.7 per cent. I am happy that Chaudhary Ranbir Singh Chair and Chaudhary Ranbir Singh Institute of Social and Economic Change of Maharishi Dayanand University are actively working in these areas. It is a befitting tribute to a great son of Haryana.

34
RIGHT TO EDUCATION FORUM

THE IDEA OF EDUCATION AS a means to social change and equality, informed the vision of our founding fathers as they drafted India's Constitution. Equality of opportunity, as outlined in the preamble of the Indian Constitution, has been widely interpreted to include equality in provision of education. The Constitution (86th Amendment) Act 2002, which made elementary education a Fundamental Right—and its consequential legislation—the Right of Children to Free and Compulsory Education Act 2009, popularly called the Right to Education or RTE Act, represent a momentous step forward in the history of our republic. The act was a ground breaking piece of legislation, the first in the world that puts the responsibility of ensuring student enrollment, attendance and completion of elementary education on the government.

The cornerstone of Right to Education is provision of free and compulsory primary education, though the aim is also to provide increasing access to learning opportunities at secondary, technical and higher levels. It was envisaged that under the RTE Act, teaching and learning processes would be stress-free. A programme for curricular reform was also envisaged to provide for a child-friendly learning system, which is at once relevant and empowering.

31 March 2016 will mark six years of the coming into force of the Right to Education. An audit is therefore appropriate, particularly to locate deficiencies that exist, and chart out a course for the future.

In the last six years, the Right to Education Act has shown promising developments. The government's budget for the Sarva Shiksha Abhiyan (SSA),

---

Note: Speech delivered at the National Stocktaking Convention being organized by the Right to Education Forum, 21 March 2016, New Delhi.

the main vehicle for the act's implementation, has increased substantially from ₹12,825 crores in 2009–2010 to ₹22,500 crore in 2016–2017. Some 3.5 lakh schools have been opened in the last decade and 99 per cent of India's rural population now has a primary school within a one kilometre radius. A survey in 2014 reported that 84.4 per cent schools now served the mid-day meals, 48.2 per cent schools had proper and functioning toilets for girls and 73 per cent schools had available drinking water. The enrolment of girls has increased slightly from 48.12 per cent in 2009–2010 to 48.19 per cent in 2014–2015 at the elementary level. For boys, the enrollment at primary level is now 52 per cent. A 55 per cent decline in dropouts was also reported in the age group 6–14 years, from 13.46 million in 2005 to 6.06 million in 2014, with the annual average primary school dropout rate declining from 6.8 per cent in 2009–2010 to 4.3 per cent in 2013–2014.

These are significant gains. Yet a critical appraisal of the functioning of the Right to Education reveals that large gaps exist in its implementation. Even with the increasing primary enrolment rates, India has the largest number of out-of-school children in the world, which is more than the out-of-school children in whole of sub-Saharan Africa. There is a huge disparity between the urban and rural education, and rich and poor children have radically different schooling experiences.

One of the most stringent criticisms of the RTE has been the quality of education being provided. The Global Monitoring Report 2012 ranked India a low 102 out of the 120 countries on the Education for All (EFA) Development Index, based on progress in universal primary education, adult literacy, gender parity and the quality of education. Some surveys have revealed that while enrolment in elementary education in our country has increased, there has been a decline in the education outcomes, with abilities in reading, writing and other comprehensive skills deteriorating among children between the ages of six and 14. For instance, only a fourth of all children in standard III could read a standard II text fluently, a drop of more than 5 per cent over five years, according to the 2014 Annual Status of Education Report (ASER). About Rs 1,15,625 crore ($17.7 billion) has been spent on Sarva Shiksha Abhiyan—the national programme for universal elementary education and a core element for implementing the RTE—over the last five years, so the decline in the quality of learning is particularly disturbing. Low learning and falling quality of education imparted to children has grave implications for the future of our society and the country. This should be a cause for serious concern to the government.

The quality of education suffers due to understaffing and lack of training of teachers. The flow of public funds has so far been focused on developing school infrastructure. Teacher training has been a neglected area. An Oxfam India policy report in March 2015 indicated that over 5 lakh sanctioned teacher's post were lying vacant and more than 6.6 lakh in-service teachers were un-trained. Around 37 per cent of primary schools were found to be non-conformant with the prescribed national pupil–teacher ratio (PTR) norm of 30:1. Moreover, around 10 per cent of schools across the country remained single teacher schools. Teacher absenteeism, which is rampant in several parts of the country, particularly impacts the disadvantaged students. The UNESCO (United Nations Educational, Scientific and Cultural Organization) EFA Monitoring Report for 2014, noted that teacher absenteeism in India varied from 15 per cent in Maharashtra to 42 per cent in Jharkhand.

We need many more good teachers, and the only way to do that is to make the remuneration more attractive, recruit better teachers, provide them with better training, and monitor their performance and availability closely.

The next major challenge is the high number of drop-outs and out of school children. Answering a question in the Rajya Sabha, on 10 March 2016, the Minister for HRD said that in 2014, some 6.064 million children remained out of school. There has been an expansion in the number of schools, but the Right to Education Forum Stocktaking Report for 2014 suggests that across the country less than 10 per cent schools comply with all the RTE norms. State and National Child Rights Commissions have been working actively with governments to reduce the percentage of children out of school. Despite such efforts, we continue to see children working at roadside restaurants, in people's homes, at construction sites, in shops and on the roads. However, to pick these children up and put them in school is hardly as easy as it sounds.

To begin with, rescue of child laborers and punishing the employer is the work of the Labour Ministry and the state police. The responsibility of bringing children to schools and providing them quality education is the work of the Education Departments. Then again, monitoring implementation of the RTE Act is the responsibility of the Child Rights Commissions in each state, which are under the Women and Child Development Department. Coordination between various implementing agencies has to be improved to develop synergies and create an environment conducive to promoting Right to Education rules.

The third issue relates to the absence of equity in education. Of the 6.064 million out-of-school children, a whooping 4.6 million or 76 per cent belonged to the Scheduled Castes, Scheduled Tribes and other religious minorities. Issues, such as those related to the 25 per cent reservation of seats for children from disadvantaged backgrounds in private schools; poor educational infrastructure in rural areas compared to urban centers; cases of discrimination on the basis of caste; and neglect of targeted elementary education schemes for the Scheduled Castes, Scheduled Tribes and other backward communities are serious in nature. Inclusive education is inherent in Right to Education and the government must address these issues expeditiously.

It is said that quantity, quality and equality are the three sides of the triangle required to ensure Right to Education. Without any one of these arms, the triangle will collapse. In this backdrop, the decline in state funding in the key social sector programmes, including education, is of particular concern. Public services like education are the key to nurture participatory growth. Financing for Right to Education remains inadequate.

Total public expenditure for education, at less than 3.5 per cent of GDP, is well below the 6 per cent commitment made in the National Education Policies. At 52 per cent, the Sarva Shiksha Abhiyan received more than half the money under school-education allocation in the latest budget, but over the last five years, the Sarva Shiksha Abhiyan budget has declined by 6 per cent, from Rs 23,873 crore ($4.4 billion) in 2012–2013 to Rs 22,500 crore ($3.3 billion) for 2016–2017. While school education is primarily the responsibility of states, the central government directly finances 60 per cent of education, through programmes such as the Sarva Shiksha Abhiyan. As many as 66 per cent of India's primary school students attend government schools or government-aided schools. Poor off-take from the schemes is another area of concern. Of the money set aside for the Sarva Shiksha Abhiyan during 2015–2016, only 57 per cent was released till September 2015, according to an Accountability Initiative report.

In addition to increasing the government investments in education, it is also essential to maintain the funding levels of other social welfare schemes, especially those operating in the rural sector, to ensure that falling incomes of parents do not impact the educational prospects of in-school children.

Legislation is one aspect of the matter. The experience gained in operating the RTE for the past six years should inform the correctives to reduce the gaps and overcome the shortcomings.

Although state education departments and local education authorities are responsible for monitoring the implementation of the Act, this responsibility needs to be taken more seriously. There is a need for having special audit mechanisms, like in the case of MNREGA (Mahatma Gandhi National Rural Employment Guarantee Act).

The immense relevance of inclusive education, particularly of disadvantaged groups, demands:

- Vibrant partnerships among the departments and organizations concerned with children of the Scheduled Castes, the Scheduled Tribes and educationally backward minorities. Government will have to set up systems for equal opportunity for children with special needs.
- Acceleration of poverty reduction programmes of the Rural Development and Panchayati Raj Departments so that children are freed from domestic chores and wage earning responsibilities.
- Ensuring that state governments get the Panchayati Raj institutions appropriately involved so that 'local authorities' can discharge their functions under the Right to Education Act. There is a need for close cooperation amongst departments concerned to ensure that so far the deprived children get their rights to education.

The transition towards a comprehensive implementation of Right to Education will come through making parents (particularly in rural areas) aware of the benefits of education for their children. This requires a change of mindset at the community level, and accountability of all entrusted with this responsibility.

Despite the shortcomings in its implementation, the Right to Education Act remains a remarkable achievement. While concerns regarding privatization of education remain, the act offers a first step towards an educational system in India that provides access, equity and inclusion for all children.

35
THE VALUE OF SCIENTIFIC TEMPER

THE THEME OF 'SCIENTIFIC TEMPER' is often taken for granted, and yet inadequately explored. What do the two terms—'scientific' and 'temper'—actually mean? Any dictionary would tell us the meaning of 'temper'—it means a frame of mind or mental disposition. The same dictionary tells us that 'scientific' means seeking knowledge through systematic observation and experiment. Its opposite is 'unscientific', which denotes acquisition of knowledge by methods that are scientific.

Thus, the simple meaning of scientific temper is a frame of mind that trains itself to seek knowledge by scientific methodology and refrains from acquiring it through other means. Its emphasis is on the 'process' as well as the 'product'.

Scientific temper means that knowledge based only on authority or legend—of superiors, elders, tradition or convention—is insufficient unless it is supported by a rational process of reasoning based on facts. Scientific temper, thus, is an attitude which involves the application of logic. Discussion, argument and analysis are vital parts of this approach. It cannot be authoritarian and must submit to reasoning based on facts and logic.

It was Jawaharlal Nehru who introduced the term in our public discourse.

'...mere applications of science and technology will not be a sufficient condition', he wrote, adding that what is needed is

the scientific approach, the adventurous and yet critical temper of science, the search for truth and new knowledge, the

---

Note: Speech delivered at the launch of the new look of Rajya Sabha TV, book release, and panel discussion, 10 January 2016, New Delhi.

refusal to accept anything without testing and trial, the capacity to change previous conclusions in the face of new evidence, the reliance on observed fact and not on pre-conceived theory, the hard discipline of the mind—all this is necessary, not merely for the application of science but for life itself and the solution of its many problems.[1]

Scientific temper is characterized by traits such as healthy skepticism, universalism, freedom from prejudice or bias, objectivity, open-mindedness, humility, willingness to suspend judgment without sufficient evidence, rationality, perseverance and positive approach to failure. A person having scientific attitude uses the method of science in his/her daily normal decision-making process.

One of the objectives of our Constitution is to make scientific temper the basis of all social interaction. This is spelt out in Article 51A: 'It shall be the duty of every citizen of India to develop scientific temper, humanism and spirit of inquiry and reform.'

Why was this done?

The answer is evident. We live in the age of science. Science has become the most powerful driver of growth and development and thus, no aspect of human life remains untouched by science. The answers to humanity's greatest challenges today—disease, hunger, environmental degradation, climate change, energy requirements and search for new technologies to overcome them—rest in our better understanding of science.

This has practical implications:

- In a competitive economy, there will be much greater demands on the scientific and technological capabilities of the country. We will need more, and better, innovations in order to remain competitive as we aspire for faster, sustainable and inclusive growth.
- Public acceptance of scientific temper and development of a critical and inquisitive attitude is a precondition for fostering and sustaining the cultivation of innovations and scientific research.
- We need to create the right ambiance and structures to encourage science research and innovation. A pre-requisite is the need to develop an enquiring attitude and an analytical approach that leads to rational thinking and the pursuit of truth without prejudice.

This should be evident to all. In reality, it is not so. Much too often there is a lack of scientific temper in our daily life. To cite a few situations:

- In our family life, we do not approve of questioning. Most parents do not like children asking questions. In schools, from nursery to high school, teachers frown upon children raising questions. In colleges and universities, asking questions is often considered 'cheeky' and an attempt by the student to cast doubt on the knowledge of the teacher.
- The same holds good for social life. It is considered 'disrespectful' to question an elder, a superior or a leader.
- This frame of mind is reflected in our attitude to matters of social custom, inherited tradition and faith. Attempts to separate myth from fact, history from mythology, belief from scientifically verified facts, are often frowned upon. Pursuant to it, occult is dubbed scientific and superstition as 'culture'.
- Such approaches have often taken unpleasant and violent turns: books have been banned or withdrawn from circulation, libraries have been burnt, individual dissenters ostracized or killed, social peace disturbed and violence inflicted on citizens.
- In each of these cases, the working assumption is that questioning will hurt sentiments, damage or destroy existing order or structures, undermine faith, disrupt social order.

Based on these dubious foundations, irrational faiths and beliefs based on unscientific prejudices and habits still persist. There is intolerance of criticism and questioning. It is ironical that the latest information technology tools are used for propagation of anti-science beliefs.

It is strange that in an India committed to modernity, we have a large number of faith or tradition-based television channels but none exclusively devoted to science or science-mindedness. It is also paradoxical that at times, even scientists succumb to practices that derogate from scientific temper. These practices raise a question: can one be scientific and un-scientific, rational and irrational, logical and illogical at the same time?

It is here that education has to play a critical role. Unfortunately, our education system is insufficiently equipped to inculcate scientific temper in young minds. Over the years, the quantum of scientific information in the country has increased, but has not brought about science-mindedness in sufficient measure.

The use of mass media as a means of transmitting science related information is perhaps the most important bulwark in our fight against ignorance and irrationality. The media, given its privileged position, has a responsibility to challenge the rampant obscurantism and superstition that afflict our society.

36
SOCIAL INNOVATION AND SOCIAL HARMONY

SOCIAL INNOVATION IS DIFFERENT FROM mere innovation, which may rightly be in the realm of technology and focus on making manufacturing more efficient and/or developing new products and services for the consumer. Our vision, instead, is wider and emanates from a desire to address the gaps in the developmental chain. It can best be defined as 'new solutions to social challenges that have the intent and effect of equality, justice and empowerment'. In other words:

- It must be new;
- It must address a social challenge;
- Its intent must be to create equality, justice and empowerment;
- Its end result must be equality, justice and empowerment.

It should thus cover technological, institutional, cultural, educational and social innovations. This is all the more relevant as the country has embarked on a decade of innovation to reflect the best of what an aspiring generation needs.

Any discussion on social innovation and social transformation is premised on the understanding that it takes place in a society where people have come together for a common purpose as a result of which there exists a modicum of social consensus and social cohesion for such transformations to take place. Consequently, it must be socially useful and must not be destructive or disruptive of social cohesion.

Note: Speech delivered at the Inauguration of the Annual National Seminar on Social Innovation, 17 November 2015, Pune.

Thus, social innovation is inseparable from the cultural, ecological, economic, political and spiritual environment in which it takes place. It cannot be pursued in isolation.

Social innovation therefore gets linked to the levels of harmony, freedom, stability and security prevailing in a society; by the same token, its promotion requires an orientation of values, objectives and priorities towards the well-being of all, and to this end purposeful strengthening and promotion of institutions, policies and practices.

Equality, equity, empowerment and social justice constitute the fundamental values of just and democratic societies. The promotion and protection of these values provides legitimacy to all institutions and all exercises of authority aimed at creating an environment in which human beings are at the centre of concern for sustainable development.

While economic progress is essential for survival and well-being, it is neither a substitute nor the panacea for the social challenges that confront us. Every society, including ours, requires its constituent parts to work in harmony.

This principle, universal in nature, was expressed succinctly some years back by the former UN Secretary General Kofi Annan. 'We must recognize,' he said, 'that stable societies are built on three pillars. Security, development, and respect for human rights and the rule of law. There can be no long-term security without development and there can be no development without security.'[1] No society can long remain prosperous or secure without due respect for human rights and the rule of law.

The operative assumption here is that respect for human rights unavoidably includes acceptance of diversity, not merely tolerance of it. This transition from tolerance to acceptance, in actual day to day practice rather than as a mantra in political discourse, is critical for making a society fully inclusive rather than selectively so.

Consequently, and given that most societies are not homogenous, 'If democracy is not receptive to various identities in a plural society, then it remains only a majoritarian democracy that under-privileges minorities'. It is for this reason that the Indian Constitution has provisions for the protection of minority rights 'as well as balancing group rights with individual rights'.[2]

These preliminary observations are necessary to delineate the societal backdrop essential for optimal creativity in a society seeking to maximize its innovative genius and also to make sure that a social consensus around equality, justice and empowerment exists, more so because there is reason today for concern about this consensus and about the emergence of a propensity for intolerance of diversity and dissent.

Infosys founder, Shri N.R. Narayana Murthy, addressing the graduating students at the Indian Institute of Science, recently asked a pertinent question. To paraphrase him: Why has there been no earth-shaking invention or technology from India over the last 60 years? Some have argued that Murthy was being too IT-centric, but the question calls for some serious soul-searching.

India has a long tradition of innovation and since Independence there have been a series of empowering social innovations in India. The innovation to use buffalo milk in place of cow's milk to produce milk powder laid the foundation for the Anand cooperative dairy model, ushering in the White Revolution in India. The introduction of cooked mid-day meals in schools was an innovation that has had a multilayered impact on the society. The Aravind Eye Care Hospital provides a vivid illustration. Since its founding in 1976 as an 11-bed hospital in Madurai, Aravind today runs six hospitals that perform more than 300,000 eye surgeries annually. This productivity is based on deep competencies, which result in cost savings that enable treating two-thirds of the poorest patients free. Yet, Aravind still earns sufficient income to enable expansion.

There are a number of other Indian innovation stories: the low cost qualitative hearing aid; the digital twin spark ignition motorcycle engine; the mitti-cool fridge; the super 30 education programme from Patna that selects and trains promising young students from socio-economically weaker sections for entrance examinations to top technical institutions; and hundreds of other innovative products and services that are using the internet or the mobile phone technology to deliver choices to a growing number of people.

Have these innovations, social or technical, become a main-stream phenomenon? Have they gathered enough momentum to make India an innovative society? What is the Indian score card on innovation? What can be done to improve it?

Aarthi Rao, in her 2012 article[3], 'What's the Matter with India?' called India a powerhouse of social innovation struggling to take the next step, lamenting that the up-scaling or conversion of the innovative starts to socially transformative levels was not sufficiently wide-spread.

The honest truth is that we lag behind many others, including our peers. The Global Innovation Index 2015[4] ranks us as 81st out of 141 countries, below Brazil at 70, South Africa at 60, Russia at 48 and China at 29.

The Index identified three areas of weakness: SMEs (small and medium-sized enterprises), intellectual property rights and higher education. Asserting that 'an economy is as innovative as its SMEs', it suggests fiscal and tax guidelines to infuse a culture of innovation and R&D in SMEs along with incentivizing innovation-driven start-ups as well as improvement in ease of business environment and infrastructure development.

In a recent article, Baba Prasad, author of the book *Nimble*, listed some of the reasons why India has failed to provide the budding entrepreneur or innovator the ecosystem, the resources or the infrastructure that Silicon Valley provides its potential entrepreneurs[5]:

- Our educational system is steeped in training implementers, not thinkers;
- There is a significant lack of appetite for taking risks, and both Indian families and educational institutions have a 'play-safe' attitude;
- There is a lack of start-up funding environment; and
- The slow pace and inefficiencies of the Indian legal system are a deterrent to innovative sprit.

Participating in a 'digital dialogue' on 5 July this year, the prime minister promised to give 'absolute support' to make enterprise and innovation easier so that India emerges as an innovation hub and keeps pace with the fast changing world. He said: 'The world is changing quicker than ever before and we cannot remain oblivious to that. If we don't innovate, if we don't come up with cutting edge products, there will be stagnation.'

The Global Innovation Index Report 2015, in its chapter on India has also identified certain strengths such as the size and sharp growth of India's economy, the presence of centres of excellence in top Indian universities, the 66 per cent increase in output of scientific publications and the leap-forging in areas of technological infrastructure, including the high penetration rate of mobile network. The report recommends that there is a need to:

- increase the number of higher education institutions as well as university-industry collaboration,
- encouraging innovations in the SMEs,
- incentivizing the development of an entrepreneurial eco-system,
- improving the ease of doing business,
- developing the physical infrastructure, and
- improving the Intellectual Property Regime (IPR).

The President of India declared the year 2010 to be the start of the Decade of Innovation with a specific focus on addressing issues of poverty. To further this national agenda, and administer governmental activity in support of innovation through assistance in human, financial, social and intellectual capital, the National Innovation Council was created to develop a 'National Roadmap for Innovation' over the next decade.

Alongside, a National Innovation Foundation—India was set up as an autonomous body of the Department of Science and Technology, Government of India. The Foundation has sought to incentivize pursuit of innovation through the Dr A.P.J. Abdul Kalam IGNITE competition at school level. The results are modest, given the size of our school-going population.

A recent report[6] of an expert's committee headed by Dr Tarun Khanna, constituted by the Niti Aayog, for determining the contours of new Atal Innovation Mission (AIM) which is a successor mechanism to the National Innovation Council, notes that 'Bringing about innovation has never been as important as today, as the global economy shifts away from the industrial economy towards the innovation economy... What is heartening is that recent economic theory suggests that government investment in R&D, knowledge-creation, and technological progress does have a role to play in fuelling innovation, productivity, capital creation, and therefore growth'.

The report recommends setting up the Innovation Mission with a three-tiered approach and dovetailing it with the National Skill Development Programmes. The committee has proposed a short term incentive based approach to redress some immediate issues; an intermediate approach to correct imbalances in education, skilling initiatives, infrastructure and business environment; and a long-term approach to create the 'culture and attitudes' needed to foster innovation and entrepreneurship.

In this context, we need to take note of what the President said on 7 March 2016 at an innovation award function:

> Midway through this Decade (2010–2020) of Innovations, we perhaps need to assess and if necessary recalibrate our approach towards harnessing the creativity of our grass-root innovators and student. Increasing the scalability of grass-root innovations necessitates a strong linkage between the invaluable knowledge bank prevalent in our society and the formal education system. To use our innovation potential for the greater good, the nodal governmental agencies must play an enabling role.

The Governor of the Reserve Bank of India, in a recent talk at IIT (Indian Institute of Technology) Delhi, listed out some ways for a nation 'to keep the idea factory open'. He suggested that the first essential is to 'foster competition in the market place for ideas' by 'encouraging challenge to all authority and tradition, even while acknowledging that the only way of dismissing any view is through empirical tests.' Imposition of a particular view of ideology is ruled out and all ideas are subject to critical examination. The second essential was: 'Protection, not of specific ideas and traditions, but the right to question and challenge, the right to behave differently so long as it does not hurt others seriously. In this protection lies societal self-interest, for it is by encouraging the challenge of innovative rebels that society develops.'

Each of these also necessitates a scientific temper and a social ambiance conducive for it.

MATTERS GLOBAL

37
THE IMPERATIVE OF WORLD PEACE

THE ENCYCLOPAEDIC PERSONALITY OF DAMODAR Dharmanand Kosambi endeared him to scholars beyond the fields of mathematics and numismatics. Amongst them was historian A.L. Basham, author of *The Wonder That Was India*, who became his lifelong friend. On Kosambi's death, Basham wrote a personal tribute and said his initial impression was that his friend had only three interests in life—ancient India, mathematics and preservation of peace; for all of them, he added, 'he worked hard and with devotion, according to his deep convictions'. This was also the view of President V.V. Giri, who chaired the Kosambi Commemoration Committee and wrote a foreword to a commemoration volume of essays published in 1974.

Kosambi was an active fighter for peace and, in the hay days of the Cold War, spent time analyzing the causes that prevented peace. He held the view that peace was a prerequisite for development and that true peace required 'true democracy', where all men are truly equal and no one claims any superiority. His focus was on peace in the global community. There is little evidence to suggest that peaceful resolution of conflicts within societies was amongst his priorities. His thought process was driven by his ideological orientation; that, in fairness, would deserve a separate discourse.

This chapter aims to explore the passion for peace, and its relevance to the world in our own times. Here, we are confronted with a contradiction of serious dimensions. A look at human history makes evident the role of violence. At the same time, the passion for peace is perennial in human history. The philosopher Lao Tzu summed up its pre-requisites in the 5th century BC:

Note: Speech delivered at the inauguration of the Dr D.D. Kosambi Festival of Ideas, 4 February 2008, Goa.

> *If there is to be peace in the world,*
> *There must be peace in the nations.*
> *If there is to be peace in the nations,*
> *There must be peace in the cities.*
> *If there is to be peace in the cities,*
> *There must be peace between neighbours.*
> *If there is to be peace between neighbours,*
> *There must be peace at home.*
> *If there is to be peace at home,*
> *There must be peace in the heart.*

The impulse was the same elsewhere, in another age. The medieval Italian scholar Marsilius of Padua commenced Defensor Pacis with a quotation, on the meaning of peace, from the 6th century Roman statesman Flavius Cassiodorus:

> Tranquillity, wherein peoples prosper and the welfare of nations is preserved, must certainly be the desire of every state. For it is the noble mother of the good arts. Permitting the steady increase of the race of mortals, it extends their power and enhances their customs. And he who is perceived not to have sought for it is recognised to be ignorant of such important concerns.

Marsilius concluded that 'we ought to wish for peace, to seek it if we do not already have it, to conserve it once it is attained, to repel with all our strength the strife which is opposed to it'.[1]

The quest for peace, as a human trait, is not synonymous with peace amongst human groups. The latter is characterized by conflict and the resultant need, through force or compact, to enforce order. The need for a final authority was felt in all groupings; the sanction for it was at times human, at others attributed to an extra-human impulse. Sovereignty in this form existed before it was conceptualized.

While peace among members of a group—society or state—was sought to be achieved through a compact or a final authority, harmony between groups or states was perceived to be a qualitatively different exercise. Domination was one form of achieving it; hence the expressions Pax Romana, Pax Brittanica, etc. that crept into political vocabulary. This was not found to be perpetual or all embracing. Hence the need for conflict management or resolution through rules of behaviour that came to be known as International

Law of Peace and War.

A methodology for conflict resolution is to be found in all societies. Kautilya refers to six methods of seeking conciliation. In modern times, the conceptual and the practical endeavour to seek peace between nations took shape in post-Renaissance Europe. Publicists like Grotius pioneered it; theoretical depth was added by philosophers like Immanuel Kant in his tract on 'Perpetual Peace', wherein he argued that peace must be established through conscious effort based on a mutuality of interest. The Kantian perception of this interest is worth recalling:

> The spirit of commerce, which is incompatible with war, sooner or later gains the upper hand. As the power of money is perhaps the most dependable of all powers included under the state, states see themselves forced, without any moral courage, to promote honourable peace and by mediation to prevent war wherever it threatens to break out.[2]

Kant was ahead of his times in considering commerce as a promoter of peace. The dominant impulse in the 18th and 19th centuries was promotion of commerce through domination and war. The other viewpoint, nevertheless, had its votaries. In 1909, Sir Norman Angell published *The Great Illusion*, wherein he argued that modern commerce made war necessarily unprofitable, even for the technically victorious country; success in war, he added, was an illusion.

Serious thinking on the futility of war, however, had to await the experience and bloodletting of World Wars I and II. In August 1945, Prime Minister Atlee committed Britain to utilize atomic energy 'not for our own ends, but as trustees for humanity in the interest of all people in order to promote peace and justice in the world'. President Truman did likewise. The Preamble of the UN Charter begins by expressing a determination 'to save succeeding generations from the scourge of war'. Removal of threats to peace thus became a primary purpose of the United Nations. Five decades later only partial success can be attributed to it and war, defined as organized violence between states, is still considered an instrument of policy to achieve objectives.

In a seminal study published in 1987, the historian Paul Kennedy surveyed the interaction between economics and strategy to study the manner in which great powers in modern history grappled with economic growth, technological innovations, the spiraling cost of weapons, and changes in the international scene and power equations. He concluded that:

> Whatever the likelihood of nuclear or conventional clashes between the major states, it is clear that important transformations in the balances are occurring, and will continue to occur, probably at a faster pace than before. What is more, they are occurring at the two separate but interacting levels of economic production and strategic power...
>
> The present large powers in the international system are thus compelled to grapple with the twin challenges that have confronted all their predecessors: first with the uneven pattern of economic growth, which causes some of them to become wealthier (and, usually, stronger), relative to others; and second, with the competitive and occasionally dangerous scene abroad, which forces them to choose between a more immediate military security and a longer-term economic security.[3]

In such a context, the effort necessarily remains confined to the management of global insecurity. Boutros Ghali's 'An Agenda for Peace' was structured on that premise. Much work has been done in the past decade-and-a-half to develop the framework for peace keeping, peace building, and conflict prevention. The approach, however, is riveted on prevention rather than cure.

In 1988, Prime Minister Rajiv Gandhi told the United Nations that 'in consequence of doctrines of deterrence, international relations have been gravely militarised' and that 'peace which rests on the search for a parity of power is a precarious peace'.[4] He proposed a time-bound Action Programme for a Nuclear-Free World and the initiation of negotiations to establish a Comprehensive Global Security System under the aegis of the United Nations.

After having ignored this and other suggestions for nuclear disarmament, an initiative has recently been taken by some establishment personalities in the United States. Concerned over nuclear weapons 'falling into dangerous hands', they have 'called for a global effort to reduce reliance on nuclear weapons, to prevent their spread into potentially dangerous hands and ultimately to end them as a threat to the world'. A world without nuclear weapons requires 'the necessary political will to build an international consensus on priorities'. This, they concede, cannot be done; 'without the vision of moving towards zero, we will not find the essential cooperation required to stop our downward spiral'.[5]

The strategic paradigm, as hitherto understood, offers no escape from the possibility of states resorting to war. This necessitates a qualitatively different approach if perpetual peace is to be made a human objective.

A new framework for world peace must begin with conceptual clarity about the meaning of words in our vocabulary. Can peace be defined as absence of conflict? If so, it could be no more than a tactical happening of a transitory nature, involving no value judgment or commitment to such a judgement. A study of the semantic history of the term itself is revealing. The impression of contention, hostility, conflict (armed or unarmed) is ever present; so is its acceptability in a certain sense. A cynical observation by Oscar Wilde is perhaps an apt reflection on human perceptions: 'As long as war is regarded as wicked, it will always have its fascination. When it is looked upon as vulgar, it will cease to be popular.'

Early in the 20th century the philosopher William James had recognized the obstacles confronting a pacifist approach. 'The war against war', he wrote in 1910, 'is going to be no holiday or camping party. The military feelings are too deeply grounded to abdicate their place among our ideals until better substitutes are offered than the glory and shame that come to nations as well as to individuals from the ups and downs of politics and the vicissitudes of trade.'[6]

A century later Robert Fisk has referred to the same problem in his monumental work *The Great War for Civilisation*:

> Governments like it that way. They want their people to see war as a drama of opposites, good and evil, 'them' and 'us', victory or defeat. But war is primarily not about victory or defeat but about death and the infliction of death. It represents the total failure of the human spirit.[7]

The truth is that, in the realm of world politics, the avoidance of war is perceived, as Hedley Bull put it, 'as a goal subordinate to that of the preservation of the state system itself...and as subordinate also to the preservation of the sovereignty or independence of individual states...the subordinate status of peace in relation to these other goals is reflected in the phrase "peace and security" which occurs in the United Nations Charter'.

So how do we go about demonstrating the vulgarity of war and war-like activities, erasing the association of ideas that lend it credibility, and exposing its implications for humanity? Can a war be waged against war?

The challenge is a formidable one.

In order to develop a rational approach, it is essential to consider the matter from four perspectives:

- The impracticality of war in the nuclear age;
- The inefficacy of power politics;
- The emergence of new imperatives for conflicts, and their implications;
- The unavoidability of inducting a sense of justice in the conduct of relations between individuals, groups and nations.

War in the nuclear age has become inconceivable. Its implications were spelt out, among others, by George Kennan in *The Nuclear Delusion* published in 1982. The impulse to acquire nuclear weapons, as a currency of power, is nevertheless pervasive and, as with all new technologies, becoming easier by the day. According to Dr Mohamad El Baradai of IAEA, 'Soon there could be 30 virtual nuclear weapon states on the horizon.' The only rational option, therefore, is to move for universal, comprehensive, nuclear disarmament through international agreements of the type already concluded with regard to biological weapons (1972) and chemical weapons (1997). In such a scheme of things, there can be no exceptions.

Power politics and the quest for dominance, hegemony or primacy would inevitably be a recipe for instability that, in the global system, cannot but induce states to resort to arms. Patterns of these may wary; the National Intelligence Council of the United States has assessed that 'the likelihood of great power conflict escalating into total war in the next 15 years is lower than at any time in the past century, unlike during previous centuries when local conflicts sparked world wars'. Local or regional wars would nevertheless continue to erupt. Every such conflict would be disruptive of development and enhance human misery. A new mechanism for conflict prevention is thus essential.

A new, and hitherto unexplored, area for future conflicts resides in the imperatives of the current and future competition for resources, of climate change and of wider environmental questions. Economic historian Angus Matterson has noted that humanity's average real income per head has risen 10-fold since 1820. The increases however have been widely divergent. Technology and resource availability have been critical to the effort. At the same time, an emerging contradiction is also becoming evident. Technology continues to improve, but declining availability of resources is generating fear, and responses bordering on panic.

The UNEP's (United Nations Environment Programme) Global Environment Outlook published in October 2007 pointed out that 'we are living beyond our means' and need to consider environment, development and energy crises as one rather than separate issues. It stressed that while governments are expected to take the lead, other stake-holders are just as important to ensure success in achieving sustainable development: 'Our common future depends on our action today, not tomorrow or sometime in the future.'

The conclusion of the UNEP report shifts the focus from the state to the public: 'while governments are expected to take the lead, other stake holders are just as important to ensure success in achieving sustainable development. The need couldn't be more urgent and the time couldn't be more opportune, with our enhanced understanding of the challenges we face, to act now to safeguard our own survival and that of future generations.'

The picture that emerges can be summed up in a set of eight prepositions:

- The new paradigm of human existence has to be premised on comprehensive security, covering both conventional and non-conventional security.
- Experience indicates that competitive security results in confrontation and conflict.
- The prospect, and intensity, of conflicts can be controlled and lessened through a globally applicable scheme of disarmament, beginning with nuclear disarmament.
- The alternative is cooperative security premised on accommodation of competing requirements.
- Such accommodation would require a point of reference, a principle that can help reconcile differences and disagreements and impede their aggravation.
- Such a principle can only be based on the concept of justice which enables us to choose between different possible arrangements that determine the division of advantages on an equitable basis, and assign rights and duties. 'When justice is destroyed,' said Manu, 'it destroys; when justice is protected, it protects.'
- A global society based on justice has no place for war since both greed and aggression would be curtailed by its operative principle.
- The actualization of such an objective cannot be left solely to state action and must involve active participation of 'other stake holders' in the civil society

There would be many who would consider such an approach utopian and impractical and would contrast it with the realistic and practical. The answer would lie in working out the implications of such 'realism'—namely, a steady march by humankind towards self-destruction. In other words, peace must be demonstrated to be good in value terms as also in practical terms since war can be demonstrated to be genuinely harmful.

In the final analysis, then, we see merit in Kosambi's vision that peace was a pre-requisite for development and that true peace required true democracy where all human beings are equal.

The struggle for world peace must therefore be a quest for equality, justice and democracy. The modalities of furthering it would inevitably be conditioned by public awareness and public action.

38

WHAT MIGHT BE HAPPENING IN WEST ASIA

IN A CONTINENT CALLED ASIA, its various geographical segments have to be named logically rather than in terms of historical accidents. West Asia is therefore as logical as East Asia, South Asia or Central Asia. Most readers would know that the terminology of the colonial period, naming regions as Near East, Middle East or Far East, made sense only from the perspective of London.

Despite this, the propensity of the West Asians to call the region Middle East is, to say the least, baffling. Is it a case of 'reinforcement of the stereotype' or, to use Antonio Gramci's phrase, 'a dilution of the consciousness of what one really is'?

Let me begin with a preposition that might sound startling. The so-called 'Arab Spring' did not happen suddenly. What is happening in some West Asian lands today by way of political turbulence has had a long gestation, was waiting to happen and is in the nature of serial volcanic eruptions, whose intensity and duration is difficult to predict.

Some questions readily come to mind. What is the nature of the turmoil and the forces propelling it? What is its impact on different segments of society and on social relationships? What is its immediate or medium-term impact on the economy? Has it influenced security perceptions of the individual states and their views on regional security? What are its implications for India, and Indian interests in the country and the region?

Some facts can be recalled to understand the context. In the first place, all the lands in North Africa and West Asia (with the exception of Iran and

Note: Asia Centre Annual Lecture, 15 February 2013, Bengaluru.

Israel) are Arabic-speaking societies, many with tribal structures still intact, overwhelmingly Muslim, who experienced colonial or neo-colonial trauma in the first half of the 20th century. The experience of each, however, was distinct. Secondly, the structures of dominance put in place after World War I, and continued with some modifications in the second half of the century, were essentially neo-patriarchal, characterized by one Arab scholar as 'the marriage of imperialism and patriarchy'. The net result of this was historical retardation or, as the Moroccan historian Abdullah Laroui put it, 'infra-historical rhythm'.

The implications of the latter were far reaching. As early as 1928, a Lebanese lady by the name of Nazira Zain al-Din wrote about the scourge of Four Veils—of cloth, ignorance, hypocrisy and stagnation. This could not but impact on the nationalist upsurge that surfaced in different places from time to time. The clash of secular and Islamist nationalist traditions also became pervasive. Writing in 1996, Bassam Tibi of Syria, calling himself a post-1967 generation man, admitted the failure of the effort 'to replace the myths of Arab nationalism by an Arab enlightenment' and by 'the erosion of the legitimacy of the secular nation-state'.[1] Similar judgments emanated from other, non-Islamist, intellectuals.

Other developments, relating to the advent of authoritarian governance combining one party and military rule, aggravated the process. It suited the regimes and also the patterns of Western dominance and strategies of the Cold War. The one exception was Palestine. It wounded the psyche of every individual in every Arab land. The grievance had merit; it was depicted poignantly by Nasser to Kennedy in 1962: 'One who did not possess gave a promise to another who did not deserve, and these two managed by power and deceit to deprive those who both owned and deserved.'[2]

Lamentation alone, however, has never been known to correct the wrongs of history, and has not done so in the case of Palestine.

In 2002, the Arab Human Development Report identified freedom, empowerment of women and knowledge as the three deficits that hampered human development in Arab countries. The public mood of pessimism was summed up in the remark that 'we, Arabs, do not have the power to do anything and there are certain alien forces that control our destiny'.

The despondency of two lost generations, in which modernity was imported as a product rather than as a process, also propelled a quest for alternatives: of an imagined past, an ideal of authenticity, an instrument of mobilization well-rooted in the consciousness of the masses. This brought forth Islamism in different manifestations. It was psychologically reassuring. As an instrument of protest, it sought democratic governance to deny the legitimacy of the authoritarian state. Rachid Gannouchi, leader of an Islamist party in Tunisia, summed it up in an essay written in exile at the end of the 20th century: 'A democratic system of government', he wrote, 'is less evil than a despotic system of government that claims to be Islamic'.[3]

The end of the Cold War and Iraq's invasion of Kuwait altered power equations. Saddam Hussain's misadventure in Kuwait left him crippled, but without loosening his hold on Iraq. An external catalyst was injected on spurious ground in the shape of the Iraq War. It progressed from 'known unknowns' to 'unknown unknowns'. Its cost in human and material terms, to both the victor and the vanquished, is still being assessed; on the side of the former, a first estimate in 2008 by Joseph Stiglitz and Linda Bilmes put it at three trillion dollars.

The war and the prolonged period of occupation and resistance to it in all its manifestations impacted on the Arab status quo but on a delayed-action fuse. The regimes that have tumbled, and those that are challenged, failed to gauge the urge for change in the majority segments of their youthful populations. The wars in Iraq and Afghanistan also demonstrated the limits of the military capacity of the United States in a non-conventional conflict.

In August 2010, through Presidential Study Directive 11, President Obama asked his government agencies to prepare for change. According to an article by David Ignatius in the *Washington Post* of 11 March 2011, the document cited 'evidence of growing citizen discontent with the region's regimes', said the region is entering a critical period of transition, and asked his advisors to 'manage these risks by demonstrating to the people of the Middle East and North Africa the gradual but real prospect of greater political openness and improved governance'.

The military and political conflicts in the first decade of the present century brought to the fore other fault lines that have left their mark on the balance of socio-political power in individual countries of the region. These have taken the shape of:

- Ethnic assertions as with the Kurds in Iraq and Syria;
- Sectarian empowerment of Shias in Iraq, and demands for rights by the Shia majority in Bahrain and Shia minority in Saudi Arabia;
- Democratic upsurges in Tunisia, Egypt and Libya, and muted rumblings

in some of the GCC (Gulf Co-operative Council) states; and
- The power struggle for Syria and its regional and global implications.

The impact of each set of challenges has been different. In Iraq, the Kurdish demand for greater role in governance in a highly centralized Arab state has been long standing. The US-led war against Saddam Hussain has resulted in a de facto autonomous Kurdish region in Iraq where the authority of Baghdad is minimal and frequently contested on matters of daily governance. In Syria, domestic political discontent against one-party rule, encouraged and assisted materially by some regional and other powers, has assumed the form of a full-fledged civil war with no end in sight. This has given Syrian Kurds a little elbow room, though without external recognition; it is likely to be complicated by neighbouring Turkey's stern policy towards its Kurdish population. The new situation in both countries has prompted apprehensions about efforts to give shape to various projects of cartographic engineering in the region, or as Hassanein Haikal put it, 'a new Sykes-Picot'.

The democratization of the political process in Iraq, in the wake of the war of 2003, projected for the first time the demographic reality of the state and resulted in the emergence of Shias as the majority politico-sectarian faction. The loss of political power by the Arab Sunnis of the country was deeply resented and continues to be contested. It also has wider geo-political ramifications. In 2004, the King of Jordan contributed, allegedly at the prompting of his chief of intelligence, the term 'Shia Crescent' to the political vocabulary of the region.

Unconsciously, perhaps, it helped highlight the geopolitical gains that accrued to Iran in the wake of the Iraq War. Iran has sustained its assistance to the Hezbullah in Lebanon; there is, however, no evidence as yet of a material Iranian impulse in the simmering of discontent in the Shia segments of the Bahraini and Saudi population, since this emanates from domestic factors and pre-date the Iraq War.

The immediate details of the political eruptions in the past two years in Tunisia and Egypt are known to most people; the backdrop is not. Since independence in 1956, the Tunisian public or people (sha'b) mostly subscribed to the ideal to a homogenous, united, modern, Francophile and secular body-politic, and a paternalistic relationship in a 'pact of obedience' to the leader (Zaim). Economic grievances did surface from time to time, but did not transform themselves into movements for rights. It is this which changed when Mohamed Bouazizi set himself on fire on 10 December 2010. Thenceforth, 'the people' became the point of reference. This did not mean homogeneity; gaps of perception on matters regional, generational and cultural have emerged and are aggravated by the demographic reality and high unemployment of around 18 per cent, according, to a World Bank study. There is an ongoing debate between Islamism and secularism, but the focus even of the Islamist Al-Nahda leaders is to establish institutions that safeguard public debate and electoral choice. And yet, as the happening of 6 February was to show, derailment is always on the cards.

Egypt is the very reverse of the relative tranquility of Tunisia, though the Tunisian protests served as an inspiration. A perceptive observer has noted that two years after the initial turmoil, 'Egyptians don't really know the balance of forces in their own homeland'. This reaffirms Leon Trotsky's observation that 'the masses go into a revolution not with a prepared plan of social reconstruction, but with a sharp feeling that they cannot endure the old regime'. The leaderless protestors in Tahrir Square and elsewhere in Egypt, fully assisted by modern communications' technology and ad hoc mechanisms of defence against police tactics, focused on toppling the Mubarak regime.

The first stage of the Egyptian revolution was essentially leaderless and reflected the aspirations of all segments of society. Its limitations became evident with the progress of events. The electoral process and the constitution-making brought to the fore the Muslim brotherhood as the most organized socio-political force on the scene. It is strong but not unchallenged; on the other hand, while both the Salafists and the liberal-secularists have mobilized against it, they do not find convergence on critical values and tactics. The most recent events thus tend to highlight nature of the challenge: how to forge a democratic system while integrating the Brotherhood and other Islamists into the political game.

Violence, until recently, was generally avoided. Ominous signs of a reversal are now emerging. A new organization, the Black Bloc, made its appearance in the last week of January, claiming to be 'formed in reaction to the Muslim Brotherhood's military wing'. In a first reaction, the Ministry of Interior has called them terrorists and ordered their arrest. A challenge is being mounted by the liberal-secularists, but not the salafists, to the legitimacy of the president himself. The Brotherhood's uncompromising position on the making of the constitution and the electoral law has hardened the political divide, which can only be addressed by the proposed national dialogue.

Events in Libya, beginning in February 2011, took a somewhat different course. The discontent against Gaddafi was used as a pretext for external interference in the shape of UN Security Council action, the declaration of no-fly zone, followed by extensive bombing of Tripoli by the French and British air forces. The mysterious refuge in Britain of intelligence chief Mousa Koussa and the cooption of other figures of the Gaddafi regime in the new set up does suggest a measure of external involvement of a clandestine nature in the progress of events. Nor were miscalculations avoided; the murder of the US Ambassador in Benghazi was to show that the nature of some of Gaddafi's opponents was not fully understood.

Two dimensions of the developments discussed above require closer scrutiny. The first relates to economic grievances. High unemployment among the youth and declining household incomes, has been a common factor of social unrest in all the affected countries. A World Bank report in September 2012 assessed that 'recent political changes will be meaningful if they lead to concrete social and economic development'. The bank has emphasized the need for transparency, good governance, job creation and competitive private sector. There is also an insistence, on the part of prospective western donors, on 'real democratic transition' taking place. A satisfying factor, from the viewpoint of the donors, is the acceptance by the new regimes of the neo-liberal economic reforms undertaken by the previous administrations.

Less explicit, but nevertheless constraining, are the requirements of rich regional donors. There is no evidence as yet of these matters having been addressed comprehensively by the new administrations; tactical commitments, however, have been made. Unease about the activities of the Muslim Brotherhood in GCC states, particularly UAE's concern about Al-Islah, has acquired a higher profile in recent months. The sole exception to this is Qatar, which maintains a multi-pronged relationship with the brotherhood.

A critical question discussed in different fora and on different planes, directly as well as elliptically, is the place of Islam in society and in state policies. In a book published in the year 2000, the American journalist Geneive Abdo wrote that 'the religious transformation of Egyptian society appeared obvious to me shortly after I stepped out in the Cairo breeze one Sunday evening in 1993', adding that 'the Islamic revival was broad-based, touching Egyptians in every social class and all walks of life'. The only outstanding question, she concluded, 'is to what degree the religious revival will take over Egyptian society'.[4]

The brotherhood, with deep roots in society and in professional groupings, subscribes to the amorphous dictum—'Islam is the solution'. Some readers would know that in terms of the political theory of Islam, governance is to be by consultation, allegiance is conditional, and dissent admissible. This, in modern terminology, would tantamount to democratic governance. The political history of Muslim societies, however, is characterized by the opposite. The choice often is between form and content. The paradox is summed up succinctly by the French-Algerian scholar Mohammed Arkoun: 'Islam is theologically Protestant and politically Catholic.'[5]

The challenge for contemporary Muslim societies, in the wake of the upsurge against autocratic governance, is to seek legitimacy, both in the light of their own cultural authenticity and the norms of the contemporary world. Local situations, even national characteristics, would shape the contours of the debate and outcomes in individual societies. Generalized perceptions of approval or otherwise would be unhelpful.

One last aspect pertains to external impulses. Since the advent of the 21st century, the region and its countries have been witness to initiatives based on innovative doctrines emanating from Western powers. Evidence of a design is compelling. Should conclusions be drawn from it?

Situations in both Yemen and Jordan too require watching since many similar forces are at work there. The GCC states—authoritarian and undemocratic, but India and Indian friendly—are in a different time zone of political evolution and the combination of enormous wealth and small populations would in all likelihood sustain the status quo for some more time. Bahrain would be an exception to this. If and when turbulence does reach the GCC, it would impact on our strategic and commercial interests significantly.

How do these developments affect us in India? Needless to say, political turbulence and economic disruption on our western flank, as in other neighbouring regions, would be an unwelcome development. Formally, a change of regime would not impact on our perceptions since Indian state practice does not admit of regime recognition. Nor is India generally given to pronouncement of value judgements on the domestic set up of other countries unless such a step is motivated by more compelling considerations of statecraft. Barring a serious divergence of views on questions of our national interest, therefore, the new regimes in these countries would not have an adverse impact on our bilateral relations. On the contrary, hard economic and geo-political interests would ensure harmonious relationships.

In the final analysis, therefore, the changes, voluntary and expressive of popular will, are to be welcomed. We know only too well that democratic institution-building requires commitment as well as patience and a temper of tolerance. To the extent our assistance is sought, it should be made available without being prescriptive. The transition to a democratic system would be genuine and durable as long as it is autonomous. Suggestions of imposition would be a negation of both.

There is, of course, another scenario to be reckoned with. What would happen if the democratization process falters, if disagreements take the shape of violent dissent, if the principle of majority rule within the framework of equal rights is not adhered to, if newly installed democratic governments fail to meet public expectations on better governance, social justice, employment and growth?

Would renewed turbulence induce external intervention—regional or extra regional?

Would it make the region resemble Pandemonium, depicted by the poet Milton as the capital of Hell, where the great Satan would be the ruling deity?

39
A CENTURY OF TURMOIL IN WEST ASIA: SOME PITFALLS OF NATIONALISM

SOME OF THE READERS MAY know that Mohiuddin Ahmad, better known as Abul Kalam Azad, was himself a man of many cultures. He was born in Makkah of an Indian father and an Arab mother, and throughout his life remained familiar with the languages, culture and political developments in western Asia, a region in our proximate neighbourhood. Happenings there in the past, as now, were and remain of interest and relevance to India and Indians. For this reason, it is essential to view them from an Indian perspective.

The year 2014, and the month of November, coincided with a momentous happening a century back. I refer, of course, to World War I that commenced in August 1914 and ended in November 1919. The centenary of the commencement of that monumental folly has been observed in many countries in Europe. Its consequences were enormous: around 17 million dead, the disappearance of the Austro-Hungarian and Ottoman Empires, overthrow of the German, the Austrian, the Russian and the Ottoman dynasties, and the emergence of new national entities.

A century later, it is useful and enlightening to dwell on the immediate and longer term impact of this on the Arab societies of western Asia with whom religiously, intellectually, and culturally Abul Kalam Azad had multi-layered affinities[1]. These, in fact, went beyond being personal; there were, instead, patterns and parallels to be discerned in the anti-colonial struggles that developed in India on the one hand and in western Asian lands,

---

Note: 43rd Maulana Azad Memorial Lecture, 11 November 2014, New Delhi.

mistakenly and parochially termed as Middle East[2], on the other. The term itself was a neologism invented by the British General T.E. Gordon and the American naval officer Alfred Mahan to describe the region between the Mediterranean and the Indian Ocean. It gained currency when the British journalist Valentine Chirol popularized it in a series of articles in 1902, published as a book a year later entitled, *The Middle Eastern Question or Some Problems of Indian Defence*[3].

This pre-occupation with safeguarding the empire in India and the approaches to it largely determined British policy in western and central Asia and in that context established an emotional bond between the anti-colonial sentiments of the freedom fighters in these regions. As Azad put it in 1923, 'India commends the spirit of every Eastern nation which is fighting for freedom, and feels chagrin for every nation which is lagging behind in these endeavours.'[4]

For this reason and despite considerable differences in the historical settings and objective conditions, it is tempting to examine the evolution of the Arab and other Asian nationalisms and their respective experiences in confronting colonial and/or imperialist domination, and shaping national entities and objectives.

Some conceptual clarity is essential to this discourse. A *nation* has been called 'an imagined community'[5], a 'community conscious of its particularistic existence'[6]. Nationalism implies 'a criterion for the determination of a unit of population proper to enjoy a government exclusively its own, for the legitimate exercise of power in the state'. It is 'a political principle which holds that the political and national unit should be congruent'.[7] It is also 'an ideological movement for the attainment and maintenance of autonomy, unity and identity on behalf of a population deemed by some of its members as to constitute an actual or potential "nation"'.[8] The two dimensions, of territoriality and ideology, may not at times appear as converging if the latter is prescriptive and non-inclusive. This would and does lead to contradictions because our world today is divided into territorial states, and the Preamble of the Charter of the United Nations testifies to it.

The beginnings of Arab nationalism in the closing decades of the 19th century, has been diligently traced by George Antonius, Bassam Tibi and others. Freedom from foreign domination was one aspect of the matter; another was the gradual awareness of possessing an identity distinct from other identities, of belonging to a 'nation'. This emanated from two processes, one purely religious and the other essentially linguistic. The latter was the older of the two and applied 'to Christians as well as Muslims, and to the off shoots of each of these creeds'.[9] Thus 'early Arab nationalism was clearly a predominantly secular ideology' with a subtle intermixture of Islam and sought to profess liberal values. This intermixture was also at times an uneasy one; one scholar has argued that 'in defining its relationship with Islam, Arab nationalism often ends where it started: with the glorification of Arabism as a commanding value in Islam'.[10]

The Arab revolt of 1916 was the first organized political action by Arab nationalists. It intermeshed with the politics of the powers aligned against the Ottomans and was impacted by it. While the Sykes-Picot Agreement of May 1916 spoke of 'an independent Arab State or a Confederation of Arab States' in the conquered Ottoman territory, the Anglo-French Declaration of November 1918 specifically mentioned 'the setting up of national governments and administrations that shall derive their authority from the free exercise of the initiative and choice of the indigenous populations'. The modification of this arrangement in the San Rimo conclave of April 1919 was viewed by the Arabs as 'a breach of faith'.[11]

Another World War I strategic device was the Balfour Declaration of November 1917. It was described by the historian Arnold Toynbee as 'the winning card in a sordid contest between the two sets of belligerents... for winning the support of the Jews in Germany, Austria-Hungary and—most important of all—in the United States'.[12] In 1923 Vladimir Jabotinsky characterized Zionism as a 'colonising adventure' whose success depended on armed force.[13] The exceptionality bestowed by the world on Israel ensured its success in 1948. The Palestinian bewilderment, and the ineptness of the Arab states, did the rest.

It is important to recall that the nation-state principle did not grow organically in the region as it did in Europe for three centuries in the post-Westphalia period.[14] The territorial entities carved out from the Arabic-speaking parts of the Ottoman Empire thus lacked historical legitimacy as political units (with the exception of Egypt) and therefore needed to create a national sentiment. They reinforced it by recourse on the one hand to sub-national, tribal, religious or monarchical identities, and on the other to supra-national, pan-Arab sentiments. The Arab political discourse used different, occasionally overlapping, expressions in the debates relating to pan-Arab nationalism. The latter was, from time to time, 'oriented towards the political utopia of a United Arab State', 'an indivisible political and economic unity' even when, in actual practice, it was characterized by 'a duality of words and deeds', as was evident from the preamble of the founding document of the Arab League in March 1945 that spoke of 'coordination, cooperation and integration...to serve the sublime objectives of the Arab Nation...on the path to the unity of their States'.

An attempt to clarify and reconcile overlapping concepts was made by the Lebanese scholar Abd al-Latif Sharara in 1957: 'If a group of men have one common language, a common history, common ideals, and are linked together by the same memories and the same aspirations for the future, the same economic and cultural interests, then such a group is a nation, no matter how many and various are its fatherlands, states and peoples. Nationalism is that emotion and common interest, combined in one feeling and one idea within the members of the nation.'[15]

The claim to be a homogenous society with an overarching character also led to a complicating factor that was not addressed sufficiently. This pertained to minority groups within states. Scholars have sought to identify different types of minorities that had or could have had an impact on national identity: minorities that are religious, ethnic or national and within them those that are sectarian, political and 'majoritarian'.[16]

Jamal Abdul Nasser and Michel Aflaq articulated the two principal versions of Pan Arabism; the first, centred on Nasser's charismatic personality in the most important country of the region and premised on his 'Three Circles', ended with Egypt's defeat in the Six Day War of 1967 while the second, more comprehensively articulated in the Constitution of the Arab Ba'th Party and its pledge for freedom of speech and assembly and a constitutional parliamentary regime, survived longer in its two mutually irreconcilable versions in Iraq and Syria. In each case, the rhetoric did not resolve the internal contradictions of the argument and did not match the capacity to deliver.[17]

Two instances of heart-wrenching introspection seeped deep into the psyche of the public and the intelligentsia. They contributed expressions to the vocabulary of modern Arabic—*al nakba* (the catastrophe) for 1948 and *al-hazima* (the rout) for 1967; the latter in particular generated serious analysis of Arab society. Its critique of Arabism focused on its social base—urban elites, merchants and army officers. Prominent among critics were the Syrian philosopher Jalal al-Azm and the poets Ali Ahmad Said 'Adonis' and Nizar Qabbani. In keeping with age-old tradition, poetry remains a powerful stimulant to sentiments and it has been observed that 'the loss of Palestine formed the tragic reality that determined the climate within which

Arabic poetry has developed since the late forties. The poetry of the last three decades has embodied the frustration, bitterness and despair eating at the heart of the Arab poets in these years'.[18]

Further afield, the Moroccan historian Abdallah Laroui described Arab society as 'living in infra-historical rhythm'. He cited with approval Syrian historian Constantin Zurayq reproach that the Arab nationalist attitude was romantic and lost in the past.[19]

Thus, the intellectual edifice of secular nationalism and modernity, called a 'dream palace' by Fuad Ajami, was seen to develop structural cracks and failed to sustain itself: 'After 1967, there was a widespread sentiment that unity was no longer the issue.'[20] A final blow to it was administered by the 1990–1991 Gulf War.

Three principal themes dominated the functioning of the Arab state system in the last eight decades of the 20th century. These pertained to (a) internal integration, (b) relations with West in its various manifestations, and (c) confronting Zionism and Israel. In actual practice, the imperatives of the first, and the pressures of the second, ensured that the third only retained a nominal, ritualistic presence.

The perception that the national took precedence over the pan-Arab and that Arab unity did not necessitate a union was emphatically articulated by an Arab leader in September 1982:

> Arab unity can only take place after a clear demarcation of borders between all countries… The question of linking unity to the removal of boundaries is no longer acceptable to present Arab mentality… We must see the world as it is… The Arab reality is that the Arabs are now twenty-two states, and we have to behave accordingly… Unity must give strength to its partners, not cancel their national identity.[21]

Despite the commonality of language, culture and to, a considerable extent, religion, the national positions of individual Arab states in regard to relations with the West were portrayed vividly in developments relating to the Baghdad Pact in 1955, the Suez crisis of 1956, the formation of the United Arab Republic in 1958, the Arab Summit of 1964, the resulting trauma of the Six Day War of 1967, the Camp David Accord of 1979, Iraq's invasion of Kuwait in 1990 and the U.S. led invasion of Iraq in 2003. In each of these, the curse of centrality in geopolitical terms was evident; in each, it was compounded by the geopolitics of oil and the imperatives of the Cold War. Most of the time it was a relationship between a centre of power and domination on the one side and a dependent and subordinate periphery on the other; it was described by the academic Hisham Sharabi as 'the outcome of modern Europe's colonization of the patriarchal Arab world, of the marriage of imperialism and patriarchy'.[22] This sustained the status quo and impeded or prevented normal political and social evolution. Much the same was said a few decades earlier (from a friendlier perspective and without the foresight of later happenings) by the Lebanese scholar and diplomatist Charles Malik who accused the West, in its dealing with the region, of a lack of responsibility, sincerity and understanding of the deeper issues at stake, apart from 'immense racial arrogance'.[23]

The dominance of tradition was evident in the slow pace of social progress. In 1928, a Lebanese lady had written about the four veils of cloth, ignorance, hypocrisy and stagnation that hampered the progress of women; 75 years later, in 2002 and 2003, the UNDP's Arab Human Development Reports still spoke of deficits of knowledge, freedom and women's empowerment as principal challenges to progress in the region. Despite the urging of the Alexandria Declaration of March 2004, freedom as a catchword was sidestepped by the political establishments in their civil or military incarnations and did not translate into more open political structures. The failure on this count left these societies entrapped in non-participatory structures of governance. These became pervasive and were evident even in societies that opted for democratic forms, if not substance, of governance in the post-2003 period. None indulged in democratic institution-building. An immediate consequence was a non-inclusive approach, and practice, of nationalism.

Alongside, and as a consequence, the erosion of the legitimacy of the secular nation-state brought forth various versions of Islamist solutions as viable alternatives. It represented to its proponents the only means of expressing popular opposition to regimes regarded as incapable of delivering wider political participation. It considered Arabism as 'a mere stage' for Islamism without a contradiction between the two.[24] It premised itself on a universally applicable principle, but restricted it to local application. It professed foundational authenticity, but in actual practice did not produce sufficient clarity on a model of governance for a nation state. The resulting dilemma was anticipated many years back by the Tunisian Islamist Rachid Al-Ghannouchi; he observed that 'a democratic secular system of government is less evil than a despotic system of government that claims to be Islamic'.[25] This pragmatic approach led him to assert, after more recent happenings in Tunisia, that 'a political transition is no time to govern with a relative majority of 51%. It is a time for consensus... Power must be shared out to prevent a putsch, to defuse any idea of despotism and backtracking'.[26]

Another, more radical, Islamist perspective has come forth from Tariq Ramadan. He depicts the Arab societies as 'rushing headlong into blind alleys' and suggests that 'the Arab world and Muslim majority societies not only need political uprisings; they need a thoroughgoing intellectual revolution that will open the door to economic change, and to spiritual religious, cultural and artistic liberation—and to the empowerment of women. What is needed is a global approach. Nothing is served by focusing on political and structural upheavals at the expense of the other, more vital matters.'[27]

A number of questions arise from the foregoing. The early advocates of Arab nationalism set out on a high note focused on cultural renaissance. In that period, their demands did not go further than the call for local and cultural autonomy within the confines of Ottoman Empire. Beyond that:

- Did the creation of nation-states from the body of a wider conglomerate induce in them sufficient sense of national identity and purpose?
- Was this perception adequately inclusive or essentially exclusive?
- Did it identify or develop an image of the *other* in relation to whom awareness of a set of socio-economic and political objectives could be inculcated and pursued as realizable targets?
- To what extent did external intervention in the region, so consistently supportive of authoritarian modes of governance, impede the acquisition of knowledge and freedom?

With the exception of Egypt, the primary and primordial identity of the Arab lands of the Ottoman Empire was essentially tribal, with some regional attributes. The regions in question were administrative units of the empire. As independent entities, no organic changes were brought about in their internal tribal structures; instead, the tribal hierarchies were integrated in the new political structures that, despite protestations to the contrary, ended up being authoritarian. This deprived them of a mass base and genuine public participation through political institutions. Aspects of this deficiency were reflected in the UNDP's second Arab Development Challenges Report 2011, which urged the need for 'a new social contract of mutual accountability (in which) the state becomes more responsive and accountable to the citizen'.[28]

The link between the citizen and the state through the mechanism of accountability (and an implicit social contract going beyond the ruler–subject relationship) is thus critical and has not been sufficiently in evidence. An analysis of the states of West Asia some years back identified among its characteristics the politics of limited association and of an essentially broad urban middle-class base, in which coercion or co-option into the state structure rather than in a 'durable resilience of the system whose legitimacy is based on the full participation of the people in the body politic'.[29] No qualitative change in this has happened (except in Tunisia), despite the turbulence in some Arab societies in recent years. As a result, the required transformation of nationalism from a political movement into a mass ideology has not taken place. Instead, there has been a propensity at times to promote or aggravate social or sectarian divisions for political gains and thereby deprive state institutions of their autonomy and national character.[30]

This deficit in traits of Arab nationalism in its national manifestations is in contrast to the characteristics of nationalism as it unfolded in some other Asian countries like India, China and Indonesia. The essential ingredient in each was mass participation and an identifiable 'other' at whom the national movement could focus its grievances. In India, in the words of the late Professor Bipan Chandra, it was 'basically the result of a fundamental contradiction between the interests of the Indian people and of British colonialism', was a 'popular, multiclass movement' that underwent 'constant ideological transformation', and 'was able to tap the diverse energies, talents and capabilities of a very large variety of people'.[31] It was supplemented and strengthened by local and regional movements of protest.[32] The legal framework put into place in the post-independence period sanctified it.

The same was also broadly true of China in its struggle against Japanese imperialism and of Indonesia's struggle against the Dutch occupation.

One last word about certain other traits of nationalism that became clearer in the 20th century. The anti-colonial and anti-imperialist phase of nationalism was one aspect of individual movements; another was the content of their strategies of governance. It was here that the ideological edges became evident. It has been argued that nationalism was amongst the transcendental fictions of the twentieth century[33], in which nationalistic self-identification was considered superior to others; also that 'appeals to our tribal instincts, to passion and to prejudice, and to our nostalgic desire to be relieved from the strains of individual responsibility which it attempts to replace by a collective or group responsibility.'[34] One particularly unedifying version was 'cultural nationalism' preaching 'authoritarian uniformity of state and faith' and fostering xenophobia.[35] Nationalism has also been viewed as 'a deeply divisive force, if it is not tempered by the spirit of tolerance and compromise or the humanitarian universalism of a non-political religion. Its stress on national sovereignty and cultural distinctiveness hardly helps to promote cooperation among people at the very same time when for technological and economic reasons they grow more and more interdependent'.[36] In many instances, militant nationalism became a reflex of despair resulting from economic failures and of unrealized aspirations along with a motivation to resurrect an imaginary past devoid of these shortcomings. From this, slippage into a religio-cultural form of strident nationalism has been found to be easy.

As against this authoritarian or cultural form, an alternate approach is that of pluralist or liberal nationalism that 'celebrates the particularity of culture together with universality of human rights, the social and cultural embedded-ness of individuals together with their personal autonomy. In this sense it differs radically from organic interpretations of nationalism, which assume that the identity of individuals is totally constituted by their national membership'.[37] Its emphasis on plurality eschews assimilation and celebrates diversity. It is multicultural in essence and aspires 'towards a form of citizenship that is marked neither by a universalism generated by complete homogenisation, nor by particularism of self-identical and closed communities.'[38] In the historically altered context of contemporary India, the thrust of this pluralist nationalism is also on the need to 'readjust state institutions to meet demands of inclusion of marginalised and disadvantaged political groups'.[39]

This, in fact, has been the Indian approach. It is premised on the ground reality of a plural society that is multiethnic, multi-religious and multilingual, a secular polity rather than a religious one, and a democratic state structure functioning on the basis of Rule of Law. Each of these ingredients constitute the core values of the Constitution; none can be abridged or abandoned without damaging the constitutional structure and endangering social harmony; nor can another set of values be grafted on the richness of Indian diversity without impinging on its uniqueness. Citizens know that Article 51 of our Constitution enjoins amongst Fundamental Duties the preservation of the heritage of composite culture. This, as Professor Upendra Baxi pointed out many years back, is a *'fundamental* obligation'.[40]

Abul Kalam Azad was a passionate believer in this diversity and the pluralist and liberal nationalism emanating from it. His approach was premised on an openness of mind, tolerant and accommodative. It found expression in a Persian couplet recited by him in one of his early speeches.[41]

Tafawut ast ma'ani shanidan man-o tu
Tu bastan-e-dar, o man fateh-bab mi shawam

What you and I hear is different. You hear the sound
Of closing doors but I of doors that open

40
RELEVANCE OF INTERNATIONAL LAW

THE RELEVANCE OF INTERNATIONAL LAW in today's rapidly changing world, and the new challenges we have to collectively address, is a good subject for serious cogitation. International Law as it is now understood and practised is of relatively recent origin. It owes its origin primarily to the Westphalian World Order forged in Europe in the 17th century. Its beginnings, modest and limited, coincide with the rise of nation states in Europe, bore its stamp and focused on common values and the reciprocity of interests.

The principles of sovereignty and legal equality of states were first enunciated by the Dutch jurist Hugo Grotius in 1625. The principles of sanctity of agreements entered into, as also the saving conditionality allowing non-compliance, lent balance to the commitments entered into by nation states.

The two World Wars presented fresh challenges to the principles and practices of international law. These related to rectification of boundaries, care of refugees and administration of the territory of the defeated enemy. Efforts to address these and related issues through the creation of the League of Nations were unsuccessful. This failure, and the horrors of World War II, led to appreciation of the necessity of international cooperation and the formation of the United Nations as a body capable of ensuring obedience to international law and maintaining peace. The Preamble of the UN Charter assert this as one of the objectives: 'to establish conditions under which justice and respect for obligations arising from treaties and other sources of international law can be maintained'.

Note: Speech delivered at the inauguration of the World Congress on International Law at Vigyan Bhawan, 9 January 2015, New Delhi.

The period since 1945 has been highly productive in regard to the growth and evolution of international law. International cooperation was widely accepted, though not universally. The first few decades in particular gave cause for optimism.

The UN assisted the process of decolonization and the effort to end Apartheid. The UN Multilateral system contributed to the enunciation of normative principles to regulate international conduct. Questions such as disarmament, social development, gender equality, population, food and water, and a host of problems relevant for the developing world were addressed. Common trans-national services related to civil aviation, maritime regulations, health, telecommunications, postal systems, refugees, world weather and food security were put in place.

193 nations are now members of the UN and subscribe to its Charter. The ambit of rules of international law has widened and includes intergovernmental organizations, corporations, non-governmental organizations as well as individuals.

The founding fathers of India's Constitution accepted these broad principles and incorporated them in the Directive Principles of State Policy. Pursuant to this, the state shall foster respect for international law and treaty obligations of organized people with one another.

The United Nation has its limitations. It is a voluntary association of sovereign nation states. These states have their own aspirations and had sought membership of the UN in their perceived self-interest.

For this reason, some parts of international law remain highly contested. These relate to the laws of warfare, to the concept of state sovereignty, and to a full range of self-serving interests of the powerful who wish to use international law to further their political, economic and security interests. A case in point is the Charter of the International Court of Justice and its 'Optional' clause.

Within the ambit of Public International Law, institutions and organizations have been used to impose unequal treaties and evolve concepts that have encouraged curtailment of sovereignty (Right to Protect), seek intrusive presence within sovereign states (Peace Keeping and Peace Building). Conflicts of laws in civil law jurisdictions, which constitutes Private International Law, seeks to address disputes between business corporations outside a unified legal framework. This has led to increasing use of commercial arbitration (under the New York Convention 1958).

There is also the growing application of Supra-National law to address global commons and such international issues relating to new technologies, evolutions in genetic sciences and problems presented by pandemics and catastrophic disaster events.

Globalization has not only increased the importance of international law but also the complexity of international legal issues. International law has grown to encompass a wide variety of fields including the prohibition of the use of force; human rights; protection of individuals during wars and armed conflicts; fight against terrorism, trafficking in drugs and other serious crimes; environment; trade and development; telecommunication; and transport.

The power structure of the organization created in 1945 clearly reflected the power realities of the world after the World War II. It was dominated by the victors of the War, who fashioned its modalities to further and facilitate the pursuit of power in political and economic terms.

Much has changed in the world since then, but the underlying realities of the power lesson remain true. If anything, the intervening years have eroded the effectiveness of the UN and its institutions, and the need for reforms has never been more urgent. The world has changed, new power realities have emerged, several new regional and trans-regional groupings have come into being, but the United Nation remains largely unaltered.

The need for reforms is widely recognized and several halting efforts have been made to change methods of work, procedures, financing arrangements, delivery mechanisms and accountability criteria, but the outcomes have been less than satisfactory. What is required is structural and systemic reforms, and that has still to happen.

There is a growing perception that there has been a decline in multilateralism. Developed countries have begun to look upon the UN and its functioning in terms of their own priorities and objectives. The UN's Charter functions in the area of money, finance, trade, expenditure, indebtedness and developmental strategies have been transferred to IMF (International Monetary Fund), World Bank and WTO (World Trade Organization). In these bodies the major economic powers, because of their voting power or the power of retaliation (WTO), have come to dominate the decision-making in these vital areas.

In the area of development, the focus is on the economic and social problems of developing countries and their internal governance issues. Here too, in the name of globalization, the thrust is on the open market, foreign investment, lowering tariffs and reducing the role of the state.

The UN's method of functioning has also changed from being a negotiating forum on hard economic issues, where substantive, legally bidding commitments were undertaken, it has increasingly become a forum for the exchange of views and where experts are invited to conduct dialogues and analyse global economic and social trends.

Another important and, in some ways, a game changing development relates to the funding of the UN. The UN finds itself starved of adequate and predictable funding. Dues have been withheld, budgetary restrictions have been imposed and assessed contributions today account for a small percentage of the total expenditure of the UN. The proportion of voluntary funding has grown dramatically and today provides a high percentage of the total. This feature has been effectively used by the major powers to impose their own priorities on the UN, by dominating its budgeting, accounting and administrative apparatus. This has resulted in the dilution of the UN's regulatory and norm-setting activities.

Although international laws and the institutions created to further its influence and application have grown significantly over the last six decades, International Law is at a crossroads and needs new direction. Its ambit has grown from interstate relations to individual rights and now covers civil society and corporations apart from state conduct. It extends to the Global Commons and attempts to address new challenges being posed by new technologies, non-state actors, unhindered information and financial flows. While it is trying to cope with transnational concerns relating to pandemics, narcotics, illegal trafficking in human beings and arms, it cannot escape addressing some fundamental issues. A few of these need to be mentioned here:

1. The nature of the state is being called into question. Today, several parts of the world are engulfed by crises of identity, political control and stability. The nation-state system is under strain, prompted by geo-political, short-term strategic compulsions and radicalized non-state actors. Colonial geographies have begun to dismantle. Military interventions in established nation states have led to instability and to the growth of sectarian and ethnic discord. Non-state actors, of different ideological persuasions, have violated borders and sovereignty at will. Some of these transgressions have received support from other powers and nation states.
2. There is a contradiction at the heart of globalization. The international economic system is becoming global, while the political structure of

the world is still based on the nation state. Goods and capital seek to flow unhindered across national boundaries. Individual nation states resist global pressures in seeking to protect their national interests. Economic globalization in its essence, as Henry Kissinger has put it, 'ignores national frontiers. International policy emphasizes the importance of frontiers, even as it seeks to reconcile conflicting national aims'.[1]

3. Values and state structures, Western in origin and proclaimed as having universal validity, are increasingly being questioned. Concepts such as democracy, human rights and international law are subject to divergent interpretations. In the absence of a consensus and a mechanism for enforcement, international law is increasingly proving ineffective.

4. The logical consequence of the promotion of democracy as a universal value necessitates its induction in the governing structures of the international system. 'A theory of legitimate power,' in the words of the political scientist David Held, 'is inescapably a theory of democracy in the interlocking processes and structures of the global system.'[2] Reforms aimed at bringing this about are essential to rejuvenate confidence in the international system, accommodate the polarities and induce movement towards a more stable world order.

Here then is the challenge to International Law and the organizations that are responsible for its implementation.

41
SOME THOUGHTS ON THE SACRED AND SECULAR IN INTERNATIONAL RELATIONS

MY CURIOSITY HAS ALWAYS DWELLED on themes secreted in the interstices of perceptions that induce state action. One of these pertains to the presence or absence of sacred and secular impulses in the enunciation of state policy and state action.

We know that each age and most societies developed and practiced their world view as part of the apparatus of governance and the achievement of the objectives of their national interest. In pursuit of this, legitimacy and empowerment was often sought from ideals considered fundamental by the society concerned. Some of these were premised on philosophical ideals, others implicitly or expressly on religious ones. Each, as Edward Gibbon put it in relation to ancient Rome, was 'useful' to the ruling establishment.

The first half of the 20th century witnessed a general secularization of the political discourse in most parts of the world. There were, nevertheless, notable exceptions. In the forties, states were founded, based on self-validating 'mythistory', overtly on religious foundations and for specific faiths. More recently, political movements premised on specific objectives or grievances of socio-political nature, have empowered themselves by this methodology and are threatening the foundations of the modern state system.

For this reason, a study of international relations also necessitates the location, if any, of the overlap and interaction between politics and religion. Instances abound in history. It has assumed a higher profile in recent times and is of contemporary relevance. In 1968, the sociologist Peter Berger wrote

---

Note: Speech delivered at the Annual International Studies Convention organized by the School of International Studies, 23 March 2015, New Delhi.

that modernization necessarily leads to a decline in religion in societies and individuals. In 1996, he felt this preposition to be false and said that, 'the world today is massively religious', and that 'there is no reason to think that the world of the twenty first century will be any less religious than the world is today'.[1] He added that although modernization may have some secularizing effects in some areas, it has also given rise to counter-secularization and that some old and new religious beliefs continue to live in individuals and that religiously identified institutions do motivate socially and politically.

Some readers may recall the monumental five-volume *Fundamentalism Project* of the American Academy of Arts and Sciences, initiated in 1987 and concluded in the mid-nineties, and the light it shed on fundamentalist movements in different religions of the world and their political fallout and impact on international relations.

These conclusions reflect emerging trends in societies of different faiths the world over. Some studies have opined that the 21st century would be the 'God's Century'.

In one of his more recently published works, Henry Kissinger has concluded that 'in our time the quest for world order will require relating to perceptions of societies whose realities have largely been self-contained'. His reference clearly is to the non-Western world and it is there that questions, even turmoil, relating to political legitimacy have of late assumed disturbing dimensions. Some though not all of these questions pertain to secularized state action and interstate relations based on professed universal values and principles enunciated or reiterated in the second half of the 20th century, principally through the United Nations system.

As a result, it has become increasingly clear that the hitherto universally accepted norms are being side-stepped, disowned, or not adhered to, by groups whose identity politics based on 'an amalgam of slogans and emotions', and deriving sustenance from the failure of political and developmental models, gives them sufficient staying power to disrupt, even destroy existing structures. Instead, they disown modernity and are selective in their espousal of democracy. They premise this on adherence to an ideal past, directly or otherwise based on their understanding of religious or religio-cultural principles and practices. An evident consequence is a de-secularization of political discourse; one result of this has been considerably enhanced levels of faith-based conflicts in different regions.

Religion in statecraft has been used for different purposes and objectives:

as an instrument of regime legitimacy, for justifying the status quo in terms of policies and postures, for a politically mobilizing role to articulate dissent. We thus come across instances of religiously relevant or religiously conditioned political action as also of politically relevant or politically conditioned religious action. Each has an impact on the circle of inclusion or exclusion.

In this perspective, a number of questions do arise. Since religious precepts having a societal impact are being used in politics by state and sub-state actors for the formulation or advocacy of state policies, what is the nature of these policies? Do they impinge on or violate constitutional, bilateral or multilateral commitments of the state? Does religion have, in any sense, a role in international relations? Is it similar to the ideological battles that characterized the world in the Cold War period? If so, what are its implications for interstate relations generally, and for regional or global stability specifically?

Answers to these appear to be in the affirmative. States and sub-state actors professing a religion-based ideology do tend to read it with varying intensity in both domestic and external policy perceptions and practices. Such projections are increasingly at variance with the accepted norms of international conduct. Local, regional and global considerations do lead to situations in which such policies are viewed as a source of tension.

What are the implications of this pattern of behaviour? It evidently replaces universal norms by particular ones. It introduces atavistic elements of varying intensity in the political discourse, sows seeds of hostility based on them, and impedes a cooperative approach 'to practice tolerance and live together in peace'. It is a violation, in word and deed, of the Charter of the United Nations and all the universal compacts and declarations emanating from it. Thus, it is a challenge to all those who live in, and want to continue living in, secular societies. On the other hand, it may be, and has been so, argued that a state may subscribe to universal norms of the international society and yet remain riveted to non-secular norms in its domestic politics. This cannot but induce latent or actual conflict of values and principles. Instances of these can be located in contemporary international practice.

Is a way out in the offing? It would depend on the ability to re-conceptualize the framework to incorporate the diversity and interdependence of contemporary societies in a cosmopolitan culture, embracing both common ideas and values. Until that comes about 'it is better', as Headley Bull put it, 'to recognize that we are in darkness than to pretend that we can see the light'.[2]

If an answer is not available in the traditional framework of IR (International Relations) theory, there is perhaps a case for looking beyond it in the social framework of members of the international community.

Secularism is a modality, not a dogma. Historically speaking, the term surfaced in the middle of the 19th century when the British publicist George Holyoake expressed it to describe his view of promoting a social order separate from religion without actively dismissing or criticizing religious belief. Since then, different societies have developed their own versions of it in theory and practice. Some of these in the Western world premised on homogenous, single-religion, citizen bodies are today facing challenges from emigrant communities of other faiths; as a result, 'this new multi-religiosity is threatening to throw western secularism into turmoil'.

It is here that the distinctive feature of the Indian approach to secularism needs to be explored for an alternate model. It does not, as Rajeev Bhargava pointed out, 'erect a strict wall of separation' between religion and state but, instead, proposes 'a principled distance' between them. It is premised on religious liberty and equality of free citizenship and is a complex, multi-value doctrine. Furthermore, and because it took shape in a deeply multi-religious society, it 'attends simultaneously to issues of intra-religious oppression and inter-religious domination'. It does not, must not, give official status to any religion or accept its hegemonic position. Instead, 'it is an ethically sensitive negotiated settlement between diverse groups and divergent values'. It is in consonance with Article 18 of the Universal Declaration of Human Rights of 1948, which stipulates that 'everyone has the right to freedom of thought, conscience and religion; this right includes freedom to change his religion or belief, and freedom, either alone or in community with others and in public or private, to manifest his religion or belief in teaching, practice, worship and observance'.[3]

Such a frame of reference, in actual implementation, would enable a society to participate in and address meaningfully the global values to which we have subscribed to in our times. It would seek to lessen the contradiction between technological globalization and 'tribalization' of the mind.

Some pitfalls in the path of such an ideal approach are identifiable. They emanate from gaps, purposeful or otherwise, between commitment and practice. At times, commitment is sought to be cushioned by clinging to the past and its aphorisms expressed in a different context; at others, public perceptions or prejudices are manipulated to put forth a mix of religion and politics in the name of strident nationalism. Both detract from, or subvert, secular values. A truly modern approach should eschew both and go beyond mere tolerance and religio-philosophical notions to positive acceptance and accommodation on the basis of equal citizenship in actual practise.

Admittedly, such an adjustment would be difficult; but so were earlier conceptual correctives in history. Mercifully, the human mind is conditioned to adapt. An eminent scholar had observed many years back that to fight the pessimism of the intellect, one must hold fast to the optimism of the will.

The present may be one of those occasions!

42
COLLECTIVE SECURITY IN THE PERSIAN GULF: AN INDIAN PERSPECTIVE

A FIRST READING OF THE general theme is somewhat confusing since, geographically-speaking, there are several 'Gulfs' to the west of India—Gulf of Aden, Gulf of Oman and Persian Gulf. Mercifully, the doubt is dispelled on closer reading! The terminological clarification given by the UN Secretariat in 1999 is somewhat helpful.[1]

The sub-themes for participants cover subjects of perennial relevance to governments, strategists, energy supply and world trade specialists, and the general public.

This chapter aims to address some aspects of the security scenario since it provides an overarching perspective to all political, economic and social activities. The context is relevant. The Persian Gulf is a body of water 989 kilometres in length and 55 kilometres in width at its narrowest point. Ever since the British withdrawal from the area in November 1970, the question of the security of the sea lanes for the flow of hydrocarbon supplies to different destinations in the world has been on the strategic and tactical agenda of the beneficiaries of these supplies. For this reason, as noted by a Saudi scholar many years back, 'Gulf regional security was an external issue long before it was an issue among the Gulf states themselves'.[2]

The centrality of the region to global supplies of hydrocarbon energy (holding 54 per cent of the world's oil reserves and 23 per cent of its gas reserves), and to its relevance as an important destination of exports from major trading nations, is evident. Thus peace, stability and security in the area

---

Note: Speech delivered at the International Relations Conference, 10 October 2015, Pune.

are critical to global security and prosperity. This establishes a convergence of local, regional and global interests.

Consequently, some questions critical to any discussion of peace and security in the region need to be addressed:

- What is the threat perception of individual countries of the littoral?
- Is it internal, or external, or both? Is there a convergence in some of these?
- Is the perceived external threat from within the region or is it extra-regional?
- Is it physical or ideological, traditional or non-traditional?
- Do extra-regional powers have an interest in disrupting peace and security in the area?

In politico-strategic terms, the eight countries of the Persian Gulf littoral are to be considered in three categories: (i) the six members of the Gulf Cooperation Council, (ii) Iran and (iii) Iraq. The political systems and ideological orientations of the six GCC states do not converge with that of either Iran or Iraq. An obvious consequence is a predilection for exclusive, rather than inclusive, security.

An early effort to make the littoral states themselves shoulder the responsibility of peace and security in the area, made in the Muscat Conference convened by Oman in November 1975,[3] was not fruitful on account of the conflicting perceptions of these states. The latter were aggravated following the Iranian Revolution of 1979 and the outbreak of the Iraq-Iran War.

In January 1980, in the context of Cold War and regional considerations, the Carter Doctrine was promulgated asserting that 'any attempt by an outside force to gain control of the Persian Gulf region will be regarded as an assault on the vital interests of the United Sates of America and such an assault will be repelled by any means necessary, including military force'. It was reiterated later in the year after the outbreak of the Iraq-Iran War: 'It is imperative that there be no infringement of…freedom of passage of ships to and from the Persian Gulf region'.[4] This approach was sustained through the period of the Iraq–Iran War though Iraqi attempts to disrupt the outflow of Iranian crude did invite blunt warnings by Rafsanjani in October 1983 and May 1984. 'We would close the Straits of Hormuz,' he said, 'if the Persian Gulf becomes unusable for us. And if the Persian Gulf becomes unusable for us, we will make the Persian Gulf unusable for others.'[5]

The formation of the GCC in 1981 and subsequent efforts to explore GCC-focused collective security arrangements alongside bilateral ones with external powers made limited progress in the 1990s. Iran, on its part, proposed in 1994 the establishment of a forum to discuss threat perceptions and security concerns amongst the littoral states; this was followed in 1995 by the suggestion of a non-aggression pact amongst them.[6]

In the past two decades a number of efforts, principally focused on the GCC, have been made to address security challenges of the region. These tend to suggest that 'a return to the *status quo ante* (e.g., the old realpolitik balance-of-power approach which depends on the US to guarantee regional stability) is no longer workable and that in order to overcome regional challenges, cooperation is needed ...(and that) most parties suggest that any new security agenda should be more inclusive (and) address not only military aspects of security, but also issues such as regional economic development, counter-terrorism, disaster response, and environmental, social and cultural topics as well. In addition, a more cooperative approach to interstate relations as a basis for a new security architecture is called for, as this is essential to an understanding of security that leaves behind zero-sum calculations of national security'.[7] More specifically, it has been suggested that 'what the Gulf needs is a series of overlapping and bilateral relationships' on the model of ASEAN (Association of Southeast Asian Nations) Regional Forum (ARF).[8]

In December 2004, Saudi Foreign Minister Saud Al Faisal drew attention to 'an urgent need for a collective effort aimed at developing a new and more solid framework for Gulf security', having a national, a regional and an international component. The national component, he said, involves 'the urgent need for comprehensive reforms in our countries with some variation in the speed of implementation depending on the individual social conditions'. The regional framework 'should be based on four pillars: the GCC, Yemen, Iran and Iraq' and the international aspect of it should involve international guarantees, underwritten by the Security Council, for the sovereignty, independence and territorial integrity of all the littoral states. 'The international component of the suggested Gulf security framework should engage positively the emerging Asian powers as well, especially China and India'.[9]

An evolution in the perception of the littoral states of the Persian Gulf is thus evident notwithstanding publicly stated disagreements, laced with atavistic premonitions, on hardcore security and foreign policy issues. A promising development has been the resolution of the Iranian nuclear question through the Iran–P5+1 Joint Comprehensive Plan of Action (JCPOA) of 2 April 2015 and the carefully worded welcome accorded to it in the US–GCC statement of May 14 and the US–Saudi statement of 4 September 2015. Also to be noted is Qatar's recent offer of hosting a GCC–Iran dialogue to address existing disputes that are 'political, regional Arab-Iranian difference rather than being a Sunni-Shiite dispute'.[10]

In this changing context, the framework proposed earlier could become the basis of discussions on comprehensive, inclusive, security. To give shape to it, threat perceptions would need to converge, beginning with an enunciation of *common threats* on non-political matters like natural or man-made disasters, response to pandemics and environmental challenges that transcend borders, counter-terrorism, drugs smuggling and related matters.

Once the foundations of a sustainable dialogue on these matters has been established, and progress made in search of acceptable responses, a more inclusive security dialogue could be initiated to identify shared interests and put in place understandings and procedures to respond to threats to peace and security. Doubts and misgivings are nevertheless likely to persist since, as the old proverb puts it, 'the wound of words is worse than the wound of swords'.

A critical impediment to any cooperative security arrangement to be entered into by the littoral states relates to the presence of foreign forces. The position of the United States, spelt out in some detail in the Senate Foreign Relations Committee Report of June 19, 2012, has been reiterated in the recent announcements made with the GCC states. Iran, on the other hand, has hitherto stressed that the region 'be free of trans-regional powers'. This impediment can only be overcome if the circle is widened and a future arrangement is premised on the participation of principal users and beneficiaries, underwritten by an international agreement or convention.

How does the foregoing impact on India and Indian interests? Some prepositions with regard to these are self-evident:

- Locating the Persian Gulf, with reference to India, is an exercise in geography *and* history. For India, the Persian Gulf littoral is proximate neighbourhood and part of our natural economic hinterland. The distance from Mumbai to Basra is 1847 nautical miles; it is 1802 to Kuwait, 1630 to Dammam, 1265 to Bander Abbas and 1046 to Dubai.
- Even before the advent of the modern age and modern means of communication, there was a vibrant trade between the west coast of

India and different points on the Persian Gulf littoral. This association generated and nurtured people-to-people contacts cherished on all sides. A good number of proverbs complementary to India are to be found in the colloquial Arabic of the lower Gulf.
- These ties were sustained in the colonial period when command of the sea ensured the supremacy of British power.
- The governments and public opinion in the littoral states are India-friendly and Indian-friendly.
- India today receives 65 per cent of its energy supplies from this region, has an overall trade of 163 billion US dollars, and a work force there of about 8 million whose remittances amounted to 35 billion US dollars in 2014–2015.
- Around 170,000 Indian pilgrims go to Saudi Arabia every year for the Haj pilgrimage.

In addition, India and GCC states have initiated important steps to engage with each other politically and strategically in a more rigorous manner, particularly in regard to combating terrorism and extremism, supply of narcotics and drugs and movement of criminal elements. There is also a growing interest in initiating and strengthening defence ties and the first steps in this regard have been taken with Qatar, Oman, Saudi Arabia and the UAE.

The GCC states look at India as a vibrant economy that could be a good destination for investments, as is evident from the India–UAE statement of 17 August 2015, and the earlier Delhi and Riyadh Declarations with Saudi Arabia. They view India as an important player on the global scene, as a large and growing market for their principal export commodity, and as a possible provider of food security and trade partner.

Iraq remains an important source of crude and has the potential for wider economic cooperation under normal conditions.

The Indian interest in a multidimensional—strategic and economic—relationship with Iran, highlighted after President Khatemi's visit in 2003, remained subdued until very recently on account of third-country considerations. The current impetus to rejuvenate these is promising.

For all these reasons, India has a vital stake in peace and stability in this sub-region and in the security of the sea lanes connecting it to the outside world. The Indian requirement is thus fivefold: (a) friendly regimes and stability in the littoral states, (b) access to the region's oil and gas resources, (c) freedom of navigation in the Persian Gulf and through the Straits of Hormuz, (d) security of sea lanes and (e) continued access to the markets of the littoral states for Indian trade, technology, workforce and two-way investments.

A first requirement is to sustain and intensify the bilateral relationships with all the littoral states of the Gulf littoral. The question of domestic stability is squarely in the domain of domestic politics of individual states and suggestions of inputs into it should be eschewed. The other two would best be achievable in an inclusive security framework underwritten by the international community through an appropriate mechanism. Together, these would facilitate the furtherance of the fifth.

Pending this, and keeping eventualities in mind, prudence suggests the creation and reinforcement of an autonomous interdiction capacity geared to India's requirement of free movement of tankers from the Persian Gulf to India, eschew marginal roles in Western security arrangements for the Gulf, and lend support, in principle, to inclusive security arrangements for the future that may be proposed for discussion.

43

TURBULENCE IN WEST ASIAN STATE SYSTEMS: ROAD BLOCKS IN THE QUEST FOR PARTICIPATORY GOVERNANCE

PERIODS OF TURMOIL, AND UNEXPLAINED happenings, are often depicted as a spectre, an impending danger. Such a spectre today seems to haunt all who look at the region of western Asia and northern Africa. The apprehensions emanate from a dangerous mix of *realpolitik* and professed ideology that challenges the status quo in the region, and has become a threat to regional and world peace.

Two years back, the world observed the centenary of the First World War. It was described by a historian as 'the first calamity of the twentieth century, the calamity from which all other calamities sprang'. One dimension of it was the Sykes-Picot Agreement of May 1916 that, together with the San Rimo arrangement of April 1919, brought into existence most of the modern state system in West Asia. In 1945, it acquired its own sub-regional system in the shape of the Arab League.

It is this edifice, of post-World War I states and of newly-induced nationalisms that now seems to be unraveling.

Analysts of the future would record the years 1948, 1967, 2003 and 2010–2011 as turning points in the modern history of West Asian lands. The first inducted Israel into the region, the second and its aftermath put an end to political Arabism, the third marked the destruction of Iraq and

---

Note: Speech delivered at IInd West Asia Conference organized by IDSA, 19 January 2016, New Delhi.

its resulting immediate and remote consequences, and the fourth signaled the commencement of the so-called *Arab Spring* or Arab Turbulence that shook the authoritarian order.

The new states in the region (with the exception of Egypt) lacked historical legitimacy and needed to create a national sentiment to reinforce the existing tribal, often fragmented, ties of cohesion within their territorial jurisdiction. This local patriotism was sought to be combined with amorphous and romantic sentiments of pan-Arabism, some of which were reflected in the 1945 Charter of the Arab League. Neither could develop an ideological underpinning that would bring forth widespread public commitment except as a formality. This was furthered by the fragility of the institutions of the new states; these were patriarchal, authoritarian and hegemonic, and evoked fear of the state rather than a commitment to its objectives and ideals.

Thus, the domestic impulses for social cohesion were insufficiently anchored, did not accommodate diversity in sufficient measure, and were susceptible to external pressure. This found its reflection in all aspects of governance which remained essentially non-participatory.

The socio-economic backdrop too was not conducive to stability and social peace. Some years earlier, three successive UNDP Arab Human Development Reports highlighted the shortcomings of knowledge, freedom and gender. The Davos Economic Forum reports on Arab Competiveness put the focus on the implications of population growth and youth unemployment and on the need for education and skill development to bring about a shift away from total dependence on a rentier economy. Pervasive rural poverty aggravated the situation.

As a consequence of the erosion of the legitimacy of the broadly secular nation-state, and the ideological vacuum created by it, various versions of Islamist solutions were presented as indigenous, more authentic, and viable alternatives. Nor was this an altogether novel recipe since religion or religious symbolism as a motivating force have been used in many societies for different purposes throughout history. Sociologists have dwelt on it at some length and, making a distinction between different kinds of politics and different senses of religion, have sought to develop a typology to classify these into *politically relevant religious action, religiously conditioned political action, religiously relevant political action* and *politically conditioned religious action*.[1]

Apart from the use and misuse of this instrumentality currently underway by many extremist groups, a few examples from the recent past can be cited. In the wake of the Egyptian defeat in the 1967 war, a perception took root that 'the Arabs had turned away from God and God has turned away from them' and this induced the Government of Egypt to distribute in the armed forces booklets explaining the meaning of Jihad. A similar step was taken by Iraq after its defeat in the 1991 Kuwait war and was visibly reflected in the new Iraqi flag. This trend was reinforced in subsequent years preceding the 2003 US-led invasion. In both instances, the purpose was empowerment. In both, subsequent developments were to show the longer term consequences; credible reports indicate that the fighting and command component of the recently formed DAISH or the Islamic State has within its ranks many officers of the pre-2003 Iraqi army.

Away from the Arab world, the most telling example of religious motivation for a political purpose was the resistance movement crafted to resist the Soviet invasion of Afghanistan in 1979. The United States, several Arab states led by Saudi Arabia and Pakistan implemented this successfully, and in the process gave birth, first to Afghan Mujahideen, and subsequently to Al-Qaeda.[2]

These external happenings of the past left their mark on Arab societies. The process varied from country to country in response to a multiplicity of impulses; a common thread was the sense of distress and a quest for a psychological refuge. Thus came about a re-Islamization of Arab societies at the grassroot level that provided, or sought to provide, solace and an ideological underpinning. A good deal has been written about this process in different Muslim societies; it has ranged from anti-imperialist sentiments and socioeconomic concerns to a re-emphasis on family values and cultural authenticity, and has covered a broad spectrum ranging from traditional segments to the youth, professional classes and the academia.[3] The new channels of communication through the internet and social media furthered the momentum. The latter also had its limitations and was not uniformly productive; one scholar has called it 'cyber-utopianism'.[4]

Despite this backdrop of an emergent social reality, the Arab Turbulence of 2010-2011 was quintessentially a non-religious, secular phenomenon that took the shape of a leaderless mass movement seeking dignity, empowerment, political citizenship, social justice and taking back the state and its institutions from rulers and their cronies.[5] Its slogans, interestingly enough, did not resort to calls for Arab unity or advocate Islam as the solution. Its most dramatic impact was the abandonment of the fear of the security apparatus of the state. At the same time, it was not united or harmonious and soon gave way to sectional interests. Uncontrolled rage did not help matters. Prospects of chaos were exploited by the counter-revolutionary forces to prevail and impose even greater control.

Why did this happen?

As also referred to earlier in the book, in a famous passage in his monumental *History of the Russian Revolution,* Leon Trotsky had observed that 'the masses go into a revolution not with a prepared plan of social reconstruction, but with a sharp feeling that they cannot endure the old regime'. The political process thus unleashed, he added, results in a 'guiding organization' without which the energy of the masses dissipates.[6]

Record shows that in the case of the countries affected by the Arab Turbulence, the emergence of such a guiding organization happened belatedly and inadequately. There was no consensus on the political and economic model to be put in place. It was 'a tale of three battles rolled into one: people against regimes; people against people; regimes against other regimes.[7] The objectives of the protesting masses ranged from modest reforms and constitutional monarchy (as in Morocco and Jordan, and in a short-lived, muted, manner in Saudi Arabia) to overthrow of the head of state (Tunisia, Egypt and Libya) to a state order based on Islamic principles (Egypt under Morsi). The call for social justice did not, however, bring forth an implementable program of action. While left-leaning groups and unions wanted higher wages and a reversal of privatization, others sought more liberal policies. One observer noted that 'the political scene in the Arab Awakening is dominated by the sociopolitical forces of the middle classes looking for a new socio-political system, one that is more just and free' but added that 'there was no dominant political or organizational force'.[8]

It is relevant to recall that the Turbulence was not as a single event, but a catalyst for long-term change whose final outcome is yet to be seen. 'The main legacy of the Arab Spring is in smashing the myth of Arabs' political passivity and the perceived invincibility of arrogant ruling elites. Even in countries that avoided mass unrest, the governments took the quiescence of the people at their own peril.'[9]

Panic characterized the initial reaction of the traditional Arab establishments whose primary objective was to maintain the status quo. Domestically and across the GCC, 'an authoritarian retrenchment and narrowing of political space' emerged.[10] Some of the GCC states took steps focused on (a) containment of the revolts in Tunisia, Egypt and Libya, (b) bringing about a counter-revolution in Yemen and Bahrain, (c) supporting the revolution in Syria.[11] The French scholar Jean-Pierre Filiu has ascribed these to the work of the 'Deep State' conducting a 'systematic war of the Arab regimes against their people.'[12]

Some questions autimatically arise here. What were the principal characteristics of authoritarian systems that were challenged by the two years of Arab Turbulence? What were its immediate and longer-term consequences? Did it have a visible impact on patterns of governance? What are its regional and global implications?

According to most observers, the authoritarian order in West Asia and North Africa was and is characterized by lack of transparency, information scarcity, nepotism, political subservience, absence of a sense of equal citizenship, ambiguous accountability, political irresponsibility and absence of rule of law. The effort in many cases to seek legitimacy through ritualistic references to religious injunctions about rule through mutual consultations and requirement of obedience to 'those charged with authority among you'[13] did nothing to alter this harsh ground reality.

Those who protested against it sought the opposite of these attributes. The response pattern, with local variations, lent credence to Machiavelli's dictum that 'men forget more easily the death of their fathers than the loss of patrimony'. Voluntary abdication from seat of absolute power is a rarity in human affairs and did not happen in West Asian lands.

Three consequences emanated from this; they persist to this day. One was initial gestures of financial largesse to their public along with an immediate resort to 'increasingly harsh measures to restrict the freedoms of their citizens to express themselves and meaningfully to participate politically and hold power accountable'.[14] Another was a decision in some of the GCC states to give generous financial packages to the countries affected by the Turbulence. A third was to intensify their military involvement in the internal conflicts in Bahrain, Yemen, Syria and Libya. Details of these are in the public domain.

The continuing intensity of domestic controls has been commented upon by an observer: 'Counter-revolutionary Egypt, Saudi Arabia and Bahrain have rejected every pro-democracy demand raised in January 2011 and have implemented new decrees to ban popular demonstrations intended to celebrate the fifth anniversary of the uprisings.'[15]

A good part of the debate on Arab Turbulence, and official pronouncements from different quarters, has focused on alleged mischief emanating from the sectarian, Sunni–Shia, conflict. Its political origins in recent years can be traced to the geopolitical consequences of the invasion of Iraq in 2003 and to the reported 2004 pronouncement of the Jordanian monarch.[16] Some of the GCC states have been its proponents in recent years. According to one scholar, sectarianism became a pre-emptive counter-revolutionary strategy.[17] This, however, clouds rather than illuminates the complex realities of regional politics. A more realistic perspective on this was provided by the Amir of Qatar who, in his UN General Assembly speech on 28 September 2015, described the existing confrontation as 'political regional Arab-Iranian difference rather than being a Sunni-Shiite dispute'.

The Turbulence in Arab lands was not immune to regional and extra-regional inputs. Bahrain, Libya, Syria and Yemen were subjected to political and or material interventions from across national borders; some of these emanated from within the region, some from immediate or proximate neighbourhood, and some from great or big powers. The objective in each case was and is to prevent, retard or reverse the change sought by a visible majority of the public. Another lecture would be required to mention the litany of 'sins' of all sides. It would suffice here to say that regime change initiatives should be autonomous to the citizens of a state; record shows that externally imposed strategies, even if used as a complement to diplomacy and deterrence, are perennially in danger of going down the slippery slope.

The picture at the end of the year 2015 was one of total disarray, a situation in which regional and global powers together with empowered local groups are engaged in political and military action in half a dozen different battlefields. The immediate concern of each is to prevail upon its adversary; little thought, if any, is being given to longer term consequences for the societies in the region. In the process, the rationale for the Turbulence takes the back seat.

It has been said that the failure to understand catastrophes is even deadlier to people than the catastrophes themselves. The requirement to comprehend the prerequisites and essentials of participatory governance were perhaps not fully comprehended by the protesting public, nor did it have a full measure of the forces aligned against it. The need to combine rage with realism went unappreciated, except in the case of Al-Nahda in Tunisia, where the requirement of a wider consensus was appreciated.

With the exception of Egypt, the primary and primordial identity of the Arab lands of the Ottoman Empire was essentially tribal, with some regional attributes. As independent entities, no organic changes were brought about in their internal tribal structures; instead, the tribal hierarchies were integrated in the new political structures deliberately by domestic and external forces that, despite protestations to the contrary, ended up being authoritarian. This deprived them of a mass base and genuine public participation through political institutions. Aspects of this deficiency were reflected in the UNDP's second Arab Development Challenges Report 2011, which urged the need for 'a new social contract of mutual accountability (in which) the state becomes more responsive and accountable to the citizen.'[18]

The link between the citizen and the state through the mechanism of accountability (and an implicit social contract going beyond the ruler-subject relationship) is thus critical for domestic cohesion and internal security but has not been sufficiently in evidence. An analysis of the states of West Asia some years back identified among its characteristics the politics of limited association and of an essentially broad urban middle-class base in which coercion or co-option into the state structure rather than (in a) 'durable resilience of the system whose legitimacy is based on the full participation of the people in the body politic'.[19]

Decades earlier, the Moroccan historian Abdallah Laroui had spelt out the requirement: 'The democratic principle means that no one in society possesses political truth, that this truth will only gradually take shape through the procedures of discussion and successive elections.'[20]

The failure to imbibe and implement this in sufficient measure is thus central to the crises that have afflicted the region.

44
ACCOMMODATING DIVERSITY IN A GLOBALIZING WORLD: THE INDIAN EXPERIENCE

A TRAVELLER FROM A DISTANT land in *mashriq-al-aqsa* comes to *Maghrib-al Aqsa* and marvels at his good fortune. His sense of history quickly reminds him that centuries earlier a great name from this land had travelled to India and recorded in some detail his impressions about the governance, manner and customs of Indians. He attained high office and also had his share of minor misfortunes.

I refer, of course, to Sheikh Abdullah Muhammad ibn Abdullah ibn Muhammad ibn Ibrahim al Lawati, better known as Ibn Batuta of Tanja.

Even in distant India, the contribution of Moroccan intellectuals to modern thought and challenges is known and acknowledged. Names like Abdullah Al-Arui and Abed al-Jabri readily come to mind; so do the contributions of feminist writers like Fatima Mernissi and Fatima Sadiqi. The challenge, in each case, was that of modernity and the contemporary responses to it. Each addressed a specific aspect of the problem; the general question was posed aptly by al-Jabri: 'How can contemporary Arab thought retrieve and absorb the most rational and critical dimensions of its tradition and employ them in the same rationalist directions as before—the direction of fighting feudalism, Gnosticism, and dependency?'[1]

This is a rich field, amply and productively explored by contemporary thinkers in Arab lands. This included the debates on Arabism, nationalism, democracy and Islam. Much has also been written about the trauma, self

---

Note: Speech delivered at the Mohammad V University, 1 June 2016, Rabat, Morocco.

or externally inflicted, experienced individually and collectively by Arab societies in the past seven decades. The misfortunes visited on Arab lands since the 19th century was in good measure a result of their proximity to Europe in the age of imperialism.

I would like to draw your attention to some terminological questions here. In many current discussions, the terms 'Arab' and 'Islam' are used together or interchangeably. But are the two synonymous? Is Arab thought synonymous with Islamic thought? Is all Arab thought Islamic or vice versa? Above all, can all Islamic thinking be attributed to Arabs?

I raise these questions because for a variety of reasons and motivations the contemporary world, particularly the West, tends to create this impression of 'a powerful, irrational force that, from Morocco to Indonesia, moves whole societies into cultural assertiveness, political intransigence and economic influence'.[2] The underlying basis for this, as Aziz al-Azmeh put it, are 'presumptions of Muslim cultural homogeneity and continuity that do not correspond to social reality'.[3]

Allow me to amplify. Islam is a global faith, and its adherents are in all parts of the world. The history of Islam as a faith, and of Muslims as its adherents, is rich and diversified. In different ages and in different regions, the Muslim contribution to civilization has been noteworthy. In cultural terms, the history of Islam 'is the history of a dialogue between the realm of religious symbols and the world of everyday reality, a history of the interaction between Islamic values and the historical experiences of Muslim people that has shaped the formation of a number of different but interrelated Muslim societies'.[4]

Readers of this book are in no need of being reminded of the truism that reasoning should proceed from facts to conclusions and should eschew *a priori* pronouncements.

What then are facts?

Wikipedia indicates the world's Muslim population in 2015 as 1.7 billion. The Pew Research Center of the United States has published country-wise and region-wise religious composition and projections for 198 countries for the period 2010–2050. It indicates that in 2010 Muslims numbered 1.59 billion out of which 986 million were in Asia-Pacific. It projects that four years from now, in 2020, the corresponding figures would be 1.9 billion, out of which 1.13 billion (around 60 per cent) would be in Asia-Pacific.

The comparative figures for West Asia–North Africa would be 317 and 381 million (19.9 per cent and 20.52 per cent) and for Sub-Saharan Africa 248 and 329 million (15.59 per cent and 17.31 per cent) respectively. Within the Asia-Pacific region, Indonesia, India, Pakistan, Bangladesh, Iran, Turkey together would account for 830 million in 2010 and 954 million in 2020.

These numbers underline the fact that an overwhelming number of Muslims of the world are non-Arabs and live in societies that are not Arab. Equally relevant is the historical fact they contributed to and benefited from the civilization of Islam in full measure. This trend continues to this day.

The one conclusion I draw from this is that in ascertaining Islamic and Muslim perceptions on contemporary happenings, the experiences and trends of thinking of the non-Arab segments of large Muslim populations in the world assume an importance that cannot be ignored. These segments include countries with Muslim majorities (principally Indonesia, Bangladesh, Pakistan, Iran, and Turkey), as also those where followers of the Islamic faith do not constitute a majority of the population (India, China, and Philippines).

Amongst both categories, India is *sui generis.* India counts amongst its citizens the second largest Muslim population in the world. It numbers 180 million and accounts for 14.2 per cent of the country's total population of 1.3 billion. Furthermore, religious minorities as a whole (Christians, Sikhs, Buddhists, Jains, and Parsis or Zoroastrians) constitute 19.4 per cent of the population of India.

India's interaction with Islam and Muslims began early and bears the imprint of history. Indian Muslims have lived in India's religiously plural society for over a thousand years, at times as rulers, at others as subjects and now as citizens. They are not homogenous in racial or linguistic terms and bear the impact of local cultural surroundings, in manners and customs, in varying degrees.

Through extensive trading ties before the advent of Islam, India was a known land to the people of the Arabian Peninsula, the Persian Gulf, and western Asia and was sought after for its prosperity and trading skills and respected for its attainments in different branches of knowledge. Thus, Baghdad became the seeker, and dispenser, of Indian numerals and sciences. The *Panchatantra* was translated and became *Kalila wa Dimna.* Long before the advent of Muslim conquerors, the works of Al-Jahiz, Ibn Khordadbeh, Al-Kindi, Yaqubi and Al-Masudi testify to it in ample measure. Alberuni, who studied India and Indians more thoroughly than most, produced a virtual encyclopaedia on religion, rituals, manners and customs, philosophy, mathematics and astronomy. He commenced his great work by highlighting differences, but was careful enough 'to relate, not criticize'.

Over centuries of intermingling and interaction, an Indo-Islamic culture developed in India. Many years back, an eminent Indian historian summed it up in a classic passage:

> It is hardly possible to exaggerate the extent of Muslim influence over Indian life in all departments. But nowhere else is it shown so vividly and so picturesquely, as in customs, in intimate details of domestic life, in music, in the fashion of dress, in the ways of cooking, in the ceremonial of marriage, in the celebration of festivals and fairs, and in the courtly institutions and etiquette.[5]

Belief, consciousness and practice became a particularly rich area of interaction. Within the Muslim segment of the populace, there was a running tussle between advocates of orthodoxy and those who felt that living in a non-homogenous social milieu, the pious could communicate values through personal practice. In this manner the values of faith, though not its theological content, reached a wider circle of the public. This accounted for the reach and popularity of different Sufi personalities in different periods of history and justifies an eminent scholar's observation that 'Sufism took Islam to the masses and in doing so it took over the enormous and delicate responsibility of dealing at a personal level with a baffling variety of problems'.[6]

It also produced a convergence or parallelism; the Sufi trends sought commonalities in spiritual thinking and some Islamic precepts and many Muslim practices seeped into the interstices of the Indian society and gave expression to a broader and deeper unity of minds expressive of the Indian spiritual tradition. The cultural interaction was mutually beneficial and an Islamic scholar of our times has acknowledged 'an incontrovertible fact that Muslims have benefited immensely from the ancient cultural heritage of India'.[7]

I mention this because I am aware, but dimly, about the role of Sufi movements and 'zawiyas' in the history of Morocco.[8] There is, in my view, room for comparative studies of Sufi practices in Morocco and in India.

It is this backdrop that has impacted on modern India and its existential reality of a plural society on the basis of which a democratic polity and a secular state structure was put in place.

The framers of our Constitution had the objective of securing civic, political, economic, social and cultural rights as essential ingredients of citizenship. Particular emphasis was placed on rights of religious minorities. Thus, in the section on Fundamental Rights, 'all persons are equally entitled to freedom of conscience and the right freely to profess, practice and propagate religion'. In addition, every religious denomination shall have the right to establish and maintain institutions for religious and charitable purposes, to manage its own affairs in matters of religion, and to acquire and administer movable and immovable property. Furthermore, all religious or linguistic minorities shall have the right to establish and administer educational institutions of their choice. A separate section on Fundamental Duties of citizens enjoins every citizen 'to promote harmony and the spirit of common brotherhood amongst all the people of India transcending religious, linguistic and regional or sectional diversities' and also 'to value and preserve the rich heritage of our composite culture'.[9]

Given the segmented nature of society and unequal economy, the quest for substantive equality, and justice, remains a work-in-progress and concerns have been expressed from time to time about its shortfalls and pace of implementation. The corrective lies in our functioning democracy, its accountability mechanisms, including regularity of elections at all levels from village and district councils to regional and national levels, the Rule of Law, and heightened levels of public awareness of public issues.

The one incontrovertible fact about the Muslim experience in modern India is that its citizens professing Islamic faith are citizens, consider themselves as such, are beneficiaries of the rights guaranteed to them by the Constitution, participate fully in the civic processes of the polity and seek correctives for their grievances within the system. There is no inclination in their ranks to resort to ideologies and practices of violence.

The same diversity of historical experience, and the perceptions emanating from it, is to be found in Indonesia that has the world's largest population of Muslims and where two Islamist parties—Nahdatul Ulema and Muhammadiyah—function legally, have large memberships, and participate in political activities including local and national elections. On a visit to Jakarta a few months ago, I had occasion to solicit their views on contemporary debates on political Islam. They said Islam in Indonesia has united with the culture of the people and their Islamic traditions have adapted themselves to local conditions. They felt Indonesian Muslims are moderate in their outlook, that Islam does not advocate extremism, and that radicalization of Islam is harmful and does not benefit the community.

Both instances cited above indicate that in countries having complex societal makeup, accommodation of diversity in political structures and socio-economic policies is not an option but an imperative necessity, ignoring which can have unpleasant consequences.

But why is the Indian model of relevance to our globalizing world?

Globalization has many facets—economic, political and cultural. All necessitate the emergence of a set of norms, values and practices that are universally accepted. A sociologist has defined it as 'the compression of the world and the intensification of consciousness of the world as a whole'.[10] An obvious implication of this would be assimilation and homogenization. In a world of intrinsically diverse societies at different levels of development, this could only result in denial of their diversity and imposition of uniformity. Such an approach can only result in conflict.

The challenge for the modern world is to accept diversity as an existential reality and to configure attitudes and methodologies for dealing with it. In developing such an approach, the traditional virtue of 'tolerance' is desirable but insufficient; our effort, thinking and practices have to look beyond it and seek *acceptance* of diversity and adopt it as a civic virtue.

We in India are attempting it, cannot yet say that we have succeeded, but are committed to continue the effort. And all right-minded people are invited to join us in this endeavour.

45
INDIA AND THE WORLD

TUNIS IS THE CITY WHERE, 700 years earlier, Ibn Khaldun was born. He wrote about the persistent human propensity to disregard changed conditions; in the process he told us a good deal about the rise and fall of political and military power. His formulation on the philosophy of history, according to Arnold Toynbee, was 'undoubtedly the greatest work of its kind that has ever yet been created by any mind in any time or place'.

The subject of this piece is 'India and the World'. Before delving into it, I wish to draw attention to a very disorderly world that all of us are confronted with today.

An eminent American strategic thinker and practitioner of the art of *realpolitik* describe the 20th century as a period of 'Megadeath and Metamyth—pawned false notions of total control, derived from an arrogant assertions of total righteousness'[1]. More recently, he wrote that 'the world is now interactive and interdependent. It is also, for the first time, a world in which the problems of human survival have begun to overshadow more traditional international conflicts'.[2]

Commenting in the same strain, but from a different perspective, a historian has observed that 'our world risks both explosion and implosion. It must change (since) the price of failure is darkness'.[3]

You will recall that in the wake of the end of the Cold War, and the expectation of an era of global cooperation for common good, a comprehensive agenda for peace was enunciated, focused on preventive diplomacy, peace-keeping, peace-making and peace-building. Other initiatives

---

Note: Speech delivered at the Tunisian Institute of Strategic Studies, 3 June 2016, Carthage, Tunisia.

came forth for addressing human security questions pertaining to economic development, social justice, environmental protection, democratization, disarmament, respect for human rights and the rule of law. Together, they helped delineate a new paradigm of security, aptly articulated in 1999 by the then UN Secretary, General Kofi Anan:

> We must broaden our view of what is meant by peace and security. Peace means much more than the absence of war. Human security can no longer be understood in purely military terms. Rather, it must encompass economic development, social justice, environmental protection, democratization, disarmament and respect for human rights and the rule of law. [4]

Although inter-state conflicts have admittedly declined, the experience of the past quarter of a century shows the manner in which the expectations of a more comprehensive corrective have been belied:

- There has been a phenomenal increase in lower intensity civil conflicts;
- There has been an increase in violence against unprotected civilians;
- Some of these conflicts have spilled across state boundaries and their principal victims are civilians;
- They have dislocated human populations and are endangering human security;
- They tend to undermine the nation state, and are creating friction between neighbouring countries.

We have witnessed the ease with which regional and sub-national conflicts have spiraled into broader conflict and become a global security challenge. These threats are increasingly emanating from non-state sources such as organized crime, organized terrorist outfits and pirates. Even more disturbing is the trend where non-state armed groups appear as parties in violent conflict.

The traditional security architecture has been slow to respond to these new realities, even as the economic prominence of new players is remarkably well understood. While emerging economies have secured a role in the global economic system, the Security Council of the United Nations remains a captive of its five permanent members (China, France, Russian Federation, the United Kingdom, and the United States). This intransigence has constrained the ability of the established security systems to address the evolving nature of security challenges.

This is the global landscape in which India has endeavoured in recent decades to address its developmental challenges and its role in the world. Some of its salient features are:

1. Twenty-five years of economic liberalization, beginning in 1991, have transformed India's economy. The average annual growth rate of 7 per cent has created wealth allowing millions of Indians to take part, and to benefit from, a globalized world. Despite this, about one-third of our population lives in extreme poverty and we face formidable challenges of education, training, human and infrastructure development.
2. Our total global trade grew from US $37.3 billion in 1991 to US $758.5 billion in 2016, a 20-fold growth in the last 25 years. There has been a phenomenal increase in India's industrial and agricultural outputs. A business friendly India is today one of the leading recipients of Foreign Direct Investment (FDI) in a range of sectors.
3. The availability of additional resources has allowed us to invest more in education and welfare of our citizens, which, in turn, has provided India with a wealth of scientific and entrepreneurial talent.
4. India is recognized as the world leader in the pharmaceutical sector and the information technology (IT) domain. Our capability in space technology and nuclear sciences has been recognized globally.
5. Strong growth has added to India's maritime and strategic capacity. Our defence capabilities have increased; so has our capacity to provide overseas security and humanitarian support to our friends and those in need. We like to resolve our conflicts peacefully through negotiations but at the same time would like to have an effective and credible deterrence capacity to protect our legitimate interests.[5]

'India is not a rejectionist power that stands outside the global order. Instead her interests lie in working to change, reform and improve the global order.'[6] This demands increased external engagement within the ambit of a non-intrusive policy.

A peaceful periphery is critical to our success and we believe that the entire South Asian region needs to grow with India for our sustainable prosperity. 'Neighbourhood first', has therefore been a key component of India's worldview, with a strong sense of priority being attached to enhancing cooperation with immediate neighbours. The South Asian Association for Regional Cooperation (SAARC) has been infused with new energy even as we have continued our bilateral cooperation with neighboring countries.

We have adopted an 'Act East' policy based on enhanced connectivity with maritime neighbours to the East. The deepening of strategic and commercial ties with the Indian Ocean Rim countries have been a priority. Our 'Link West' approach has invigorated cooperation with West Asia and the Persian Gulf littoral. We consider the Middle East Peace Process as the key to resolve long pending issues and prevent further radicalization of the region. We have sought enhanced connectivity with Eurasia through initiatives such as the Chabahar port and related infrastructure, and the Turkmenistan–Afghanistan–Pakistan–India (TAPI) pipeline, a project whose initiation I personally attended last year with leaders from the other partner states.

Our relationships with the major powers have expanded exponentially in the last two decades. We share a strategic relation with the United States and our cooperation has deepened across a range of activities on the foundations of a convergence of our economic and political views. With Russia, we have traditionally had good relations, which have expanded significantly in energy and defence co-operation sectors. With China, the bilateral trade has expanded considerably with new avenues of economic cooperation being created. With Japan a range of cooperation activities are being implemented, especially in the infrastructure sector.

We have reached out to our friends in Africa through initiatives such as the India Africa Forum Summit, held last year in New Delhi. We convened a conclave of South Pacific islands to explore issues of mutual interest and define India's contribution in their growth and development goals. With other emerging economies we have collaborated, such as under the BRICS forum, to develop more equitable global governance systems.

The agenda of global issues, and of multilateral diplomacy, remains a matter of perennial interest to us. India has been a major contributor to international peacekeeping operations under the United Nations flag, has engaged with our partners in shaping the Sustainable Development Goals (SDGs) agenda, and continues to work with like-minded countries to make the global financial and trade systems more equitable and transparent, and to address our common challenges, such as environmental degradation. India took the lead at the recently concluded COP 21 at Paris to forge an international consensus and has become one of the strongest advocates of clean energy, particularly solar energy and energy innovation.

We do believe that as one-sixth of the humanity, and in keeping with the growing capacities and aspirations of our people, India has a much larger role to play in charting a more equitable and sustainable future for our world. For this reason we believe that any global forum which does not include India has limited relevance.

West Asia and North Africa are not unfamiliar regions to India. Historical ties, cultural bonds, shared interests and concerns characterize our relations. We have a vital stake in the stability, security and economic well-being of this region and are willing to expand our strategic and economic partnership. There are several areas where our interests converge. Our bilateral trade with the region in 2014–2015 was about US $49.58 billion[7] and is expected to grow further despite the economic slowdown. We also look to this region for ensuring our energy security and for commodities such as phosphates. This region, with its young population and natural resources, has tremendous growth potential. It can act as a bridge between the three continents of Asia, Africa and Europe. Indian companies have started to increase their investments in the region. There is a considerable potential for expanding trade in the areas of automotive components, automobiles, engineering products, IT, pharmaceuticals, bio-technology and healthcare sectors.

There are also areas of common concern. Terrorism has emerged as a principal global challenge. Tunisia as a country, like my own, has suffered the horrors of this scourge of humanity. Terrorism today has global reach, no city remains safe. There is a new level of threat to pluralist and open societies. Old structures of terrorism also remain. There are countries that still use it as an instrument of state policy. There can be no distinction between good and bad terrorists. A terrorist is a terrorist; one who commits crimes against humanity cannot have any religion, or be afforded any political sanctuary.

International terrorism can only be defeated by organized international action. We need to restructure the international legal framework, such as by adopting a Comprehensive Convention on International Terrorism to deal with the challenges of terrorism. Societies that stand for peace and share values of humanism have to increase their cooperation in intelligence sharing. We should strengthen efforts to prevent supply of arms to terrorists, disrupt terrorist movements, and curb and criminalize terror financing. We have to help each other secure our cyber space, and minimize the use of internet and social media for terrorist activities.

Relations between India and Tunisia have been friendly and free of discord. We share common principles and have a similar approach on many issues. India had extended strong support to the Tunisian struggle for freedom, and today, India stands ready again to provide all possible support as you embark on a path of freedom and democracy.

Tunisia can also be a hub for our trade with both Europe and Africa. Tunisia can leverage our expertise and proven capabilities in production of pharmaceuticals, especially generic medicines at affordable cost, advancement in healthcare sector, science & technology and provision of high quality education at reasonable cost to its advantage. I see a prosperous and peaceful future as our commercial and political interactions deepen. It will open a new era of peace and prosperity, not only for our two countries but the entire region.

NOTES

5: Prudence and the Moral Imperative

1. Brzezinski, Zbigniew. *Out Of Control: Global Turmoil On The Eve of the 21st Century*, New York, 1993, pp. ix–xv.
2. Brezezinski, Zbigniew. *Strategic Vision: America and the Crisis of Global Power*, New York, 2012, p. 189.
3. Eban, Abba. *Diplomacy for the Next Century*, Yale, 1998, pp. 152, 170.
4. Mishra, Pankaj. *From The Ruins Of Empire: The Revolt Against The West And The Remaking Of Asia*, London, 2012, p. 8.
5. Oommen, T.K. *Understanding Security: A New Perspective*, New Delhi, 2006, p. 151.
6. Booth, Ken. 'Human Wrongs in International Relations', *International Affairs*, London, 71(1), 1995, pp. 103–126.
7. Bobbitt, Philip. *The Shield of Achilles: War, Peace, And The Course Of History*, New York, 2003.

6: Citizens and State Conduct

1. *Nandani Sunder & Ors v. State of Chattisgarh* (2011) 7 SCC 547: '18. Such misguided policies, albeit vehemently and muscularly asserted by some policy makers, are necessarily contrary to the vision and imperatives of our constitution which demands that the power vested in the State, by the people, be only used for the welfare of the people—all the people, both rich and the poor -, thereby assuring conditions of human dignity within the ambit of fraternity amongst groups of them. Neither Article 14, nor Article 21, can even remotely be conceived as being so bereft of substance as to be immune from such policies. They are necessarily tarnished, and violated in a primordial sense by such policies.'
2. Roy, Anupama. 'Ideas and Vision: Introduction' in *Human Rights and Peace: Ideas, Laws, Institutions and Movement*, ed. Ujjwal Kumar Singh, New Delhi, 2009, p. xvi.
3. Bingham, Tom. *The Rule of Law*, London, 2010, p. 161, citing Professor Sir Francis Jacobs.

4. Barker, Ernest. *Church, State and Education,* Michigan, 1957, p. 169.
5. Lohia, Ram Manohar. 'The Concept of Civil Liberties' in Ujjwal Kumar Singh, op. cit., p. 210.
6. Dhar, P.N. *Indira Gandhi, the 'Emergency', and Indian Democracy,* New Delhi, 2000, p. 222.
7. Gudavarthy, Ajay in Ujjwal Kumar Singh, op. cit., p. 255.
8. Rawls, John. *A Theory of Justice,* USA, 1999, pp. 3–4.
9. The Prevention of Torture Bill 2010 was introduced in the Lok Sabha and passed by it on 26 April 2010. The Rajya Sabha referred it to a Select Committee on 31 August. Its report was presented on 7 December 2010. No further action was taken by the government and the Bill lapsed with the dissolution of the 15th Lok Sabha.
10. Mehta, Pratap Bhanu. *The Burden of Democracy,* New Delhi, 2003, pp. 113–115.
11. A.G. Noorani & South Asia Human Rights Documentation Centre. *Challenges to Civil Rights Guarantees in India,* New Delhi, 2012. This publication analyses in particular the role of the criminal justice system in India in the erosion of civil rights and focuses on preventive detention, extra-judicial killings, counter-terrorism and human rights, the death penalty, narcoanalysis, undertrials and videoconferencing, anti-conversion law, impunity and AFSPA. Also, for an overall assessment, Ashish Nandy. 'From the Age of Anxiety to the Age of Fear' in Rajesh Chakrabarti, *The Other India: Realities of an Emerging Power,* New Delhi, 2009, pp. 94–100.
12. Ministry of Home Affairs, Government of India. *Annual Report 2013–14,* p. 83, paragraph 6.6.
13. Seth, Leila. *Talking of Justice: People's Rights in Modern India,* New Delhi, 2014, p. 69.
14. Working Group on Human Rights in India and the UN. *Human Rights in India Status Report* 2012, New Delhi, December 2012, pp. iv and 178.

7: Democracy and Dissent

1. Jain, Ujjwal Kumar. 'Ram Manohar Lohia's Concept of Civil Liberties' in Anupama Roy, *Human Rights and Peace: Ideas, Laws, Institutions and Movement,* ed. Ujjwal Kumar Singh, New Delhi, 2009, p. 210.
2. Kelkar, Indumati. *Dr. Rammanohar Lohia: His Life and Philosophy,* New Delhi, 2009, p. 60.
3. Ibid., p. 73.
4. Tolpadi, Rajaram. 'Context, Discourse and Vision of Lohia's Socialism', *Economic and Political Weekly* (EPW), Vol. xiv No.40, 2 October 2010, pp 71–77.
5. Lohia, Rammanohar: 'The Caste System' (December 1961) in *Collected Works of Dr. Rammanohar Lohia, Volume 2,* Hyderabad, 2011, p. 322.
6. Ibid., p. 217.
7. Shankar, B.L. and Valarian Rodrigues. *The Indian Parliament: A Democracy at*

Work, New Delhi, 2011, p. 343, citing the speech of 28 December 1955.
8. AIR 1955 All 193, 1955 CriLJ 623, 27 August 1954. Some other cases relating to Dr Lohia's contention on freedom of expression were cited by the Supreme Court in paragraphs 22, 33, 34, 88 and 89 of the judgement of 24 March 2015 cited below.
9. Kelkar, op. cit. pp. 380–381.
10. Yadav, Yogendra. 'On Remembering Lohia' in *EPW*, Ibid., p 47.
11. Sheth, D.L. and Ashis Nandy. *The Multiverse of Democracy*, New Delhi, 1996, pp. 20-23.
12. 'Social cascade' has been defined as 'large scale social movements in which many people end up thinking something or doing something because of the beliefs or actions of a few early movers who greatly influence those who follow.' 'Group polarization' occurs 'when a deliberation group ends up taking a more extreme position than its median member took before deliberation began.'—Cass R. Sunstein. *Why Societies Need Dissent,* Harvard, 2003, pp. 54 and 112.
13. Supreme Court of India Writ Petition (Criminal) No. 167 of 2012 AIR 2015— *Shreya Singhal v. Union of India,* 24 March 2015.
14. Mehta, Pratap Bhanu. 'Do not disagree—*Blaming NGOs reveals the diminishing space for dissent in our democracy*', http://archive.indianexpress.com/news/do-not-disagree/917869/, accessed on 9 May 2015.
15. 'Strategies to Quash Dissent' in *EPW*, Vol. L No. 17, 25 April 2015; 'Open Intimidation' in *EPW*, Vol. L, No. 29, 18 July 2015, p. 8.

8: International Human Rights Day

1. Cassese, Antonio. *Human Rights in a Changing World*, Philadelphia, 1990.
2. T.S. Elliot's poem 'The Hollow Men'.
3. Human Rights Council, Working Group on Universal Periodic Review. Compilation prepared by the Office of the High Commissioner for Human Rights in accordance with paragraph 5 of the annex to Human Rights Council resolution 16/21, Thirteenth session, 21 May–4 June 2012.
4. http://www.countryreportcard.org/, accessed on 9 May 2016.
5. https://www.hrw.org/asia/india, accessed on 9 May 2016.
6. https://www.amnesty.org/en/countries/asia-and-the-pacific/india/report-india/, accessed on 9 May 2016.

9: Role of Women Legislators in Nation Building

1. Kamala Nehru, Sarojini Naidu, Anasuya Sarabhai, Aruna Asaf Ali, Sushila Nayyar and Miraben are a few illustrious women associated with the freedom movement.
2. M.K. Gandhi in 'Young India', 17 October 1929.
3. Election Commission of India, General Elections, 2014 (16th Lok Sabha), Table No.23, Participation of Women Electors in Poll.
4. Lok Sabha USQ No. 4136, 13 August 2015.

5. There are only 66 women members out of 543 members elected to the 16th Lok Sabha and 31 out of 242 members in the Rajya Sabha.
6. Since 1952, Lok Sabha has had only 591 women members while Rajya Sabha has had a total of 185 women members (including 20 nominated members).
7. Bihar, Haryana and Rajasthan have 14 per cent women in their respective assemblies, whereas there is no women representation in Mizoram, Nagaland and Puducherry.
8. Women in National Parliaments (Situation as of 1 December 2015), http://www.ipu.org/wmn-e/world.htm, accessed on 9 May 2015.
9. Election Commission of India, General Elections, 2014 (16th Lok Sabha), Table No. 20, Performance of National Parties and Table No. 26, Participation of Women in National Parties.
10. Cammisa, Anne Marie and Beth Reingold. 'Women in state legislatures and state legislative research: Beyond sameness and difference', *State Politics & Policy Quarterly*, Vol. 4, 2004, pp. 181–210.
11. Rosenthal, C. S. 'Gender Styles in Legislative Committees', *Women and Politics*, 21, 2001, pp. 21-46.

10: Public Investment and Subsidies on Agricultural Inputs and the Upliftment of Agrarian Economy

1. NITI Aayog, Government of India. 'Raising Agricultural Productivity and Making Farming Remunerative for Farmers', Occasional Paper, 16 December 2015.
2. Appu, P.S. *Land Reforms in India: A Survey of Policy, Legislation and Implementation*, New Delhi, 1996.
3. Singh, Manmohan. 'Inaugural Address' in *Indian Journal of Agricultural Economics*, Vol. 50, No. 1, January–March 1995, pp. 1–8.
4. http://www.livemint.com/Politics/tVWn9xU6Nqgt3ZLZJcHvBO/The-state-of-Indias-farmers.html, accessed on 10 May 2016.
5. Sainath, P. 'How States Fudge the Data on Declining Farmer Suicides', rediff.com, 1 August 2014.
6. http://indianexpress.com/article/opinion/columns/lead-from-the-centre/#sthash.Iu8nfptj.dpuf, accessed on 10 May 2016.
7. Chand, Ramesh, P.A. Lakshmi Prasanna and Singh, Aruna. 'Farm Size and Productivity: Understanding the Strengths of Smallholders and Improving their Livelihoods', *EPW*, Vol. XLVI, No. 26 & 27, 25 June 2011, p. 5–11.
8. Singh, Karam. 'Agrarian Crisis in Punjab: High Indebtedness, Low Returns and Farmer Suicides' in *Agrarian Crisis in India,* ed. Narasimha Reddy and Srijit Mishra, New Delhi 2010, pp. 261–280.
9. http://www.financialexpress.com/article/budget-2016/column-budget-2016-hoping-for-agri-recovery/217276/, accessed on 10 May 2016.
10. http://indianexpress.com/article/opinion/columns/lead-from-the-centre/#sthash.Iu8nfptj.dpuf, accessed on 10 May 2016.

11. Sharma, Vijay Paul. 'India's Agricultural Development under the New Economic Regime: Policy Perspective and Strategy for the 12th Five Year Plan', W.P. No. 2011-11-01, Indian Institute of Management, Ahmedabad, November 2011.
12. Varshney, Ashutosh. 'Self-Limited Empowerment: Democracy, Economic Development and Rural India', *Journal of Development Studies,* Vol. 29, No. 4, 1993, pp. 127–215.
13. Lall, Rajiv. 'The good, the bad and the ugly of India's rural transformation', *Business Standard*, 19 November 2013.

12: Role of the Judiciary: Some Thoughts on its Criticality

1. Barak, Aharon. 'A Judge on Judging: The Role of Supreme Court in a Democracy', 116 *Harvard Law Review* 19, 2002–2003.
2. Cardozo, B.N. *The Nature of the Judicial Process*, Yale, 1928, p. 3.
3. Ibid., p. 11.
4. Bingham, Tom. *The Rule of Law*, London, 2010, p. 93.
5. Sachs, Albie. *The Strange Alchemy of Life and Law*, New York, 2009, p. 173.
6. Chatterjee, Partha. 'Secularism and Tolerance' in *Secularism and its Critics*, ed. Rajeev Bhargava, New Delhi, 1998, p. 358.
7. Sen, Amartya. 'Secularism and Its Discontents' in Bhargava, Ibid., p. 484.
8. Sorabjee, Soli. 'Nationalism Can't be Manufactured by Reciting Verses', *The Sunday Standard*, 20–26 March 2016, p. 11.
9. Andhyarjina, T.R. 'Basic Structure of the Constitution revisited', *The Hindu*, 21 May 2007. Also, *The Kesavananda Bharti Case: The Untold Story of the Struggle for Supremacy by Supreme Court and Parliament*, New Delhi, 2011—*passim*.
10. S.R. Bommai v. Union of India (1994), 3 SCC (Jour) 1, 11 March 1994, para 252. Also, paras 153(viii), 176, 177, 304, 434(10).
11. Sen, Ronojoy. *Articles of Faith: Religion, Secularism and the Indian Supreme Court* New Delhi, 2010, p. xxix.
12. Jacobsohn, Gary Jeffrey. *The Wheel of Law: India's Secularism in Comparative Constitutional Context*, New Delhi, 2003, p. 146.
13. Cossman, Brenda & Kapur, Ratna. 'Secularism: Bench-Marked by Hindu Right,' *Economic & Political Weekly*, Vol. 31, No. 38, 12 September 1996, pp. 2613-2630.
14. Padhy, Sanghamitra. 'Secularism and Justice: A Review of Indian Supreme Court Judgments', *Economic & Political Weekly*, Vol. 39, No. 46/47, 20-26 November 2004, pp. 5027-5032.
15. Report of the Expert Group on Diversity Index, Submitted to Ministry of Minority Affairs, Government of India, 2008.
16. *Bommai,* para 182.
17. Pannikar, K.N. *Colonialism, Culture, and Resistance,* New Delhi, 2007, p. 95.
18. Ibid.
19. Dhavan, Rajeev and Nariman, Fali S. 'The Supreme Court and Group Life: Religious Freedom, Minority Groups, and Disadvantaged Communities' in

Supreme But Not Infallible—Essays in Honour of the Supreme Court of India, New Delhi, 2000, p. 278.
20. Austin, Granville. 'The Supreme Court and the Struggle for the Custody of the Constitution', Ibid., p. 13.
21. Jacobsohn, op cit., p. 103.

13: The Intellectual and Society: Role and Responsibility

1. President Radhakrishnan's Speeches and Writings, Second Series, Publications Division, Government of India, New Delhi,1969, p. 185.
2. *On the Improvement of the Understanding – The Chief Works of Spinoza*, New York, 1951, vol. II, p. 7.
3. Bertrand Russell. 'Philosophy's Ulterior Motives' in *Unpopular Essays*, London, 1951, p. 74.
4. S. Radhakrishnan. *Religion and Society*, London, 1947, p. 10.
5. Ibid., pp 227-229.
6. Journal of Parliamentary Information, Vol. xiii, No. 2, October 1967, p. 139.
7. Cited in Edward W. Said. *Representations of the Intellectual*, New York, 1996, pp. 35–36.
8. Theses On Feuerbach, XI, Marx/Engels Archive.
9. Cited in Jerome Karabel. 'Towards a theory of intellectuals and politics', *Theory and Society*, 1996, Vol. 25, pp. 205–233.
10. Arnold J. Toynbee. *A Study of History: Abridgement of Volumes I-VI* by D.C. Somervell, London, 1956, p. 394.
11. Noam Chomsky. 'The Responsibility of Intellectuals', *The New York Review of Books*, 23 February 1967.
12. Said, op. cit., p. 102.
13. Johnson, Paul. *Intellectuals*, London, 1988, pp. 2 and 342.
14. Said, op. cit., p. xiv.
15. Kapur, Devish.'Ideas and Economic Reforms in India: The Role of International Migration and the Indian Diaspora', *Indian Review*, October 2004, Vol. 3, No.4, pp. 364 and 382.
16. Kothari, Rajni. *Rethinking Democracy*, New Delhi, 2005, p. 166.
17. Mehta, Pratap Bhanu. *The Burden of Democracy*, New Delhi, 2003, passim.
18. Kothari, op. cit., passim.
19 Vahanvati, Goolam E. 'Rule of Law: The Siege Within' in Mool Chand Sharma and Raju Ramachandran (eds), *Constitutionalism, Human Rights and the Rule of Law – Essays in Honour of Soli J. Sorabjee*, New Delhi, 2005, p. 168.
20. Pratap Bhanu Mehta is trenchant on this score: 'The Court's concern for its own authority has led it to read the political tea leaves with care. The judicialization of politics and the politicization of the judiciary turn out to be two sides of the same coin…The Supreme Court, strikingly, has given up any formal pretense to the doctrine of the separation of powers' – 'The Rise of

Judicial Sovereignty' in Sumit Ganguly, Larry Diamond and Marc F Plattner (eds), *The State of India's Democracy,* Baltimore, 2007, pp. 113 and 115.
21. Guha, Ramachandra. *India After Gandhi*, Picador India, New Delhi, 2007, p. 691.
22. State of Democracy in South Asia: A Report by the SDSA Team, New Delhi, 2008, pp. 140–141, 149–158.
23. Bhaduri, Amit and Medha Patkar. 'Industrialisation for the People, by the People, of the People', *Economic & Political Weekly*, 3–9 January 2009, Vol. XLIV, No.1, pp. 10–13. Also, Prabhat Patnaik in *Frontline*, 28 March–10 April, 2009, Vol. 26, No.7, pp. 4–6 in the cover story 'Time for Change', pp. 4–22.
24. Sen, Amartya. 'Capitalism Beyond the Crisis', *The New York Review of Books*, 26 March 2009, Vol. 56, No. 5.
25. *Economic & Political Weekly*, 31 January–6 February 2009, Vol. XLIV, No. 5, p. 5.
26. Administrative Reform Commission, Fourth Report, 16 January 2007, pp. 126–127 and 172–194.
27. Justice J.S. Verma. 'Recent Judicial Trends in Enforcement of Freedoms – Indian Experience' in *The New Universe of Human Rights*, New Delhi, 2004, p. 35.
28. Report of the Expert Group on Diversity Index, Ministry of Minority Affairs, New Delhi, 2008, p. iv.
29. Oommen, T.K. *Nation, Civil Society and Social Movements: Essays in Political Sociology*, New Delhi, 2004, pp. 175, 183, 184.
30. Said, op. cit., pp. 100–101.

14: Identity, Citizenship and Empowerment

1. Mujeeb, M. *The Indian Muslims*, London, 1967, p. 555.
2. Roy, Asim. *Living Together Separately: Cultural India in History and Politics*, ed. Mushirul Hasan and Asim Roy, New Delhi, 2005, p. 25.
3. Mahajan, Gurpreet. *The Multicultural Path*, New Delhi, 2002.
4. Engineer, Asghar Ali. 'Secularism in India: A Minority Perspective' in Chakrapani, Rajesh. *The Other India: Realities of an Emerging Power*, New Delhi, 2009, p. 30.
5. Puri, Balraj. *Muslims of India Since Partition*, New Delhi, 2007, pp. 18-19.
6. Said, Edward W. *Covering Islam,* New York, 1981, p. xv.

15: The Art and Culture of Islam in India

1. Chand, Tara. *Influence of Islam on Indian Culture*, Allahabad, 1922, p. i.
2. Lapidus, Ira M. *A History of Islamic Societies*, Cambridge, 1988, p. xx.
3. Habib, Irfan. *Medieval India: The Study of a Civilization*, New Delhi, 2008, p. 96.
4. *The Tuzuk-i-Jahangiri or Memoirs of Jahangir,* New Delhi, 2003, Vol. II, p. 20.
5. Chand, Tara. *The Influence of Islam on Indian Culture*, Allahabad, 1922, pp. 141–142.

16: Challenges for a Homeless Language: Urdu in Present-day India

1. Nehru, Jawaharlal. *Letters to Chief Ministers 1947-1964*, Vol. 3, pp. 341, 342, 350.
2. Ahmed, Firoz Bakht. 'Urdu Needs a Kiss of Life', *The Crest, Mumbai*, 30 October 2010.
3. Rawls, John. *A Theory of Justice*, Harvard, 1999, pp. 3–4.

17: Physical Integration and Emotional Inconsonance

1. Menon, V.P. *Story of the Integration of Indian States*, p. 490.
2. Menon, ibid.
3. Ambedkar, B.R. Speech in Constituent Assembly, 25 November 1949.
4. Kothari, Rajni. *Re-Thinking Democracy*, New Delhi, 2005, p. 8.
5. Khan, Rashiduddin. *Bewildered India: Identity, Pluralism, Discord*, New Delhi, 1995, p. 295.
6. Verghese, B.G. *Rage, Reconciliation and Security: Managing India's Diversities*, New Delhi, 2008, p. xiv.
7. Ibid., p. 216.
8. Jayal, Nirja Gopal. 'Regional threat to federalism', *India Today*, 26 March 2012.

18: Identity and Citizenship: An Indian Perspective

1. Castells, Manuel. *The Power of Identity*, 2nd edition, Wiley-Blackwell, 2010, p. 6.
2. Sen, Amartya. *Identity and Violence: The Illusion of Destiny*, London, 2006, p. 169.
3. Soroush, Abdolkarim. *Reason, Freedom and Democracy in Islam*, Oxford, 2000, p. 156.
4. Waldron, Jeremy. 'Cultural Identity and Civic Responsibility' in Kymlica, Well and Norman, Wayne, *Citizenship in Diverse Societies*, Oxford, 2000, p. 157.
5. Guha, Ramachandra. *India After Gandhi: The History of the World's Largest Democracy*, London, 2007, pp. ix–xx.
6. Kautilya. *The Arthashastra*, ed. Rangarajan, L.N., Penguin, 1992, p. 140.
7. Jayal, Nirja Gopal. Citizenship and Its Discontents: *An Indian History*, New Delhi, 2013, pp. 16, 273–275. Also, Rao, B. Shiva (ed.). *The Framing of India's Constitution—A Study*, 2nd revised edition, 2012, p. 150.
8. Barker, Sir Ernest. *Principles of Social and Political Theory*, Oxford, 1951, p. vi.
9. *Constituent Assembly Debates*, Volume X, 25 November 1949, Volume X, p. 979.
10. Kothari, Rajni. *Rethinking Democracy*, New Delhi, 2005, p.98.
11. Patnaik, Prabhat. 'Independent India at Sixty Five', *Social Scientist*, New Delhi, Jan-Feb 2013, Volume 41, No. 1–2, pp. 5–15.
12. Gutmann, Amy. *Identity in Democracy*, Princeton, 2003, pp. 3–7, 37.
13. Kothari, Rajni. 'Rise of the Dalits and Renewed Debate on Caste' in Chatterjee, Partha. *State and Politics in India*, Oxford, 1999, p. 444.

14. Apporvanand, 'Democratisation of Communalism', *DNA*, Mumbai, 23 September 2013.
15. Menon, V.P. *The Story of the Integration of Indian States*, New Delhi, 1956, p. 469.
16. Khan, Rasheeduddin. *Bewildered India-Identity, Pluralism, Discord*, New Delhi, 1995, p. 295.
17. 'Report of the Expert Group on Diversity Index'. Submitted to Ministry of Minority Affairs, Government of India, 2008, pp. vii–viii.
18. Kymlica, Will. *Multiculturalism: Success, Failure and the Future*, Minority Policy Institute, Europe, February 2012, pp. 1–2.
19. Mahajan, Gurpreet. *The Multicultural Path: Issues of Diversity and Discrimination in Democracy*, New Delhi, 2002, pp. 15, 17, 217–218.
20. Guha, Ramachandra. 'Politicians and Pluralism: The inclusive ideals of the Republic must not be lost sight of', *The Telegraph*, Kolkata, 7 September 2013.

20: History and Historians

1. Macaulay, Thomas Babington. 'Essay on History', *Edinburgh Review*, 1828.
2. Carr, E.H. *What is History?*, 1961, pp. 30 and 52.
3. Khaldun, Ibn. *The Muqaddimah*, New York, 1981, pp. 5 and 24.

21: Indian Muslims: Quest for Justice

1. Kundu, Amitabh. 'Post Sachar Evaluation Committee - Final Report', presented to the Ministry of Minority Affairs, Government of India, on 29 September 2014, pp. 170–181.
2. Noorani, A.G. *The Muslims of India*, New Delhi, 2003, p. 13.
3. Arkoun, Mohammed. *Rethinking Islam: Common Questions, Uncommon Answers*, Boulder, Colorado, 1994, p. 13.
4. The Qu'ran. S XIII.11.

22: Mohammad Mujeeb: An Intellectual's Locution of Dissent

1. Mohammad Mujeeb. 'Speaking for Myself' in *Islam and the Modern Age*—Special Issue on Prof. Mohd. Mujeeb—Volume XXXIV, No. 3–4, August–October 2003, pp. 27–28.
2. Mujeeb. 'Conscience', Ibid., p. 40.
3. Mujeeb. 'The Status of Individual Conscience in Islam', Ibid., p. 107.
4. Mujeeb. *The Indian Muslims*, London, 1967, p. 56.
5. Lambton, Ann K.S. *State and Government in Medieval Islam*, Oxford, 1981, pp. 110–111.
6. Mujeeb. *The Indian Muslims*, op. cit., pp. 79-80.
7. Ibid., p. 101.
8. Ibid.

9. Mujeeb. 'The Status of Individual Conscience in Islam', op. cit.
10. Mujeeb. *The Indian Muslim.* op. cit., p. 302.
11. Mujeeb. Ibid., pp. 163-165.
12. Ibid., pp. 264–265.
13. Ibid., pp. 271–272.
14. Ibid., pp. 277, 280–281.
15. Ibid., pp. 448–451.
16. Ibid., pp. 456–457.
17. Ibid., pp. 460 and 463.
18. Mujeeb, 'Freedom and Obligation in Islam', op. cit., p. 141.
19. Datta, V.N. 'Mohammed Mujeeb: A Portrait from Memory 1902–1985', *Islam and the Modern Age,* Vol. xxxiv, Nos. 3–4, August–October 2003, pp. 11–23.

24: Faith and Interfaith: An Imperative of Our Times

1. Thapar, Romila. *A History of India: Volume 1,* New Delhi, 1990, p. 87.
2. Gibbon, Edward. *The Decline and Fall of the Roman Empire,* Vol. I, 1952, p. 12.
3. Falsafi, Nasrullah. *Zindagani-i-Shah Abbas,* Tehran, 1358 H, p. 286.
4. Moahapatra, Kalpana. *Political Philosophy of Swami Vivekanand,* New Delhi, 1996, p. 8.
5. Engineer, Asghar Ali. *Jihad and Other Essays,* 2013, pp. 98–100.

25: Insecurity and the State: Emerging Challenges

1. Field Marshal Cariappa Memorial Lecture, 2001.
2. Field Marshal Cariappa Memorial Lecture, 1995.
3. Walker, David. 'General Cariappa encounters White Australia', *Journal of Imperial and Commonwealth History,* Volume 34(3), 2006.
4. Oommen, T.K. *Understanding Security: A New Perspective,* New Delhi, 2006, p. 151.
5. Rousseau, Jen Jacques. *The Social Contract or Principles of Political Right,* London, 1948, p. 103.
6. The Princeton Project on National Security: Final Report, 2006, p. 51.
7. Khaldun, Ibn. *The Muqaddimah: An Introduction to History,* Princeton, 1981, p. 5.

26: Intelligence for the World of Tomorrow

1. Tzu, Sun. *The Art of War,* New York, 1971, pp. 144 and 147.
2. Cited in Prouty, Fletcher. *The Secret Team: The CIA and Its Allies in Control of the United States and the World,* New York, 2008, p. 508.
3. Popper, Karl. *Conjectures and Refutations: The Growth of Scientific Knowledge,* Routledge & Kegan Paul, 1963, p. 38.
4. Johnston, Rob. *Analytic Culture in the U.S. Intelligence Community,* 2005, p. 11.
5. Bobbit, Philip. *The Shield of Achilles: War, Peace and the Course of History,* New

York, 2003, pp. 813 and 816.

27: India and the Great War

1. Kissinger, Henry. *Diplomacy*, London, 1995, pp. 201–202.
2. Cited by Hay, William Anthony. 'When Lamps Went Out', *Wall Street Journal*, 22 March 2013.

28: Golden Jubilee Commemoration of the India-Pakistan War of 1965

1. Kux, Denis. *The United States and Pakistan 1947-2000*, Washington, 2001, p. 159.
2. Srivastava, C.P. *Lal Bahadur Shastri*, New Delhi, 1995, pp. 226–228.
3. 'Secretary of State Dean Rusk': Interview by Paige E. Mullhollen, Foreign Affairs Oral History Project, L.B. Johnson Library, 28 July 1969, p. 100.
4. Nawaz, Shuja. *Crossed Swords*, Karachi, 2008, pp. 235– 238.
5. Kennedy, Paul. *The Rise and Fall of the Great Powers*, New York, 1989, p. 539.

29: Science and Technology

1. Lord May of Oxford. 'Threats to Tomorrow's World', Address to the Royal Society, 30 November 2005.
2. Sen, Amartya. *The Argumentative Indian*, New York, 2005, Preface.
3. Russell, Bertrand. *Unpopular Essays*, London, 1950, p. 125.
4. Oppenheimer, Robert. Remark attributed to him during his trial in 1954.

30: Higher Education—Challenges and Imperatives for Change

1. Newman, Cardinal John Henry. *The Idea of a University*, 1858, Preface.

31: Human Development and Inequality

1. Iyer, Krishna. 'Of justice, justices and justicing', *The Hindu*, 12 September 2008.
2. Baxi, Upendra. 'Justice V.R. Krishna Iyer – Legal Luminary', *Indian Express*, 24 January 2009.
3. Iyer, Krishna. 'Political State and Civil Society', *The Hindu*, 15 February 2002.

32: Socio-Economic Parameters

1. Ambedkar, B.R. Speech in Constituent Assembly, 25 November 1949.

33: Challenges in Indian Agriculture

1. Chaudhary, Ranbir Singh. Speech in Constituent Assembly, 6 November 1948.

35: The Value of Scientific Temper

1. Nehru, Jawaharlal. *Discovery of India*, 1946, p. 512.

36: Social Innovation and Social Harmony

1. Speech by former UN Secretary General Kofi Annan, 2010.
2. Akhter Majeed, Forum of Federations Newsletter, October–November 2007, pp. 10–23.
3. http://nextbillion.net/whats-the-matter-with-india/, accessed on 25 May 2015.
4. https://www.globalinnovationindex.org/content/page/GII-Home/, accessed on 25 May 2015.
5. http://www.livemint.com/Companies/1TT1Yf8qxHw6gQyuj8X6TK/Indian-innovation-Why-we-need-to-look-beyond-Silicon-Valley.html, accessed on 25 May 2015.
6. http://niti.gov.in/mgov_file/report%20of%20the%20expert%20committee.pdf, accessed on 25 May 2015.

37: The Imperative of World Peace

1. Marsilius of Padua. *Defensor Pacis*, 1980, pp. 3 and 5.
2. Kant, Immanuel. *Perpetual Peace: A Philosophical Essay – First Supplement*, Section 3.
3. Kennedy, Paul. *The Rise and Fall of the Great Powers,* New York, 1987, pp. 538–540.
4. Gandhi, Rajiv. Address to UN General Assembly, 9 June 1988 (Document A/S – 15/PV.14, 15 June 1988).
5. Proposal by George Shultz, William Perry, Henry Kissinger, Sam Nunn in *Wall Street Journal*, 4 January 2007, http://online.wsj.com/article/SB116785152515666636.html.
6. James, William. 'The Moral Equivalent of War', 1910, http://constitution.org/wj/meow.htm (last accessed on 11 July 2016).
7. Fisk, Robert. *The Great War for Civilization,* London, 2005, p. xxxi.

38: What Might Be Happening in West Asia

1. Tibi, Bassam. *Arab Nationalism: Between Islam and the Nation State*, New York, p. ix.
2. The Palestine Problem: Correspondence between President Gamal Abdel-Nasser to President John F. Kennedy on the subject of the Palestine problem, Information Department, Cairo, 1961, p. 9.
3. Gannouchi, Al-Rachid. 'Secularism in the Arab Maghrib', ed. Azzam Tamimi and John L. Esposito, *Islam and Secularism in the Middle East*, London, 2000, p. 123.
4. Abdo, Geneive. *No God But God: Egypt and the Triumph of Islam*, New York, 2000, pp. ix and 1999.
5. Arkoun, Mohammad. *Islam: To Reform or Subvert*, New Delhi, 2009, p. 379.

39: A Century of Turmoil in West Asia: Some Pitfalls of Nationalism

1. Evidence of this is to be found in his speech of 27 October 1914, in Calcutta.

Its theme was 'Ittehad-e-Islami', Sahitya Akademi, *Khutbaat-e-Azadi*, New Delhi, 1974, pp. 13–36.
2. Lewis, Bernard. *The Multiple Identities of the Middle East*, London, 1998, p. 3
3. Koppes, Clayton R. 'Captain Mahan, General Gordon, and the Origins of the Term "Middle East"', *Middle Eastern Studies*, Volume 12, No. 1, January 1976, pp. 95-98. An even earlier instance of this was the preference for the division of Persia in spheres of influence in first decade of the 20th century; cf Wilson, Arnold. *S.W. Persia: A Political Officer's dairy 1907–1914,* London, 1941, p. 10.
4. Presidential Address to Special Session of Congress, 15 December 1923.
5. Anderson, Benedict. *Imagined Communities; Reflections on the Origin and Spread of Nationalism*, London, 1991, pp. 5–6.
6. Tamir, Yael. *Liberal Nationalism*, New Jersey, 1993, p. 63.
7. Kedourie, Elie. *Nationalism*, 4th edition, 1993, p. 1 and Gellner, Ernest. *Nations and Nationalism*, New York, 2006, p. 1.
8. Smith, Anthony D. 'Theories of Nationalism', *Asian Nationalisms*, ed. M. Leifer, London, 2000, p. 1.
9. Antonius, George. *The Arab Awakening*, London, 1938, pp. 15–18.
10. Enayat, Hamid. *Modern Islamic Political Thought*, London, 1982, p. 114.
11. Antonius, op. cit., pp. 428–436, 305
12. Toynbee, Arnold J. Foreword to Robert & Hadawi. *The Palestine Diary*, Volume 1, New York, 1972, p. xiii.
13. Beit-Hallahmi, Benjamin. *Original Sins—Reflections on the History of Zionism and Israel*, New York, 1993, p. 103.
14. Hobsbawm, E.J. *Nations and Nationalism since 1780*, Second Edition, 1992, p. 12 and the reference to three stages of awareness designated as phases A, B and C. Hobsbawm also assesses the likely decline of the sentiment of nationalism with the decline of the nation-state in a globalizing world of multiple identities (p. 192).
15. Sharara, Abd al-Latif. 'The Idea of Arab nationalism' in Haim, Sylvia G. *Arab Nationalism—An Anthology*, London, 1962, p. 228.
16. Kumaraswamy, P.R. 'Problems of Studying Minorities in the Middle East,' *Alternatives, Turkish Journal of International Affairs*, Volume 2, Number 2, Summer 2003.
17. Tibi, Bassam. *Arab Nationalism: Between Islam and the Nation State*, New York, 1997, pp. 20–25, 211–214
18. Sulaiman, Khalid A. *Palestine and Modern Arab Poetry*, London, 1984, p. 213.
19. Laroui, Abdallah. *The Crisis of the Arab Intellectual*, London, 1976, pp. 24, 153–154, 177.
20. Ajami, Fuad. *The Arab Predicament: Arab Political Thought and Practice since 1967*, 1981, p. 37.
21. Excerpts from an interview given by Saddam Husayn to a Kuwaiti editor, cf Dawisha, Adeed. 'Arab Nationalism in the Twentieth Century', New Jersey, 2003, p. 277.
22. Sharabi, Hisham. *Neopatriarchy: A Theory of Distorted Change in Arab Society*,

New York, 1992, p. 21.
23. Malik, Charles. 'The Near East: The Search for Truth', in *Foreign Affairs*, January, 1952.
24. Sayyid Qutb in 1953, cited in Sivan, Emmanuel. *Radical Islam*, New York, 1985, p. 30.
25. Al-Ghannouchi, Rachid. 'Secularism in the Arab Maghreb' in Azzam Tamimi and John L. Esposito (ed.). *Islam and Secularism in the Middle East*, London, 2000, p. 123.
26. Mandraud, Isabelle. 'Tunisian Islamists take moderate view', *The Guardian Weekly*, 4 July 2014, p. 10.
27. Ramadan, Tariq. *Islam and the Arab Awakening*, New York, 2012, p. 142.
28. UNDP. 'Arab Development and Challenges Report 2011: Towards the Developmental State in the Arab Region', Cairo, 2011, pp. iv, 1-14.
29. Dawish, Adeed & Zartman, William. *Beyond Coercion: The Durability of the Arab State*, New York, 1988, pp. 282–283.
30. Harling, Peter. 'Failure of the Modern Middle East Nation State: Taking Iraq Apart', *Le Monde Diplomatique*, October 2014.
31. Bipan Chandra & Others. *India's Struggle for Independence*, New Delhi, 1989, pp. 22–26.
32. Pandey, Gyan. 'Peasant Revolts and Indian Nationalism: The Peasant Movement in Oudh 1919-1922' in Ranjit Guha. *Subaltern Studies I*, New Delhi, 1982, pp. 143–195.
33. Brzezinski, Zbigniew. *Out of Control: Global Turmoil on the Eve of the 21st Century*, New York, 1993, p. 19.
34. Popper, Karl. *The Open Society and Its Enemies*, London, 1962, p. 49.
35. Tamir, op. cit., p. 83, citing H. Kohn.
36. Kohn, Hans. *Nationalism: Its Meaning and History*, New York, 1955, p. 90.
37. Tamir, op. cit., p. 79.
38. Mahajan, Gurpreet. *The Multicultural Path: Issues of Diversity and Discrimination in Democracy*, New Delhi, 2002, pp. 217–218.
39. Kaviraj, Sudipta. 'Nationalism' in Jayal & Mehta. *The Oxford Companion to Politics in India*, New Delhi, 2010, p. 331.
40. Baxi, Upendra. 'The Constitutional Discourse on Secularism' in Baxi, Alice Jacob and Tarlok Singh. *Reconstructing the Republic*, New Delhi, 1999, p. 217.
41. *Khutbaat-e-Azad*, Kanpur, 29 December 1925, pp. 211–233.

40: Relevance of International Law

1. Kissinger, Henry. *World Order*, New York, 2014, p. 368.
2. Held, David (ed.). *Political Theory Today*, Stanford, 1991, p. 234.

41: Some Thoughts on the Sacred and Secular in International Relations

1. Berger, Peter. 'Secularism in Retreat', *The National Interest* 46, Winter 1996, p.3.

2. Bull, Hedley. *The Anarchical Society*, London, 1995, p. 308.
3. Bhargava, Rajeev (ed.). *Secularism and Its Critics*, New Delhi, 1998, passim.

42: Collective Security in the Persian Gulf: An Indian Perspective

1. UN Editorial directive ST/CS/SER.A/29/Rev.1 of 14 May 1999.
2. Badeeb, Saeed M. *Saudi-Iranian Relations 1932-1982*, London, 1993, p. 123.
3. Chubin, Shahram. *Security in the Persian Gulf 4—The Role of Outside Powers*, London, 1982, pp. 152–153.
4. Michael A. Palmer. *Guardians of the Gulf: A History of America's Expanding Role in the Persian Gulf, 1833-1992*, New York, 1992, pp. 106, 109.
5. Ramazani, R.K. *Revolutionary Iran–Challenge and Response in the Middle East*, Baltimore, 1986, pp. 15–16.
6. Foreign Minister Velayati's speech of September 1, 1994 in the Conference on Disarmament (CD/PV 690, pp 8-14); also Gary Sick and Lawrence Potter. *The Persian Gulf at the Millennium*, New York, 1997, pp. 239 and 246n36.
7. 'EU–GCC Partnership: Security and Policy challenges', *Al Jisr Workshop*, Conference Overview Paper, Berlin, 16–17 March 2010, pp. 2–3.
8. McMillan, Sokolsky and Winner: 'Towards a New Regional Security Architecture', *The Washington Quarterly*, Summer 2003, pp. 167-175.
9. The International Institute for Strategic Studies (IISS). *The Manama Dialogue*, London, 5 December 2004.
10. Statement by Amir of Qatar in UN General Assembly, 28 September 2015.

43: Turbulence in West Asian State Systems: Road Blocks in the Quest for Participatory Governance

1. Arjomand, Said Amir. *The Political Dimensions of Religion*, New York, 1993, p. 2.
2. Hegghammer, Thomas. *Jihad in Saudi Arabia: Violence and Pan-Islamism*, New York, 2010. The author concludes the book with a 2005 quote from a Saudi intelligence officer: 'We encouraged our young men to fight for Islam in Afghanistan. We encouraged our young men to fight for Islam in Bosnia and Chechnya. We encouraged our young men to fight for Islam in Palestine. Now we are telling them you are forbidden to fight for Islam in Iraq, and they are confused.'
3. The process, in the case of Egypt, was graphically traced well before the Turbulence by Geneive Abdo in her book—*No God But God: Egypt and the Triumph of Islam*, New York, 2000.
4. Al-Rasheed, Madawi. 'No Saudi Spring: Anatomy of a Failed Revolution', *Boston Review*, 1 March 2012.
5. Gerges, Fawaz A. (ed). *The New Middle East: Protest and Revolution in the Arab World*, New York, 2014, pp. 4–15.
6. Trotsky, Leon. *The History of the Russian Revolution*, Vol. 1, London, 1932, pp. 16–17.
7. Hussain, Agha and Malley, Robert. 'The Arab Counterrevolution', *The New*

York *Review of Books*, 29 September 2011.
8. Elakawi, Zaki Sami. 'The Geopolitical Consequences of the Arab Spring', *Open Democracy*, 24 November 2014.
9. Manfreda, Primose. 'Definition of the Arab Spring', 25 November 2014, http://middleeast.about.com/od/humanrightsdemocracy/a/The-Arab-Spring.htm.
10. Kamrava, Mehran. 'The Arab Spring and the Saudi-led Counterrevolution', *Orbis*, Winter 2012, p. 97.
11. Madawi Al-Rasheed in Gerges, *op. cit.*, p. 354.
12. Book review of *From Deep State to Islamic State-The Arab Counter Revolution and its Jihadi Legacy, The Economist*, London, 8 August 2015.
13. Qur'an, xlii.38 and iv. 59.
14. Khouri, Rami G. 'The Dark Heart of 2015's Legacy Across the Middle East', *Agence Global*, 2 January 2016.
15. Nakhleh, Emile. 'Arab Spring: Five Years on Counterrevolution and Fading Euphoria', 5 January 2016, http://lobelog.com/the-arab-spring-five-years-on-counterrevolution-and-fading euphoria/.
16. Black, Ian. 'Fear of a Shia Full-Moon', *The Guardian*, 26 January 2007.
17. Hashemi, Nader. 'Towards a Political Theory of Sectarianism in the Middle East: The Salience of Authoritarianism Over Theology', citing Madawi Al-Rasheed 27, October, 2015, http://www.mei.edu/content/map/toward-political-theory-sectarianism-middle-east-salience-authoritarianism-over-theology.
18. UNDP. *Arab Development and Challenges Report 2011: Towards the Developmental State in the Arb Region*, Cairo, 2011, pp. iv, 1–14.
19. Dawish, Adeeb and Zartman, William. *Beyond Coercion: The Durability of the Arab State*, New York, 1988, pp. 282–283.
20. Laroui, Abdallah. *The Crisis of the Arab Intellectual: Traditionalism or Historicism*, Berkeley, California, 1976, p. 28.

44: Accommodating Diversity in a Globalizing World: The Indian Experience

1. Abu Rabi, Ibrahim M. *Contemporary Arab Thought: Studies in Post −1967 Arab Intellectual History*, London, 2004, p. 265.
2. Gilsenan, Michael. *Recognizing Islam: Religion and Society in Modern Middle East*, London, 1982, p. 19.
3. Al-Azmeh, Aziz. *Islam and Modernities*, London, 1993, p. 4.
4. Lapidus, Ira M. *A History of Islamic Societies*, Cambridge, 1988, p. xx.
5. Chand, Tara. *The Influence of Islam on Indian Culture*, Allahabad, 1922, pp. 141-142.
6. Mujeeb, M. *Indian Muslims*, London, 1967, p. 120.
7. Nadvi, Abul Hasan Ali. *Muslims in India*, Lucknow, 1980, p. 76. The Arabic version of this monograph was published by the Nadwatul Ulema, Lucknow, 1976.
8. Julien, Charles-Andre. *History of North Africa – Tunisia, Algeria, Morocco*, London,

1970, p. 210. Also, Willis, Michael. J. *Politics and Power in the Maghreb – Algeria, Tunisia and Morocco from Independence to the Arab Spring*, London, 2012, pp. 17, 163, 178.
9. Constitution of India, Articles 25, 26, 29, 30, 51A(e) and (f).
10. Robertson, R. *Globalization: Social Theory and Global Culture*, London, 1992 p. 8.

45: India and the World

1. Brzezinski, Zbigniew. *Out of Control: Global Turmoil on the Eve of the 21st Century*, New York, 1993, p. 203.
2. Brzezinski, Zbigniew. *Strategic Vision: America and the crisis of Global Power*, New York, 2012, p. 1.
3. Hobsbawm, Eric. *Age of Extremes: The Short Twentieth Century 1914-1991*, London, 1994, p. 585.
4. Kofi Annan. 'Towards a culture of peace' in *Letters to future generations*, UNESCO, Paris, 1999.
5. Address by National Security Adviser A.K. Doval at Munich Security Conference, New Delhi, 21 October 2014.
6. Speech by former NSA, Shivshankar Menon, New Delhi, 21 September 2015.
7. Of which about US $31.07 bn with West Asia (excluding GCC) and US $18.5 bn with North Africa—Data from Government of India, Department of Commerce, Export Import Data Bank.

INDEX

Abbas, Khwaja Ahmad, 134, 154–157
   and censorship issues, 155
Abdo, Geneive, 250
accountability, 179–182, 285
act of commission, 39
act of omission, 39
A.D. Gorwala Report of 1951, 8
Administrative Reform Commission (ARC), 19
'Adonis,' Ali Ahmad Said, 256
Aflaq, Michel, 256
Age of Extremes: The Short History of the Twentieth Century, 166
agriculture
   agricultural income, 62
   average annual growth rate, 217
   challenges in Indian, 218–219
   fertilizer subsidy and its associated inefficiencies and misuses, 63–64
   Green Revolution benefits, 62
   policy intervention recommendations, 65–66
   production performance in India, 63–67
   public fund allocation to, 63
   share in GDP growth, 216
   as a source of livelihood, 61
Ahmad, Mohiuddin (Abul Kalam Azad), 253–254, 261
Ajami, Fuad, 257
Akbar, emperor, 105, 148–149
al-Azm, Jalal, 256
al-Din, Nazira Zain, 246
Alexandria Declaration of March 2004, 258
Al-Ghannouchi, Rachid, 258

Al Ghazali, 146
Aligarh Muslim University (AMU), 96–97
Al India Majlis-e-Mushawarat, 139
Ali Sardar Jaafri Committee, 1990, 111
Al-Jahiz, 104
Al-Kindi, 104
al-Latif Sharara, Abd, 256
Allen, Richard, 112
Al-Masudi, 104
Al-Qaeda, 281
Ambedkar, B.R., 5, 11, 22, 48, 117, 127, 159, 211, 214
   vision of 'one person, one vote, one value,' 24
American Humane Association for Protecting Children and Animals, 4
Amnesty International Report 2014/15, 55
Anand, Mulk Raj, 156
Anand cooperative dairy model, 231
Angell, Sir Norman, 239
Anglo-French Declaration of November 1918, 255
Annan, Kofi, 168, 230
Annual report of our National Human Rights Commission for 2011–2012, 54
Antonius, George, 254
'Appeal for Inter- Communal Harmony,' 131
Arab Ba'th Party, 256
Arab Development Challenges Report 2011, 259, 285
Arab Human Development Report, 246
Arab nationalism, 254–256, 259–260
Arab revolt of 1916, 255

Arab Spring, 245, 280. *see* Arab Turbulence
Arab Turbulence, 279–285
Arasaratnam, S., 138
Aravind Eye Care Hospital, 231
Aristotle, 196
Arkoun, Mohammed, 142, 250
Armed Forces Special Powers Act (AFSPA), 42
Articles of Constitution
   Article 18, 271
   Article 19(2), 49
   Article 29, 113
   Article 32, 73
   Article 226, 73
   Article 19(1)(a), 49
   Article 51A, 18, 226
   Article 350A, 97, 113
   Article 51A(f), 74
   Articles 14, 15 and 16, 76
   Articles 19 and 25, 48
Atal Innovation Mission (AIM), 233
Auliya, Khwaja Nizamuddin, 160

Bachchan, Amitabh, 157
Background Paper on Electoral Reforms, 23
Badauni, 106
Baghdad Pact, 1955, 257
Bakhsh, Khuda, 92
Bakhsh, Maulavi Mohammad, 92
Balfour Declaration of November 1917, 255
Balkanization, 117, 119
Balkan war, 183
Bandyopadhyaya, Narayanan, 106
Bania, Marwari, 46
Baradai, Dr Mohamad El, 242
Barani, 106
Barcelona Report, 2004, 167
Barker, Ernest, 38, 126
Basham, A.L., 237
Baxi, Upendra, 207, 261
Begum, Gül Badan, 106
Bengal Famine of 1942–1943, 61
Bentinck, Lord William, 199
Berger, Peter, 268
Bhakra Nangal Project, 215
Bhargava, Rajeev, 271

Bhaskar, Ira, 112
Bhopal gas tragedy, 90
bilateral relationships, 274–277
Bilmes, Linda, 247
Bobbitt, Philip, 36, 176–177
Bommai judgment, 75–78
Booth, Ken, 36
Bose, Subhas, 45
Bouazizi, Mohamed, 249
Brass, Paul, 111
Brown, Percy, 105
Brzezinski, Zbigniew, 29
Bull, Headley, 241, 270
Butterfield, Herbert, 30

Calcutta University Act, 1857, 199
Camp David Accord of 1979, 257
Cariappa, Field Marshal K.M., 165–166
Carr, E.H., 136
Carter Doctrine, 274
Cassiodorus, Flavius, 238
Castells, Manuel, 125
The Caste System, 46
censorship of films, 155
Chand, Tara, 102, 107
Chandra, Bipan, 260
Charter of the United Nations (UN), 6, 29, 35, 239, 264–265, 270
Chipko movement, 90
Chirol, Valentine, 254
Chomsky, Noam, 84
citizenship of a modern state, 124–125
civil liberties, 38–39, 45
civil rights, 39
civil society, 10, 31
civil society movements, 7
Clarke, Arthur, 168
climatic changes, 172
Code of Conduct, 10
Colvile, Sir James William, 200
Committee on Judicial Accountability, 37
Commonwealth War Graves Commission, 185
competitive federalism, 13
Comprehensive Global Security System, 240
computer security, 177

Congress Socialist Party, 46
conscience, 5, 10, 27, 30, 145, 152–153, 197, 271
   collective, 44, 56
   public, 26
Constitution-making process, 117–130
Constitution of India, civil liberties and human rights in, 38–43
Constitution (86th Amendment) Act 2002, 220
Convention against Torture and Other Cruel, Inhuman, 41
Convention on the Elimination of all forms of Discrimination against Women, 41
Convention on the Elimination of all forms of Racial Discrimination, 41
Convention on the Rights of Persons with Disability, 41
Convention on the Rights of the Child, 41
cooperative federalism, 13–14
corruption, 19–21, 88–89
corruption, problem of, 8–9
corruption control mechanism, 21
Corruption Perception Index, 9, 19
counterfactuals, 136
Covenant of the League of Nations, 1919, 35
criminal justice system, 8
cyber-utopianism, 281

Damodaran, A.K., 28
Davos Economic Forum reports on Arab Competiveness, 280
Dayal, John, 157
Declaration of Principles on Tolerance, 160–161
Degrading Treatment or Punishment, 41
Dehlavi, Pandit Kailash Narain Kaul Bedil, 74
Delhi Declaration, 277
democracy, 22
democracy, functioning of, 12, 26
democratic rights, 39
dharma, 5
dialogues, 161–162
diplomacy, 29–30, 34–36

Directive Principles of State Policy, 129, 264
Directive Principles of State Policy in Part IV of the Constitution, 53
dissent as a right, 48–49
distributive justice, 4
Disturbed Areas Act (DAA), 42
domestic jurisdiction, 6
Drafting Committee of Constitution, 11–12, 22
Draft National Pact, 132
Dr A.P.J. Abdul Kalam IGNITE competition, 233
Dreze, Jean, 88
Dubey, Muchkund, 34
Dulles, Allen, 176

Eaton, Richard, 92
Eban, Abba, 30
editor's job, 68–72
   changes in role and position, 70–71
   in digital medium, 71–72
   journalistic ethos and values, 69–70
   Press council guidelines, 68
Egypt, 248–249, 255, 280–282, 284
Einstein, Albert, 48
elected candidate, 24–25
electoral procedures and practices, 23, 25–27
Eliot, T.S., 52
Engineer, Asghar Ali, 95, 161
Equal Opportunity Commission, 140
ethics in public life, 10

faiths or belief systems, 158–162
Fazl, Abul, 106
federalism, 12–13
   essential nature of, 15
federation, 12
Filiu, Jean-Pierre, 283
First-Past-The-Post (FPTP) system, 23, 26, 128
First Report of the Ethics Committee of the Rajya Sabha, 1998, 9
First World War, 183–186
   casualties, 184
fiscal federalism, 13, 15
Fisk, Robert, 241

foreign-policy pronouncements, 33–34
foreknowledge, 175
free, just and humane society, 4
Fundamentalism Project, 269
Fundamental Rights and Directive Principles of State Policy, 40

Gaddafi regime, 250
Gandhi, Indira, 33
Gandhi, Mahatma, 5, 7, 18, 45, 57, 214
Gandhi, Prime Minister Rajiv, 240
Gandhi, Rajiv, 28
Gandhian approach, 5–6
Gandhian dictum, 21
Gannouchi, Rachid, 247
GCC (Gulf Co-operative Council) states, 248, 250–251, 274–277, 282–284
Ghali, Boutros, 240
Gibbon, Edward, 123, 137, 159, 268
Giri, President V.V, 237
Global Citizenship Country Report Card, 55
Global Innovation Index Report, 2015, 232
globalization, 265, 271
global security and prosperity, 273–274
Global Trends 2025, 167
Gordon, T.E., 254
governance, 7
Gramci, Antonio, 245
Green Revolution, 62, 217
Grotius, Hugo, 263
Grow More Food Campaign, 62
Guha, Ramachandra, 87, 96, 112, 125
The Guilty Men of India's Partition, 46
Gujral Committee, 111
Gulati, Ashok, 64
Gulf War, 1990–1991, 257
Gupta, Ashin Das, 138

Habib, Irfan, 104
Haikal, Hassanein, 248
Hasan, Abul, 105
Havel, Vaclav, 83
Hazare, Anna, 90
Held, David, 267
higher education, 201–205
historians, 135

history
  distinction between memory and, 135
  of India, 137–138
  writing and teaching, 136–137
History of the Russian Revolution, 3
Hobbes, 169
Hobsbawm, Eric, 166
Holyoake, George, 271
Hooda Ji, Bhupinder Singh, 215
human development, 207–208
Human Development Report, 2011, 208, 213
humaneness, 4
humane society, 4
human rights, 7, 21, 38–39, 51, 56, 206–207
  institutional structure for the attainment and enforcement of, 53
  monitoring and safeguard mechanisms in India, 54–55
  violations, typology, 54
Human Rights Watch World Report for 2015, 55
Hussain, Saddam, 247–248
hydrocarbon energy, 273

Ibn Khurdadbeh, 104
Ignatius, David, 247
India–GCC states relations, 276–277
Indian Muslim community, 92–101, 139–143
  problems confronting, 140
Indian People's Theatre Association, 156
Indian political system, 211
Indian states, integration of, 116–117
India–Pakistan War, 1965, 187–190
inequality of human development, 208, 212–213
insecurity, 166–173
Integrated Production Programme, 62
intellectuals, roles and responsibilities in a society, 81–85
  on communal, economic or regional issues, 89
  in contemporary India, 85–90
  against corruption, 88–89
  on economic amelioration, 87–88

in functioning of the institutions, 85–87
to protect and safeguard the environment,
    90–91
with regard to rights, 89
intelligence
    information, 175–176
    misuse of, 178
Intelligence Community, 180
Intelligence Services Act 1994, 180
interfaith dialogue, 158–159
International Covenant on Civil and
    Political Rights, 41
International Covenant on Economic, Social
    and Cultural Rights, 41
International Law, 263–267
International law of Peace and War, 238–239
international relations, sacred and secular
    impulses in, 268–272
Iqbal, Allama, 98, 107
Iranian Revolution of 1979, 274
Iran–P5+1 Joint Comprehensive Plan of
    action (JCPOA), 276
Iraq-Iran War, 274–275
Islam, 92, 99, 103, 106, 142
Islamic art and culture, 102–107
    calligraphy, 106
    Persian influence, 105
    pre-Moghul and Moghul periods, 105–
    106
Iyer, Justice Vaidyanathapura Ramakrishna,
    206–209

Jahangir, emperor, 105
James, William, 124, 241
Jan Dhan, Aadhaar and Mobile (JAM), 64
Jansunwai, 89
Jennings, Ivor, 117
Johnson, Paul, 84
Johnston, Rob, 176
Jordan, 251
judiciary, 73–78
Juzjani, 106

Kalila wa Dimna, 104
Kant, Immanuel, 239
Kao, Rameshwar Nath, 174

Kapoor, Raj, 157
Kargil Review Committee Report, 181
Kashmir problem, 187–188
Kautilya, 126, 170, 175, 239
Kay, David, 178
Kennan, George, 242
Kennedy, Paul, 190, 239
Khaldun, Ibn, 137, 196
Khalidi, Omar, 110
Khan, Aitamad, 151
Khan, Khafi, 106
Khan, President Ayub, 189
Khan, Syed Ahmad, 150
Khanna, Dr Tarun, 233
Khilnani, Sunil, 117
Khuda Bakhsh Oriental Public Library, 92
Kissinger, Henry, 34, 183–184, 267, 269
Knowledge Commission, 195
Kosambi, Damodar Dharmanand, 237
Kosygin, Prime Minister Alexei, 189
Kothari, Rajni, 86, 118
Koussa, Mousa, 250
Kufi, Ali bin Hamid, 106
Kuhn, Thomas, 195
Kundu, Amitabh, 89
Kundu Report, 140
Kymlicka, Will, 124

Ladurie, Emmanuel Le Roy, 138
Lahori, Iqbal, 150
Lall, Arthur, 32
Lall, Rajiv, 66
Lao Tzu, 237
Lapidus, Ira, 103
Laroui, Abdallah, 257, 285
Law Commission Report of 1999, 23
Law Commission Report on Electoral
    Reforms, 1999, 25–26
Libya, 250
Lippman, Walter, 166
Livingston, W.S., 15
Lohia, Ram Manohar, 38, 45–46
    advocacy of issues, 46
    on state government, 47
'Look East and Act East' policy, 138
Ludhianavi, Sahir, 112

Mahabharata, 4
Mahajan, Gurpreet, 94, 125
Mahan, Alfred, 254
Mahatma Gandhi National Rural Employment Guarantee Act (MNREGA), 224
'Make in India' programme, 67
Malihabadi, Josh, 7, 19
Malik, Charles, 258
Man and Development, 3
Mander, Harsh, 88
Mansur, Ustad, 105
Marden, B.J., 196
Marsilius of Padua, 238
mass consciousness, 3–4
Matterson, Angus, 242
Mehta, Pratap Bhanu, 86
Menes, King, 136
Menon, V.P., 116–117
Milton, John, 173
Mishra, Pankaj, 30
Mixed Compensatory Proportional Representation on the German model, 25
Montagu–Chelmsford Reforms of 1919, 185
Mookerji, Radha Kumud, 138
morality, 34
Moulavi, Vakkom Abdul Khader, 210
Mujeeb, Mohammad, 92, 144–153
  critique of the religious thought, 149–150
  debate between orthodoxy and dissent, 145–148
  interest in Sufism and Sufis, 148
  moral sense, 145
  views on the orthodox Muslim positions, 152–153
multiculturalism, 130
Murthy, N.R. Narayana, 231
Muslim Brotherhood, 249–250
Muslim Personal Law, 96–97
Muslim societies, challenge for contemporary, 251–252

Nadwi, Sheikh Abul Hasan Ali, 141
Nandy, Ashish, 86, 169

Narain, Sunita, 90
Narang, Gopi Chand, 112
Narayanan, K.R., 28
Narlikar, Jayant, 194
Narmada River Valley project, 90
Nasser, Jamal Abdul, 256
National Commission to Review the Working of the Constitution, 23
National Human Rights Commission, 53
National Human Rights Commission (NHRC), 42
National Integration Conference, 118
national interest, 31
nationalism, 254, 256, 258, 260–261, 271
nationalist movements, 185
National Knowledge Commission, 2008, 201
National Rural Employment Guarantee Act (NREGA), 88
National Security Council of the United States, 167
National Skill Development Programmes, 233
negotiations, 32–33
Nehru, Jawaharlal, 38, 45, 61, 116–117, 154, 196, 225
nepotism, 8
Newman, Cardinal John Henry, 200
N.N. Vohra Report of 1995, 8
Non-Cooperation Movement, 132
nuclear disarmament, 240, 243

Objectives Resolution, 1947, 48
Office of the UN High Commissioner for Human Rights, 52
Oommen, T.K., 31, 90, 168
operational secrecy, 181
Operation Gibraltar, 187–188
Oppenhiemer, Robert, 197
Ottoman Empire, 253, 255, 259, 284
Oxford Centre for Islamic Studies, 123

Pachauri, Dr R.K., 172
Pal, Bipin Chandra, 131
Panchatantra, 104
Panchayati Raj system, 212

pandemic, 171–172
Pani Panchayat, 90
Panneerselvan, A.S., 69
Parivartan, 89
Parthasarathi, Gopalaswami, 28–29, 31–32, 36
Patel, Sardar Vallabhbhai, 116–117, 128
Patnaik, Prabhat, 88
peace, promotion of, 237–244
People's Union for Civil Liberties and Democratic Rights (PUCDR), 39
People's Union for Civil Liberties (PUCL), 39
Persian Gulf, 273
pluralism, 93–94, 130
P.N. Haksar Memorial Lecture, 3
political corruption, 7
political federalism, 12–15
Praja Socialist Party, 46
Prasad, Baba, 232
Premchand, Munshi, 157
Progressive Writers' Association, 156
Protection of Civil Rights Act, 1955, 53
Protection of Human Rights Act, 1993, 41–42
the Protection of Human Rights Act, 1993, 53
public conscience, 26
Public Interest Litigation (PIL), 89
Public International Law, 264
Public Safety Act (PSA), 42
Punchi Commission, 118
Puri, Balraj, 96

Qabbani, Nizar, 256
Qasim, Mulla Abul, 151
Qazwini, 106

Radhakrishnan, Sarvepelli, 81–85
Rafsanjani, 274
Rai, Lala Lajpat, 131–134
Rajagopal, Shri, 214
Raj Ghat, New Delhi, 5
Ralegan Siddhi, 90
Ranganath Mishra Commission, 97
Rao, Aarthi, 231

Rawls, John, 35, 39, 69, 73
Ray, Asim, 94
73rd and 74th Constitution Amendment Acts, 58
representative-ness of the elected representative, 24
Resolution 211, 189
resource federalism, 13
Richelieu, Cardinal, 32
Right of Children to Free and Compulsory Education Act 2009, 220
Right to Education (RTE) Act, 220–224
criticisms of, 221–224
'Right to Information' movement, 7
Riyadh Declaration, 277
Rousseau, 5, 169
RTI Act, 88
Rule of Law, 6, 9, 18–19, 38, 86–87, 93, 261
Rumsfeld, Donald, 168
rural politics in India, 66
Rusk, Dean, 189
Russell, Bertrand, 81, 197
Russell, Richard, 155
Russian Revolution of 1917, 184
Ryle, Gilbert, 33

Sachar, Bhim Sen, 16
Sachar Committee Report, 139
Sachar Report, 96
Sachs, Judge Albie, 74
Said, Edward, 84, 91, 99
Samad, Abdus, 105
San Rimo arrangement, 279
Santhanam Committee, 8
Sarkaria Commission, 118, 121
'Sarmad,' Sheikh Mohammad Saeed, 151
Sarva Shiksha Abhiyan, 202–203, 220, 223
Saxena, N.C., 88
Schimmel, Annemarie, 105
science policy of India, 193–198
scientific temper, 225–228
Second Ballot System, 25–26
secularism, 74–76, 78, 271
Seeley, John, 135
Sen, Amartya, 34, 66, 69, 74, 88
'Seven Social Sins, 5

Shahjahan, emperor, 105
Sharabi, Hisham, 258
Shastri, Prime Minister Lal Bahadur, 188–189
Shia Crescent, 248
Shikoh, Dara, 107
Shills, Edward, 83
Shiva, Vandana, 90
Silent Valley project, 90
Sindhi language, 108
Singh, Manmohan, 8
Singh Ji, Chaudhary Ranbir, 215
Sinha, Satyendra Narayan (Chhote Sahib), 11
Six Day War of 1967, 256
Snow, C.P., 175
social harmony, Lala Lajpat Rai's perceptions, 131–134
social innovations, 229–234
societies, 16–17
Sorabjee, Soli, 75
Spinoza, Baruch, 81
state, primary duty of, 31, 39
State Human Rights Commissions, 53
state responsibility, in terms of constitutional obligations, 40
States Reorganization Commission, 108
Steering Committee on Science and Technology, 194
Stern, Fritz, 184
Stiglitz, Joseph, 247
Suez crisis of 1956, 257
Sufism, 104, 106–107
Supra-National law, 264–265
Supreme Court of India, 37
Swan, Abram de, 109–110
Sykes-Picot Agreement, 279
Sykes-Picot agreement of May 1916, 255

Tagore, Rabindranath, 45, 117, 124
Tarkunde, Justice Vithal Mahadeo, 37
Tashkent Agreement, 189–190
Taylor, Charles, 125
Tehri Dam project, 90
terrorism, 170–171

Third Report of the Ethics Committee, 2002, 10
Tibi, Bassam, 254
Tilak, Bal Gangadhar, 131
tolerances, 75
Toynbee, Arnold, 255
transparency, 7
tribalization, 271
Troksky, 176
Trotsky, Leon, 3, 249
Trubowitz, Peter, 31
Tunisia, 248–249, 258–259, 284

UN Convention against Corruption, 18–19
UNDP's Arab Human Development Reports, 258
UN General Assembly, 172
UN General Assembly resolution 65/206, 55
UN General Assembly Resolutions, 160
UN High Commissioner for Human Rights, 52, 54
United Arab Republic, 257
United Nations Development Programme's (UNDP) Human Development Index, 41
United Nations Environment Programme, 243
United Nations (UN), 264–266
Universal Declaration of Human Rights, 35, 51, 53
    characteristics of, 51
Universal Declaration of Human Rights, 1948, 41
Universal Declaration of Human Rights of 1948, 271
Universal Periodic Review of Human Rights, 43
Universal Periodic Review on India for 2012–2016, 54
university education, 200–205
University Grants Commission (UGC), 195
University of Calcutta, 199
UNMOGIP (United Nations Military Observer Group in India and Pakistan), 188

UN Multilateral system, 264
UN Refugee Conventions, 55
UN Security Council, 188, 250
UN Special Rapporteur on Violence against Women, 43
UP Special Powers Act, 14 of 1932, 47
Urdu language, declining popularity of, 108–115
  percentage of Urdu speakers, 109
  in terms of Urdu literacy, 110–111
  ways for promotion and development of Urdu, 111–114

Vakkom Moulavi Foundation Trust, 210, 214
Varshney, Ashutosh, 66
Verghese, B.G., 120
virtue in public life, 17–18
virtuous society, 17
Visveswaraya, Sir Mokshagundam, 195
Vittal, N., 88
Vivekananda, Swami, 160

West Asia, 245–252
Westphalian principle, 53
Westphalian World Order, 263
White, Sir Harold, 165
White Australia policy, 165
White Revolution, 231
Windsor, Philip, 30
women legislators in nation building, 57–60
  contribution to democratic governance, 60
  representation in local bodies, 58
Wood, Sir Charles, 199
World Bank, 265
World Trade Organization (WTO), 265
Wotton, Sir Henry, 34

Yadav, Yogendra, 23
Yaqubi, 104
Yashpal Committee Report, 2009, 201
Yemen, 251

Zionism, 255, 257
Zurayq, Constantin, 257